D0079420

Adam Usk's Secret

THE MIDDLE AGES SERIES

A complete list of books in the series is
available from the publisher.

Adam Usk's Secret

Steven Justice

PENN

UNIVERSITY OF PENNSYLVANIA PRESS

PHILADELPHIA

Published by
University of Pennsylvania Press
Philadelphia, Pennsylvania 19104-4112
www.upenn.edu/pennpress

Printed in the United States of America on acid-free paper
1 3 5 7 9 10 8 6 4 2

Library of Congress Cataloging-in-Publication Data
Justice, Steven, 1957–
Adam Usk's secret / Steven Justice. — 1st ed.
p. cm. — (The Middle Ages series)
Includes bibliographical references and index.
ISBN 978-0-8122-4693-3
1. Adam, of Usk, active 1400. Chronicon Adae de Usk, A.D. 1377–1421. 2. Adam, of Usk, active 1400—Literary art. 3. Written communication—England—History—To 1500. 4. Great Britain—History—Richard II, 1377–1399—Historiography 5. Great Britain—History—House of Lancaster, 1399–1461—Historiography. 6. Wales—History—1063–1536—Historiography. I. Title. II. Series: Middle Ages series.
DA235.J87 2015
942.03'—dc23 2014028639

For Anne Middleton

Contents

Introduction

Literary criticism not long ago offered itself the cheering thought that it might stop chasing symptoms and "just read," that it might attend to what books know and advertently say rather than poke at what they inadvertently disclose.[1] These impulses arrive from time to time; a generation ago, Paul de Man suggested that we might try "mere" reading;[2] and cultural studies in its dogmatic moods preferred surface to depth.[3] But the trenchancy, good faith, and fresh intelligence of this instance was liberating, and the field responded.[4] "Just reading" proposed a return to literature's "surface," and so, despite its different program, it was welcomed by those who hope for a return to the literary—to what once was disparaged, and now is celebrated, as "form."[5] Both the disparagement and the recelebration were understandable.[6] From the 1930s to the 1980s, from new criticism to deconstruction, pretty much everyone claimed that literature mediated not the world but (at most) itself—its desires, its logic and machinery, its conditions of possibility, and its limits—and that this reflexiveness was its special excellence and that of its practitioners. But giving literature a mastery so minuscule and absolute had trivialized it, sealed it from the world. In such airless weather, the return of "history," back in the 1980s and 1990s, stirred a breeze. A new historicism brought the chance to study literature's complicities and accidents, to treat it as the correlative, and sometimes the plaything, of power. This paradoxically revived it, gave it the world back again. But its successes were guaranteed in advance; it could not remain intriguing for long or long hold off the drift to "symptomatic reading."[7] For reasons I will sketch later, the search for symptoms is one ideal type of reading, and the point of gravity to which anything resembling it naturally drifts. Its constitutional earnestness is such that it can always find a symptom. Even the absence of symptoms can be symptomatic. (There seems to be nothing there? Of course there does!) These new historicisms worked to feel surprise at discovering the secrets books kept, even though they habitually discovered the same secrets. Looking back, one feels it must have taken some imaginative discipline to be surprised at literature's concealments, not only because they varied so little, but because concealment—hiding complexities behind the pose of simplicity, pointing in directions it pretends not to look—is what literature is best at. A work well made knows how to allow the pleasures of discovery; that is a part of its art. Symptomatic reading was bound to grow tedious: there is scant grace and scant satisfaction in snatching away what it is busy offering; scant satisfaction, too, in achieving what can always and by stipulation be achieved. So it is easy to understand the relief that criticism felt when it told itself it could stop.

~

All to the good. But then you find yourself reading ("just reading") a work that seems so absorbed in what it wants *not* to say that its very syntax twitches and snaps under the effort of control:

> But the king, unknown to me before this in his power, and his laws—from here on I feared him, and took the bit through my jaws.[8]

This is Adam Usk writing in 1401: a civil lawyer, once an academic, now advisor to Henry IV; then, shortly after writing these words, a papal bureaucrat and episcopal aspirant; and then a vagrant, schismatic, traitor, double agent, and improbable repatriate. (His life will be sketched in Chapter 1.) This sentence concludes a recollection of his Oxford days, when he led southern and western students in bloody conflict with the northerners. In the sentence preceding, he has stepped boldly into a public role (as "the principal leader and patron of the Welsh faction"), encountered retaliation ("we could not be stopped until many of our number had been indicted for treasonable insurrection"), and collapsed submissive ("we barely managed to gain our liberty from a jury before a king's justice"). In this one, he treats his belated recognition that punishment hurts as the achievement of adult political wisdom, and declares that in this new and chastened maturity he assumed an abject and painful discipline of silence. (Both the silence and the pain are suggested by the "bit" in his jaws.[9]) But even his silence proves inept: the sentence goes haywire, loses track of its grammatical object, and shuts the episode down before it can conclude. His profession of silence still conveys the sound of thoughts unspoken.[10]

That is Usk throughout. His bold starts tumble into anticlimax; he interrupts what he starts to tell and omits what he might have told. Just as he reaches what we want to know, he shrugs past it: "And so (why draw this out?) although Richard had fully deposed himself, the sentence of that deposition . . . was openly and publicly and solemnly recited."[11] *Why draw it out?* Because Usk had accompanied Bolingbroke's invasion and drunk in his tent, because he had helped prepare the deposition and accession, because as he watched Richard renounce the crown he knew everything that had been done to bring him to that point; because drawing it out might tell what only he could have told instead of what we already knew. Usk's nervous, second-guessing manner seems to be trying to tuck back what would spill out, aborting discourse in little panics. His editor calls Usk a "reticent" chronicler, anxious and withholding.[12] He lets us glimpse his intimacy with great men and great events: in the field with Bolingroke's invasion,[13] consulting with the putsch on its legal grounds for claiming the throne,[14] preparing a legal memorandum for the king,[15] dining with lords.[16] With maddening consistency, these moments shut down prematurely, or gutter into inconsequential anecdote. Watching these lurches of avoidance, you conceive suspicions for which there is no other cause, asking: what it is that he cannot tell?

Usk is reticent; so is the world he describes, flourishing portents that prove opaque or useless. While he was in Bruges, a fireball "larger than a large barrel" sailed through the air, hit a bell-tower, split, and dropped before the doors of Bardolf and Northumberland, "a very great presage of their ruin,"[17] but did not cause them to alter their disastrous plan or Usk to question its wisdom. Events apparently on the brink of speech only succeed in wearing the look (like Usk) of knowing more than they tell. He is an aficionado of literary oracles: he records the prophecies of "John of Bridlington" with a straight face,[18] the prophecies of Merlin likewise.[19] But instead of yielding knowledge, these lure him down rabbit-holes: reading the chronicle of Martinus Polonus while visiting a monastery,[20] he copies out a prophetic legend (226), which then reminds him of the Antichrist's advent (226-28), which in turn leads him to copy one hundred fifty-two verses on the "Fifteen Signs of Doomsday" (228-36). By that time, the narrative occasion has rather lapsed.

When Usk enters his chronicle, he comes shaded in isolation, trailing clouds of unspecified fear and desire. He wakes to the auditory aftertrace of a nightmare:

> On my soul, the night before, a voice woke me from from my sleep, sounding in my ears, "On my back the sinners built &c.," "The just Lord &c.," as in the Psalm, "Oft have they fought." This led me to wake fearing that some misfortune would befall me that day, and I fearfully committed myself especially to the guidance of the Holy Ghost.[21]

And he wanders at night to savor bitter similitudes:

> I lodged near the papal palace, and often studied the ways of the wolves and dogs, rousing myself of a night for the purpose. The dogs would bark, standing at the doors to protect their masters' houses, and the wolves would pick off the smaller ones as prey even from the midst of the larger. When they were

> carried off, they hoped to be defended by these larger ones, and so cried the more powerfully; the latter would bark more loudly from their places but bestir themselves not at all. And I reflected that this is just the sort of league that obtains between the strong ones of the country and exiles in foreign woods.[22]

It is easy enough to infer what these are about: the dream in the first passage woke him to a day that saw initiatives bruited in parliament against Welshmen like himself, and the Roman dogs in the second reminded him of English ill-treatment abroad. These inferences, however, explain everything but what needs explaining, the chilly and tight-lipped half-disclosure.

What is his secret? You might guess that it would be the frenzied violence of the political regime he helped install: its tenuous and unconvinced gestures at legitimacy, its cynicism, its casual savagery. These, we have been told, are the open secrets no one felt he could tell in Lancastrian England. But the chronicle tells them as matter of common knowledge:

> [1399:] [Bolingbroke] proclaimed that while his army would head for Chester, he would spare the people and the countryside, since they had made their submission to him. . . . But he wasted it completely, sparing neither field nor crop.[23]
>
> [1400:] Many found with them were led to Oxford, and there they were hanged and beheaded. I saw their corpses, dismembered like the bodies of animals taken in the hunt, brought to London—some in bags, some on poles slung between two men's shoulders—and then pickled in brine.[24]
>
> [1402:] On Mardi Gras, one William Clerk . . . , deprived first of his tongue, because he had spoken against the king (he put these things on others) and second of his hand, with which he had written them, and third, by the penalty of talion, because he did not prove his false declarations, at the Tower is beheaded.[25]

Violence is no secret. Indeed, it is so common that in these episodes it starts to look like the screen: they end so abruptly as to suggest that political mayhem and political bootstrapping are public facts, safe to recall, that block the view of some other nastiness behind. There is a flicker of subjective presence in excess of what is explained in these scenes, as also in the half-remembered echo of a dream and the insomnia that wanders out in the streets to rehearse its thoughts. He offers plenty of explanations, but the less his explanations explain, the more they look like camouflage.

~

Usk's chronicle is an eerie and aversive and captivating work. Reading its surfaces *as* surfaces cannot do much with its rustle of hasty concealment: you cannot intelligently apprehend them without asking what secret they hide. But there is no punchline in which they reveal it: so willy-nilly you treat what you find there as symptoms pointing to what they do not mean to disclose.

Of course "surface" (if we like that metaphor) is concerned here, since one would not look for the book's secret if his book itself did not suggest on its surface that one should. Forgive the obvious point, but if a symptom appears, it appears there. At the same time, the metaphor itself is incautious: language of surface and depth can describe something everyone can recognize, but cannot help in understanding how it works. Medieval theory spoke better, not of a surface, but of a literal sense—a sense that is made, *constructed* as the allegorical senses had to be. The clue that something nonliteral, allegory or symptom depending on the period and temper of the exegete, awaits discovery must be a property of the work's design even if it is not itself designed. Literary criticism has the tools to isolate how a work asks its reader to look beyond what it tells, by what devices it does and with what effects; literary description can help trace what shape an explanation would need before it could settle what the mystery unsettles. The narrative secret has long been recognized as a routine device of composition;[26] even if the presence of *this* secret is only inadvertently betrayed, criticism can describe the conditions of it.

~

In fact, criticism's recent cultivation of "surface" and its recent cultivation of "form" alike have the effect of showing how many features new-critical and deconstructive and psychoanalytic readings shared with the historicist readings that tried to displace them. One of these is a confidence that the ambitions and worries and desires of literary criticism are interesting. You don't come by that confidence so frequently now. It is touching to look back on a time when critics could choose titles bespeaking a heroic self-conception: *Criticism in the Wilderness*, "The Critic as Host," *Agon*, *The Reach of Criticism*, *The Critical Difference*. This self-admiration was often noted and mocked by older, more conservative critics in the 1970s and 1980s; but then their generation had assumed "A Burden for Critics," deployed an *Armed Vision*, assumed custody of *The Liberal Imagination*. The conviction that criticism was a captivating topic was not invented in the 1970s. But it is not certain that it has survived into the 2010s. If we look at the intensity of the old debates—should we read surfaces? should we seek symptoms?—and then look by contrast at the relatively painless way "surface reading" has assumed a place in our routines, the question most apt to suggest itself is not, What can we learn from the intense self-contemplation of literary criticism?, but What is it about literary criticism that keeps such options alive? Followed far enough, this leads to the further question, What kind of knowledge does criticism discover?

Usk proves useful as a sort of laboratory in which the desires of scholarly inquiry can be isolated and observed as they existed, not just before literary criticism began to cultivate that heroic self-regard, but before it was conceived as a discipline. He provokes interpretative desires (the wish to find the secret, the wish to declare that there is no secret, the wish to ignore the secret or to specify the mechanisms by which its presence is announced); he plays with these desires; but he also doubles them, performs within his narrative the analytic moves that literary criticism would centuries later preen itself on mastering. His vague portentousness mimes in advance the conviction that there is a secret that belongs to no one in particular, that is simply history's adventitious product. He anticipates, introjects, and performs as melodrama the critical moods that treat an impersonal secrecy as ideology's fleeting glance at itself. For that is precisely what his book seems to tease with. My first chapter offers a schematic instance. There is one fact about Usk's career as an ambitious ecclesiastic, a fact now solidly established, that he passes over unmentioned. This has been attractively advanced as a candidate for Usk's secret; but it can be shown that it is not that secret. Subsequent chapters pursue evidence that seems always to remain a step ahead of investigation. These chapters discover a number of things undiscovered before now both in Usk's chronicle and in the events it chronicled. Not least of these things is that the work itself offers a kind of theory of secrecy as such—or, more specifically, a theory of historical action and historiographical beauty, a theory built around secrecy, defeat, and compulsive desire, around plans and projections routinely disappointed but autistically resistant to the lessons of disappointment. The shame of defeat makes you resolve not to be mocked again by events, and therefore to judge more carefully, to seek out a fuller and more finely differentiated understanding of events and their courses. The predictive and prescriptive conclusions sought in history are lessons history proves unable to teach; but so is the lesson that such lessons cannot be learned. The hope that a historical understanding refined enough may be "equipment for living" comes to look naive, unequal to the real cunning of history; but then the idea that history is complex proves to be more naive still, since it turns out that events defeat knowledge not by their cunning but by their crudity and obviousness.

As a theory meant to account for historical action or historical reading, this is evidently preposterous, but there is no suggestion that it is meant to account for them. It is left to be discovered in the action of the chronicle, which is not an evidentiary dossier on its behalf but a sequence of narrative and descriptive effects orchestrated by it. At its heart is not an idea but a mechanism for producing sensation. Usk has noticed how reading, writing, and action all involve habits of forecast: forays of anticipation and conjecture navigate the present sentence or present circumstances with guesses at what should follow. Both historiography and prophecy magnify this habit into observability and show it to be the victim of its own desires. Usk's prose demands these forays, and then turns them against the mind that makes them: his prose works its effects by an obviousness it persuades readers not to credit, so that it can surprise and shame them with what they already know. By these means he renews rhetorical habits that seem dead and formulaic, turns the excess that frequently drains rhetoric of its emotional effect into a paradoxical source of such effect, stunning by the sheer oversupply of its premeditation.

That is one reason I chose Usk: by these means he calls criticism to account in one of its most casual and confident maneuvers, asking on what grounds we can conclude that an author has *not* foreseen our conclusion and that we learn about him what he does not know about himself. He coaxes out our most unwary critical moves and mirrors them back to us.

There is a second reason I chose Usk: my enthusiasm for his literary genius: a genius constrained, unsubtle, unpleasant, imperfectly disciplined, and indisputably minor, but genius all the same. In place of the information we might have hoped for from a figure so well placed, we get feints, flashes of garish ornament, narrative culs-de-sac, sudden plangencies, theatrical sighs, moans of dire but vague distress. The stark tones he uses to paint a world supplied with intense feelings but not with selves to feel them and his pointless implicit theory of history together create a kind of art. Its range of resources is limited—formal and acoustic patternings, the transient and unanchorable moods they float, their forms and notions of beauty, sensations evoked and the devices evoking them, aesthetic models inherited and aesthetic models confected—but it pushes them as far as they will go. And I will try to insist on the importance of the fact that these are things we can *know* about Usk: the act of writing, its products, and their aesthetic properties are as real as, though not realer than, laws and institutions; they also are as concrete, as finite, as local in their production and consumption, and therefore as historical.

The body of commentary on Usk is strikingly intelligent and very, very small. Two names should be mentioned now. Andrew Galloway's pages on Adam Usk constitute by degrees of magnitude the most intelligent literary comment on this work; he alone has appreciated its unsettling stylistic accomplishment.[27] Inevitably I disagree with him about almost everything, but his trenchancy and independent-mindedness produce literary-historical description at its best, and illustrate the dignity of that act. To the prolific and exacting Chris Given-Wilson, every scholar of Usk (and of late-medieval England) is in debt. His edition of the chronicle is exemplary in all dimensions. His facing translation, in the tradition of Southern's Eadmer and Butler's Jocelin, avoids awkward and literalized forms for an elegant recreation of sense and tone. There are miraculously few mistakes and fudges. Anyone wanting to read Usk in translation should use it, but it is, speaking strictly and without irony, too good for my purposes. I stick to pedantically literal translations of my own.

~

A note on quotations. Because Usk's orthography is consistent and interestingly eccentric, I give quotations from his chronicle just as they appear in Given-Wilson's edition. Latin quotations from all other sources are silently regularized, replacing consonantal *i* and *u* with *j* and *v*, "nichil" with "nihil," "eciam" with "etiam," and so on; and sometimes they are silently repointed for clarity. All translations not expressly attributed are mine. I use anglicized or otherwise adapted forms of such foreign names as conventionally have them, especially Welsh ones; hence "Glendower" and not "Glyn Dŵr," just as "Rome" and not "Roma"—indeed the more so, as I know no Welsh.

Chapter 1

The First Secret

I have said that Adam Usk seems to keep a secret, and I have proposed to look for it. One answer has anticipated me. Independently and almost simultaneously, two scholars (mentioned at the end of the Introduction) discovered that Usk omitted from his story an important autobiographical detail. One of them, Andrew Galloway, has brilliantly defined the curious tonal effects of Usk's prose:

> By turns, his Chronicle reeks of pride, rebellious criticism, guilt, and penance, especially the last. The literal social meanings and bases of his penitential moments are, however, blurred in favor of delineating the writer's penitential posture abstracted from political choices and experiences.[1]

And he has explained them as effects of a secret from which Usk would deflect our attention: schism and treason. In midlife, this faithful servant of the English king and the Roman pope transferred his allegiance to the antipope at Avignon and bet on his king's defeat at the hands of Owen Glendower's Welsh rebels.[2] The shame of his pointless treachery, Galloway argues, produces a dissociating guilt; this guilt in turn picks out the writer in a beam of intense but unspecific responsibility whose glare obscures his real defections.

If this indeed were the secret behind Usk's discursive hiccups, then we could stop here, but it is not. Neither his gloomy comments on the schism nor his tics of style derive from his dalliance with Avignon. More than that, though he conspicuously neglects to report this dalliance, he conspicuously neglects to hide it as well. Explaining why this secret is not "Adam Usk's secret," and indeed is no secret at all, offers a neat occasion to summarize the known facts of his life and of his chronicle's composition.

~

Usk began writing it in 1401.[3] From the parish of St. Mary's, Usk, in Wales, which supplied his cognomen (he also was "Adam Porter"),[4] he had built a successful career on patronage and education. Edmund Mortimer, earl of March, sent him to Oxford,[5] where he studied the learned laws and began briskly swapping benefices.[6] Early on, in 1381, he sought commission as a notary at the hands of Pileus de Prata, cardinal-priest of St. Praxed's, who was in England that spring.[7] In 1387, *extraordinarius* in canon law at Oxford, he saw the appellant lords march past after the battle at Radcot Bridge.[8] He took his degree in civil law by about 1393, and held the chair in that subject until 1395, when he resigned it to Henry Chichele.[9] He practiced as advocate in the court of chivalry and in the archbishop of Canterbury's consistory court;[10] Archbishop Arundel replaced Mortimer as his primary hope of preferment.[11] Usk's presence in the 1397 parliament (presumably in Arundel's entourage), his service on various commissions,[12] and the rank of his clients[13] show his prominence at this time. His service at Henry IV's accession shows it more dramatically: Usk, who had joined Bolingbroke and Arundel when they returned to England, accompanied them on the campaign from Ravenspur to Bristol, then served among those "bishops and doctors" charged with determining the grounds on which Bolingbroke would claim the throne. After the accession, he continued consulting for the king,[14] and continued to practice in Chivalry and the Arches.[15] His prominence at this time is revealed also by the occasions on which he could embarrass himself: he makes a false step in conversation with the ambassadors of Rupert of Bavaria, the new emperor, with Bishop Trefnant standing at his elbow.[16]

At this high point in his career, Usk began writing his chronicle. He wrote quickly. This point will be important; it is worth describing the unique manuscript in which it survives.

In a will dated 20 January 1430 and proved on 26 March that year, Usk left to his kinsman Edward ap Adam a copy of Higden's *Polychronicon*, most of which survives as British Library MS Additional 10104.[17] Higden's compilation had driven its rivals from the field of universal history in late fourteenth-century England;[18] it is an utterly unsurprising book for a civilian like Usk to have owned.[19] It survives now in over a hundred manuscripts; in the early fifteenth century, there must have been thousands. As the work circulated, it accumulated continuations carrying its narrative forward from the 1340s where Higden had left it. Usk's copy included what John Taylor calls the (C) continuation, bringing the narrative to the death of Edward III; in Usk's copy, this extends to fol. 154.[20] On the remainder of the final gathering, and on another gathering never bound with the volume—34 folios altogether—is Usk's continuation of the (C) continuation, beginning in 1377 with Richard II's accession and continuing, though only desultorily after 1414, through the middle of 1421.[21] His portion, what we call "the chronicle of Adam Usk," is formally distinguished from Higden's *Polychronicon* and the (C) continuation only by the intervention of a blank page.[22]

These leaves comprise the fair copy of his manuscript, made in that volume of the *Polychronicon* by scribes in his employ. They let us follow the rhythm of his career and of his authorship closely through 1401-2.[23] His scribes worked from written drafts.[24] Combined with the sequence of their hands, anticipatory references to future events and to passages later in the chronicle show that each campaign of composition took place immediately after the events reported, and was copied immediately as well.[25] The first scribe copied a long section of just over sixteen leaves (thirty-three manuscript pages, yielding sixty-two pages in the printed edition) that report events through Henry IV's second parliament in March 1401. The first sentence of this section assumes Richard's fall from power on 30 September 1399, and its second page (155v) seems to speak of Richard's death sometime in early 1400;[26] these leaves anticipate later events, but none later than 10 March 1401, so that the writing of this section can be dated to a period of at most about three months at the beginning of that year. The second scribe's work begins with report of the earl of Warwick's death, on 1 April 1401; these pages look back at one point to an event that transpired on 20 March and forward to one around 30 June.[27] This section covers only about three manuscript pages, and the next section, only a few lines of text, reports the return to France of Richard's queen Isabella on 28 July, while the next scribe copies a little less than a manuscript page, with events beginning in "autumn" and concluding apparently in late October. And so on. It is therefore possible to locate his composition during this period with some precision.

He draws this period formally to a close. On fol. 172b, a passage copied by the sixth of his scribes announces a new undertaking. He surveys his life to that point, and addresses God, who

> granted me, from the infinite riches of your grace, to complete my studies at Oxford, and the three-year course of the doctorate and the seven years' service as advocate in the court at Canterbury, a position both honorable and beneficial, and who have helped me in all other duties of mine whatever, from my youth right up to my old age and decrepitude.

(He was about fifty.) He asks consolation in

> my departure for Rome, along with my journey there and also my return to the land of my desire, undertaken so as to be counted among the number either of the advocates or of the auditors, . . . to your honor and glory and to the flourishing of both the interior and the exterior man.[28]

Twelve years would elapse before he wrote the next sentence, which looks back on that journey as something long past:

> Why delay? On the eleventh kalends of March in the year of our Lord 1401 [= 19 February 1402], the compiler of these presents, as he had purposed with God's permission, having boarded ship in London at Billingsgate, with a favorable wind blowing and the sea plowed up with the rudder . . . directing his steps toward Rome, crossed to land within a single natural day.[29]

So in 1402, Usk left for Rome, and did not resume writing his chronicle until he found himself back in England, in 1414.[30]

Everything through his farewell to England, everything before the story of his Roman journey, was written before Usk left England on 19 February 1402. He left for Rome to seek the next, highly plausible step in advancement, "to be counted among the number either of the advocates or of the auditors." This ambition was fulfilled on arrival: "within two weeks" he was "chaplain to the pope and auditor of the sacred palace. To him"—that is, to Usk, who often refers to himself in the third person as "the compiler (or notator) of these presents"—"the pope himself, within eight days, committed thirty great cases that had been delated to him, to be brought to a close by his application."[31] It has been suggested that Usk left England in haste and under a shadow. But he was following a path familiar to ecclesiastical careerists.[32] Adam Orleton had been auditor of the palace under Pope John XXII, and was provided to the see of Hereford in 1317 and translated to Winchester ten years later; Usk, we will see, thought about Orleton's successes.[33] There were contemporary instances. In summer 1398, the pope provided to the see of Bangor first Lewis Aber and then, when that provision was blocked, Richard Young, both auditors.[34] Richard Scrope, auditor of the palace in the mid-1380s but in 1398 the archbishop of York, owed his spectacular rise to this route.[35] It had its risks: the crown's jealousy over episcopal appointments and the statute of provisors meant that the pope's provision might be resisted, and his candidate resented.[36] But it was by no means a path taken only by those under cloud of suspicion: Andrew Barret, who Harvey suggests must have been trusted by Richard II, received Llandaff in 1395, after a decade's service as auditor in the Rota; and Henry Bowet's provision from curial service to Bath and Wells in 1401 was evidently not displeasing to Henry IV, on whose council he, like Young, regularly sat.[37] Some of these men later flourished a pert independence, and Scrope died a rebel. But what they did after receiving the pallium shows the confidence of action their networks of affiliation allowed them to assume. The aspiring bishop could do worse in those days, and for centuries after: four hundred years later, Lacordaire declined appointment to the Rota lest he be stranded as a church bureaucrat.[38] Usk asked nothing better than to be so stranded.

Once in place, he was one of about a dozen to whom appeals to the pope could be delegated. Their decisions were gathered as precedents that lived in the personal libraries of canonists and civilians.[39] Usk's judicial work would largely have involved contested benefices and provisions and appeals from diocesan rulings. Auditors could influence provisions: when the bishop of London died, they as a body nominated his successor, and the pope initially agreed.[40] Rules against influence-peddling and conflict of interest show they had influence to peddle. So does the oath of secrecy they took, which made the keeping of secrets a defining virtue of their post.[41] And so does the fury of gossip and faction that plagued the institution.[42] Auditors were visible, influential: one might find himself giving the initial sermon at a papal election and processing in a papal coronation.[43] The auditors were papal chaplains ex officio, and Usk's recollections of the ceremonies at which he assisted show how intimately he worked with the pope: in 1405, he received at Candlemas white candles "for the king and queen of England"; he held the ashes for the pope on Ash Wednesday, and later, for the pope's annual Easter distribution of the *agnus Dei* wax ("lambs, made of white wax and blessed"), he "held the basin, so often emptied, and kept for my own those which remained at the end."[44] The pope teased him,[45] and once offered use of his personal physician.[46] He also offered patronage: Boniface IX and Innocent VII, he says, both tried to make him bishop in 1404.[47] He had taken a good professional path like other Englishmen distinguished in the learned laws.

Both provisions failed. Boniface tried providing him to Hereford on John Trefnant's death, but—as usual, he names himself in the third person—

> through the envy of the English who resisted this and slandered him with poisonous letters to the king (from which he suffered great misfortunes by land and sea for four years, an exile), what he carried away was not promotion but abasement and the extremest poverty, deprived of his benefices and goods, among foreigners, like Joseph, and hearing a language he did not understand—

"although," he concludes, "he was rewarded with gold for his counsel."[48] (We will hear more about all this.) Then Innocent agreed to the auditors' suggestion that Usk be provided to replace Guy Moon at St. David's.[49] That, too, failed:

> But when this business became known, some people—who loudly complained to the king and to the cardinals holding English benefices, threatening these latter that, if they permitted this, they would lose those benefices because of the king's anger—even swore that the king should send the compiler of these matters to prison and the gallows. They also prohibited merchants from providing me money, under pain of their partners' expulsion from England. This was the great obstacle to the business, which was thus quashed.[50]

Obviously he has left something out. What was said against him in England, and why? Later, in his profitable French "exile," we see him keeping company with Lord Bardolf and the earl of Northumberland, rebels against Henry and allies of Glendower; the thought may have struck observers that his sympathies were suspect.[51] But the cadence of detail suggests something more humdrum. After mentioning the failure of his provision to Hereford, he says that "in the meantime" (*interim*) parliament had straitened sanctions in the Statute of Provisors, which reserved for the king and lords presentation to benefices.[52] It was not a good moment for papal provision, or for deciding cases in the rota about collations of benefices reserved to the pope.[53] When he wrote the king protesting "the detraction practiced by the envious,"[54] he recalls that he had left for Rome with Henry's permission, *obtenta licencia*. (Just before he left, two mainpernors pledged that he would seek nothing against Provisors.[55]) He recalls to the king his earlier service, warns him against detractors, seeks advancement—and, transparently, tries to excuse his accepting the auditorship, by insisting that the position was unpaid, taken after prayerful consideration and in hopes of being useful to his king.[56]

These are minor obscurities. What follows, the story of a career upended, is obscurer still. During the Roman riot of August 1405, his banker skipped town,[57] and the next summer, financially broken by this embezzlement and by "the ingratitude of friends, as will be told below" (it never is), Usk crossed the Alps.[58] He tells little of how he occupied himself. He entered France, and traveled through Dijon, Champagne, Paris, Amiens, and Bruges; warned to avoid England "because the king was threatening my death," he awaited assistance for two years, "though in vain."[59] His benefices were granted to others. He traveled more ("Flanders, France, Normandy, Brittany"), did legal piece-work ("I passed through lands, in counsel to many bishops, abbots, and noblemen, earning enough from that"); he was twice cheated and robbed ("even my trousers"), but still prospered, receiving on the same day as his disastrous loss an ample "one hundred twenty crowns."[60] He browsed monastery libraries and took notes; he mixed with company of doubtful utility.[61] Finally he returned to England on the most disadvantageous terms:

> And so the compiler of these matters swore before the [Lancaster] king of arms that he would pretend to be Owen

> [Glendower]'s man and pass with his people to him in Wales; from there, he would seize the opportunity to defect from him to my Lord of Powys, under whose protection he would await the king's pardon. And thus it happened; and this oath saved his life.[62]

He hid in forests, "tortured by many great dangers . . . , and suffering several sleepless nights in fear of hostile attack";[63] safe-conduct finally in hand, he left Glendower "secretly at night." He made a chaplain's pathetic living at the manor of Welshpool, saying Mass for food, "unvisited by my ungrateful kin and former friends; and, God knows, as distressed in circumstances as I was in my heart."[64] In 1411, at the instance of Lord Powys and David Holbach, the king pardoned him.[65] In England, "as if born anew," he reassembled some fragments of his career: "I began to recompose some little bit my state," though thankless protégés declined to return his favors.[66] Archbishop Arundel took him back into service; "servants, books, clothes, and hearth I reacquired, like a second Job—blessed be God," he adds idiotically, "eternally and beyond."[67] He started writing again. After accounts of Agincourt and Harfleur, the chronicle's episodes grow spotty, and end altogether with the aftermath of the Dauphin's slaughter of the English at Baugé in 1421. As noted, his will was dated in January of 1430 and proved in March; so in the early months of that year, he died an anticipated death.

~

That is what he tells. What he leaves out, as Galloway and Given-Wilson showed, can be quickly related. In 1407—between his mysterious departure from Rome to undertake itinerant lawyer's work and his move to England briefly to practice espionage—Usk received provision as bishop of Llandaff from the Avignon pope Benedict XIII, recognized only as a schismatic "anti-pope" by England and of course by the Roman pope whom Usk had served. Such reversals of allegiance were not unheard of during the papal schism: Cardinal Pileus de Prata, from whom the young Usk tried to receive notarial commission, himself left the Roman for the Avignonese adherence in the 1380s.[68] Given-Wilson confirms Usk's defection with other evidence, including a notation in Benedict's register and evidence that Usk had been declared traitor in England.[69] Appointment as Avignonese bishop of Llandaff was a merely speculative good: as long as Wales was under English dominion, the see would be occupied by the Roman adherent. Only if the French-Welsh alliance defeated England would he possess it, and so his acceptance of the see entailed allegiance to Glendower and treason against Henry IV.

For Galloway Usk's defection, with the unspecific guilt that seeps from it, is a symptom of the medieval intellectual's impossible self-understanding and consequent self-surveillance: a chronic and diffuse self-accusation by which Usk's place in the clerical rank isolates him simultaneously from it and everyone; his eerie "penitential" preoccupation with corruption and failure distract him from his more particular and unnerving treachery to pope and king. Galloway's essay culminates with a discussion of a long, mysterious passage; his precise sense of style and effect show themselves in its selection, and in his diagnosis of its motility and mystery. Galloway quotes the passage in full (in Maunde Thompson's translation, which is garishly beautiful) and so will I (in my own, which is not):

> *Two popes through .xxii. years.* One thing there is in these days which I relate with pain: that two popes, like a monster in nature, who for twenty-two years now have most impiously torn the seamless tunic of Christ (contrary to that passage in Solomon: "One is my dove"), have stirred up the world, with error of souls and various terrors of torment. And alas, if it is true that I now bring back to my memory, that passage of the Gospel, "You are the salt of the earth. But if the salt lose its savour, wherewith shall it be salted? It is good for nothing any more but to be cast out, and to be trodden on by men."[70]

> *Venality in the priesthood.* And so because of a priesthood grown venal, did not Christ, making a whip, cast out those buying and selling in the temple? And therefore I fear that, punished and ground down, we will be cast out from the priesthood, as I note that in the old covenant, after such venality had dishonored the priesthood, the cloud of smoke, the unquenchable fire, and the sweet savor ceased in the temple. But why draw it out? The Virgin Mother herself, according to Apocalypse, fled with her son to the desert from before the beast sitting on the throne. But here Plato orders me to be silent, since nothing is more certain than death, and nothing more uncertain than its hour.[71]
>
> *Adornments of the church at Usk.* And so (blessed be God) to the church of my origin, the church of Usk, now that I am learning to die, my memorial—a suitable missal, gradual, tropary, sequentiary, and antiphonal (all newly composed, with the new additions and notes), and a full set of vestments with three copes elegantly worked with my badge (of a naked man digging on a black field) commending me to the prayers of worshippers there—; this I leave. Further on, if God grants it, proposing to elaborate this same church with a more decorous reconstruction in honor of the Blessed Virgin;—but not thinking that this is to my praise, because I pray that this record of my foolishness here not be seen during my lifetime.[72]

Galloway observes that, in "the thoughts' slow funneling toward death," Usk erects a highly visible and very concrete object of criticism, the papal schism, and incorporates himself into that object while simultaneously diffusing it, first into generic critique and then into a still vaguer apocalyptic, finally evaporating specificity altogether in the penance of the private self. This reading is the best comment on Usk as a writer ever committed to print. But it claims that the passage "hints at political contexts that cannot be directly acknowledged": "its abrupt transitions and simmering attention to the Schism point us toward uncovering one more of those secrets and conflicts in Adam's intellectual professionalism that, in their cumulative rather than specific effect, produced his display of a penitential self divided from but continually coexisting with a politically and socially participatory self"—the secret in question being his Avignon allegiance, which Galloway now reveals.[73]

But the passage is even stranger than his discussion shows. These lines, so sure that they are afraid, cannot work out what they are afraid of: when they try to settle the fear on one object, it skitters off onto another. Usk worries that God will punish priestly sin, but he interrupts this reflection, first with a shrug that the point is too obvious to make ("But why draw it out?") and then with a shudder that it is too dangerous to risk ("Plato commands me to fall silent"). And then his explanation of that risk—Plato commands silence, "*since* nothing is more certain than death"—is evident nonsense: the hope of evading death in the short term, not the impossibility of evading it in the long term, would motivate prudential self-protection. The redoublings, motives avowed and then ducked, drive the suspicion of a secret even more deeply to some other dread still unrevealed: the spectacular non sequitur suggests that emergency tactics have engaged to draw the eye away from his fear, as if even revealing fear is a fearful thing. The tone settles on something Galloway thinks pablum, a form of anxiety so comfortably familiar that there is nothing pertinently anxious about it: "learning to die," mortification and amendment of life, repair and adornment of his parish church, and humility that ostentatiously flinches at their mention. It is hard to tell why this anxiety should be less trenchant than the others. Indeed, the reaction is identical: the final aversion from owning his gift to the church doubles back in the same panic of self-censorship that we saw before, fluttered by one of those syntactic disturbances that bespeak a failure of self-possession: the hope expressed of further bequests interrupts itself with the supervening hope that "the record of my foolishness here"—itself an awkward phrase to which we will return—will not be seen, and, in its haste to move on, forgets to dispense a main verb. Of course there is the secret of his schismatic apostasy; on that basis Galloway could insist that straying into the discourse of mortification tries to distract the reader from the secret being kept.

~

But if the schismatic adherence is his secret, Usk is inexplicably reckless about keeping it. He scatters clues by which readers could guess, and have guessed, his Welsh and Avignonese allegiances. His first editor, who knew nothing of the entry in Bishop Hallum's register, guessed that Usk supported Glendower; so did A. B. Emden, and so did R. R. Davies.[74] A history of the Welsh church guessed at the schismatic provision, and the *Fasti ecclesiae anglicanae* ambered that guess in its footnotes.[75] Presumably Galloway and Given-Wilson looked for evidence because they guessed it too. It is not just Usk's tone of persecuted Welshness and his unblushing ambition that raise the suspicion. He offers details that presuppose schismatic adherence, details that purposed concealment would be most alert to suppress. His assertion that while in territories under Avignon's sway he acquired "gold" from offering "counsel" suggests that he was undertaking representation of clients in the courts of the Avignon pope; the arrangement brokered with King Henry—that Usk should earn his pardon by spying on Glendower—is incomprehensible without supposing that everyone knew Glendower had reason to trust him. His purpose in supporting the Welsh cause is implied in how he abandoned it: "In the end, the earl [of Northumberland] was induced to return to Scotland and from there to England, with seals devised to deceive him with the promise that he would have the reign for himself; he promised me great advancement to persuade me to return with him."[76] Though he says nothing about Benedict XIII or Llandaff or arrangements with the French, he openly assumes them. Active and anxious suppression of these facts would require something more systematic and purposeful, something more attentive than would allow hints to fall so carelessly. Secrets hidden this poorly are not secrets.

And of course they were not hidden. His apostasy and treason were known to the king; to Bishop Hallum; to the sheriff of Wiltshire, and to those who heard him proclaim Usk's forfeiture; to Adam atte Hull and Robert Webbe, distrained for tithes now forfeit;[77] to the Lancaster king of arms, to Robert Holbach and the lord of Powys.[78] His adherence to Glendower had been an open secret for years: William Lovell had in 1404 warned a correspondent in England against using Usk as a curial contact since "he is not wholly pure of Glendower, and so neither in this nor in any business do we generally hold converse with him."[79] Indeed, it is hard to imagine how silence might benefit him, since by the time he wrote he had already suffered and recovered from the consequences of his defection. Both Given-Wilson and Galloway appreciate the problem, suggesting that what he evades is not detection but shame. But then he points straight at the shame. Much of this will come to our attention later,[80] but we see an instance of it in the desire, expressed in the passage just discussed, to withhold from circulation this "record of his foolishness here."

~

Now one could object that that is just the suspicious thing: calling our attention to a shame it is hard to take seriously deflects that attention to a shame rather easier to credit: it points toward "one more of those secrets," his cynical adherence to Avignon.

But the passage about the papal schism cannot be explained by his defection to Avignon, because it was written in 1402, before his departure for Rome, and long before his defection to Avignon, in the period when he hoped reasonably to become a bishop of the Roman allegiance. So his schism, even if concealed, could not explain the feeling of concealment in passages written years before it. Shifts are of course available to save the appearances. One might allow that perhaps Usk fostered a hearty allegiance to the Welsh cause even as he served its English lord, an allegiance he felt as presentiment of the defection that would come;[81] or that the very nature of ambition for an intellectual worker in this milieu made him a producer who needed to hawk his wares. But even if we adopt some such suggestion, the strategy it describes can be called private, but, without some cause for deliberate suppression, hardly "secret," and can hardly explain bustles of nervous concealment.

Finding nothing, we are thrown back on the suspicions generated by the narrative gaps Usk puts on display, the rhetorical abruptions that arrest his story in mid-course and avow an unexplained silence, his contradictions—that is, on rhetorical resources the work makes use of, rather than on some content it tries to suppress. Any occlusions we find will have to be inferred from the work itself—from its apparent (and therefore visible) *acts* of occlusion.

~

There is one secret, Usk's first as a chronicler, that we do know for certain, though it prompts rather than ends my inquiry. That is the chronicle itself. "I pray that this record of my foolishness here not be seen during my lifetime": the assertion means that his *Polychronicon* continuation is to remain secret while he lives. There is every reason to think that he means it.[82] Galloway notices this as well, of course, and elsewhere calls Usk's chronicle "perhaps the first 'secret history' since Procopius."[83] This is more a witty description than an identification, since Usk would not have heard of Procopius.[84] But he needn't have. A practice that in the nature of the case is only fractionally documented was the private compilation of a manuscript in which one would record one's thoughts for oneself. For obvious reasons, these usually did not enjoy fame. One great instance in the Latin tradition was the spiritual commonplace-book of Guigo, first prior of the Chartreuse; his most recent editor thinks that Guigo must have foreseen a posthumous readership, but he made no provision for it, and both the unframed state of the text and its very narrow circulation attest to its authentically private function.[85] In the early seventeenth century, Augustine Baker, the English Benedictine, composed a *Secretum* whose name he explains: "the present treatise of mine is termed

'Secretum' and to be imparted but to few and those such as may be fitting to know of such secrets."[86] Another specimen, and the probable source of Baker's title, was a late medieval cause célèbre. In mid-career, Petrarch wrote a brilliant, severe dialogue with himself, which he called *Secretum meum*: "you, my little book, will flee the press of men and remain contentedly with me, not forgetting your name—for you are *my secret*, and that is what you shall be called."[87] Only hints of the work leaked during his lifetime; it was read only after his death, but read widely then.[88] There is even a late Middle English translation, after Usk's time.[89] The moralizing lament Usk utters in the passage under discussion—"nil sit cercius morte, nil incercius hora mortis," "nothing is more certain than death, nothing more uncertain than the hour of death"—is used by Petrarch in almost precisely the same form; though the sharing of a commonplace so common is no proof of anything.[90] There is no improbability in thinking that Usk might have known this work. Assuming that he did would yield a potential source for Usk's interest in depicting a compulsion to do what one knows, even while doing it, ought to be left undone; this interest we will discuss later.[91] There is still less improbability that he knew *of* Petrarch's *Secretum*; knowledge of that would show a source for the idea of conceiving a book as a secret reserved to oneself, something that would be circulated only after his death.

The one is possible, the other more possible still. But there simply is no evidence for either, no evidence that he had read or that he had heard of Petrarch's work. Nor is there need for such evidence. Whether he had some model before his eyes makes little difference. If we credit his remark, then Usk's first secret is not a fact that his book conceals—even the fact of his schismatic and treacherous apostasy—but the book itself, the *secretum* that would (as Petrarch puts it) "remain with him" for the course of his life, to "recall in obscurity what in obscurity was said." The *Secretum* gives Petrarch his place of retreat from a literary life perpetually on view to a public, a life ostentatiously lived in literary exchange with others; and it offers a private space where he can speak clearly with himself about just that ostentation. Usk's "secret," the work meant for his eyes alone, confirms the solitariness of the life he portrays, and throws the self-consciousness of his isolation into relief. He does not portray a life lived in any sense with others. Friends are mentioned only after they have betrayed him;[92] there is gratitude to patrons, and piety toward his parish church, but no confidences and no expectation of confidants. The work does not imagine that secrets might be entrusted to anyone.

But this circumstance has a consequence more obvious and flat-footed than this: if Usk meant to keep his chronicle a *secretum* during his own life, then provident self-protection cannot explain secrets kept *in and from* the chronicle, unless he feared a threat which was threatening indeed, dire and near to hand. The next chapter considers such a possibility.

Chapter 2

The Story of William Clerk

In the last chapter, something that looked like a secret Usk had deliberately concealed proved to be written all over his book, a treacherous and self-aggrandizing act he had reason to regret but not to hide. Deeds done, however, are not the only cause of guilt. Might Usk's secret have to do not with something he had done, but with something he could too easily do, or even something he knew and could too easily say? Writers who fear censorship come to regard their own pages with the censor's eye.[1]

Under the year 1401, Usk tells of an unlucky conversation in which John Trefnant, bishop of Hereford, silenced him. Wenzel IV, king of Bohemia, had been deposed as German emperor, and Rupert of Bavaria substituted for him. The new emperor sent "solemn ambassadors" to England in hopes of a marriage alliance, and

> to these I said privately, "Surely the King of Bohemia, once elected, holds the empire? So whence this new election of yours, when the first has not been quashed?" One great clerk among them answered me, "Because he was useless, and was still uncrowned by the pope, the electors did this." Then I said, "According to the chapter *Venerabilem*, from *De lectionibus*, this function distinctly and solely pertains to the pope, because

> he transferred the empire from the Greeks to the Germans."
> Then the bishop of Hereford told me to be quiet.[2]

Trefnant intervened in chatter gone awry. Awry how? Those who have wondered have assumed that Usk offended the Germans,[3] but their "great clerk," unoffended, continued the conversation by sharing with him some witty verses ("in which I rejoice") on simony.[4] This obliviousness to offense suggests that the bishop's nervousness lay elsewhere.

The context shows where. Immediately preceding this paragraph is the story of William Clerk that I quoted in the introduction and here give in full:

> On Mardi Gras, one William Clerk—scribe of Canterbury, born in the county of Chester—having been condemned by the Court of Chivalry, and deprived first of his tongue, because he had spoken against the king (he put these things on others), and second of the hand with which he had written them, is, third, by the penalty of talion, because he did not prove his false declarations, at the Tower, beheaded.[5]

The connection with Usk's faux pas will emerge, but this passage brings its own problems. Those who have thought about it seem quietly to have agreed that this never happened, or at least that its report has been mangled beyond recovery. That Given-Wilson's impeccably documented edition does not trouble to footnote this paragraph silently classes it with absurd stuff like the birth of a two-tailed, two-headed calf.[6] Paul Strohm, commenting on this episode in passing, is circumspect about its reliability, allowing that it may be an "invention"; later he attributes composition of the chronicle to Usk's "later years."[7] Their doubts are easily understood because the story is improbable on its face. The Court of Chivalry had jurisdiction over matters arising from knightly service and the laws of war. Parliament, it is true, had complained for years that Chivalry habitually operated outside its sphere of competence, but these complaints concerned its tendency to become an alternative venue for lawsuits.[8] The Court of Chivalry did have competence over treasonable acts committed in England in open war by those of knightly status. But Clerk was a scribe, not a knight. Usk says that Clerk was executed for the crime of writing, which would make him the only man in late medieval England who was.

It is easy to suspect that the scene is fantasy, not only because it seems hard to credit, but also because it is structured as fantasy. What its details of date and venue claim for historicity, its symmetry and grim compression seem to deny. His trial, torture, and death—William Clerk's entire existence in public history—take one sentence, whose verb-final construction labors to sustain a merely syntactical suspense. The threefold action is at once clinical and fairy-tale: first (*primo*) amputation of tongue, next (*secundo*) hand, and then (*tercio*) head. The few concrete details emerge with startling clarity from an account otherwise cloudy as a parable. Clerk's members, seen in sharp focus at the moment of their removal, are all that is seen; he becomes a bodily form only during his disassembly. His name suggests occupation and status, redundantly confirmed by his identification as "scribe"; the only biographical detail is his Cheshire origin, which has its own force. There is a chilling artfulness in this. As Strohm shows, you could hardly find a better "disciplinary parable": the victim, from Ricardian Cheshire, has been "dangerously placed" in Canterbury; the gruesome death of a "Clerk" is therefore a shot across the bow "of an entire lettered class."[9]

Clerk's execution and Usk's interview with the Bavarians have just one point of connection: both involve assertions about kingship and legitimacy peremptorily censored. Clerk's execution, spare and incredible, imparts to Trefnant's rebuke its tang of urgency: indiscretions on such topics can be costly. Strohm treats the story as a Lancastrian dream of judicial preemption with "much to offer a regime interested in silencing opposition and wielding punishment theatrically," though each such preemption inadvertently hosts alternative possibilities.[10] So Clerk's quick brutal death begins to look like Lancastrian desire exposed as a continual risk to

Lancastrian ideology itself, precipitated into painful awareness in Usk's subjective experience of it. Writing as a "Lancastrian partisan," perhaps, Usk's account of himself shows how easily the fantasies of discipline and punishment generate *even in oneself* the thoughts that solicit punishment: he who sharpens the sword of torture may be preparing it for his own neck, when in the press of speech he utters notions the preparation itself has engendered. The story's sheer improbability then marks its fantastical condensation of desires and fears, in which the régime could convince itself that blood spilled theatrically enough and often enough would somehow legitimate it, somehow argue strength rather than weakness.

But the story is not fantastical. Clerk's death happened, and the artifice of the passage reveals something more chilling than the lurid description of a fantasized death: the lurid description of a real one.

Reasons for skepticism vanish on inspection. No entropic memory from "later years," this was written at most within a year of the alleged event (it appears in the section Usk composed before leaving England in February 1402), and probably within four months.[11] Of course its difficulties inhere, and one might therefore dismiss it as a lie, a distortion, a fantasy embroidered around some more plausible event ignorantly apprehended. But Adam Usk was one of the few men in England at this time to whom these explanations do not apply: were he lying, distorting, or fantasizing, he could have done better. For Chivalry was a court of civil law, where Usk practiced;[12] by June, within about a couple of months of William Clerk's alleged case, he represented Lord Grey of Ruthin in a suit brought there; Usk first mentions it just before telling Clerk's story.[13] His proximity to the case, his access to routinely good information, and his expertise in civil law make such explanations inefficient: it is not a story he would have invented deliberately or inadvertently. The curiosities of this case, far from disauthenticating what he writes, do the reverse.

These details clarify and bolster Usk's account. Others are clarified by it.[14] Usk dates the trial to Mardi Gras, which in 1401 fell on 15 February. Eleven days earlier, on 4 February, the earl of Northumberland was commissioned to hear and determine "divers unaccustomed cases and business concerning the estate, fame and condition of the king's person and the dignity of the crown, although they are such that by their nature they cannot be discussed or determined by pretext of the office of constable or by the common law of the realm but only by the king's hearing or permission."[15] Northumberland was constable, and Chivalry therefore his court; this commission prescribes the very irregularities that have made Clerk's execution by that court shortly after seem improbable. Parliament was at that point in session, adjourning finally on March 10. Before adjournment, a common petition complained of grave abuses by which the Court of Chivalry was imprisoning men over whom it had no jurisdiction. We are now talking about criminal matters: the complaint was that the Court of Chivalry was both holding men in emergency detention (which the grammar implies would have been in itself grounds for complaint) and making them answer appeals, trying and sentencing on criminal charges.[16] Put Usk's account together with the parliamentary petition, and it seems that Henry turned to the Court of Chivalry to punish criticism it pleased him to regard as treasonable; he got what he asked for; but he then granted a parliamentary request that Chivalry not again be used in this way. As far we know, it was not so used again.

The execution of William Clerk, scribe of Canterbury, should be accepted as historical fact.

~

The previous chapter started with what seemed clear and deliberate omission of a pertinent fact, but watched the structure of concealment melt and film into insubstantiality. This one started with a story whose power lay in its menacing unreality, but has watched it become real. The result is the same. As inquiry feels back along the clues trailed by Usk's narration and builds context around it, it becomes less plausibly a symptom of Lancastrian regulatory lust or of anything else. But while the factuality of Clerk's history must weaken any thought that it sprang from fantasy, it could strengthen the thought that other fears sprang from it. We may ask it some questions.

First: Why did Henry turn to the Court of Chivalry in this case, and why did it provoke opposition? Compare an event four years later. In the wake of the 1405 rebellion, several of the accused were tried and executed by Chivalry. These trials provoked no opposition: no one disputed that the men thus dispatched were in open rebellion,[17] and in such an emergency the Court of Chivalry must have seemed appropriately summary. It could convict peremptorily on notoriety, and on the king's record (a device for a time unavailable at common law).[18] The king could therefore direct the court to find that Archbishop Scrope's treason spoke for itself. But this case can suggest what might have led Henry to call on its services in different circumstances four years earlier. Despite the presumptive guilt of the archbishop, Henry could not persuade his own justices to try him; they could not judge a bishop, they said, and Henry turned to Chivalry when he failed to bend them.[19] This suggests the possibility that Henry sent William Clerk's case to Chivalry because he could not obtain conviction under the common law—not because of the defendant's rank, but because of some problem with the charge or its evidence.[20] The great statute of treasons (1352) had carefully defined the scope of treason prosecution: mere words of criticism, unless inciting or supporting harm meant to the king or his family, were not treason.[21] Henry had promised strict construction of this statute when he sought the throne, and thus found his hands briefly tied at common law. (He was working actively to free them at this time.)[22] But not in the Court of Chivalry, which was not constrained by the English statute and which therefore offered a move around its flank.[23]

Second: What was Clerk's crime, and why did Henry cash in chips to punish it? Usk says that Clerk was beheaded "by penalty of talion . . . because he had not proved his false accusations" against the king. Talion was the Roman principle that punished malicious false accusers with the sanctions they had sought against their victims.[24] Clerk, then, was accused of having written something that falsely charged the king with a capital crime. One assertion made about Henry in these years, which he treated with unremitting severity, fits this description.[25] According to the *Eulogium historiarum* (for our purposes it does not matter whether this happened), Henry confronted Roger or Richard Frisby, leader of some Franciscans who opposed his rule, and told him what he had told all England, that he was not a usurper, but a validly elected king. Frisby responded, "An election is null and void when a legitimate possessor is alive. And if he is not alive, you killed him. And if you killed him, you forfeit any title or right you may have to the kingdom."[26] To this, Henry replied, "By this head of mine, you will lose that head of yours."[27] Frisby's argument had two parts: if Richard is alive, no one can claim his throne, and if he is dead, then Henry, as traitor and murderer, forfeits any right to it.[28] Usk's mention of *talio* implies that William Clerk died because he had said and written a version of the latter, which is the best evidence of something then said about Henry that could be construed as charging him with a capital crime and therefore redound by talion on the accuser's head. Thus, Usk says, Clerk, failing to prove "his false accusations," suffered by talion the punishment to which the accusations, if proved, would theoretically have made Henry liable: if Henry had rebelled against and killed his rightful lord, then Henry was guilty of treasonable murder and deserved to die.

This makes clearer the connection in Usk's mind between this story and the rebuke by Bishop Trefnant that follows it: while Clerk's utterance echoes the second of Frisby's points against Henry IV, Usk's banter inadvertently echoes the first. Given-Wilson, as I have said, calls Usk "reticent," approaching candor but flinching from it, "anxious to steer a course between what he knew to be the truth and what it was judicious to divulge."[29] It may be, in other words, that the secret bespoken by this suggestive juxtaposition is his dangerous knowledge of the legal and moral tenuity of Henry's claim to the throne Usk helped him to, and about the savagery awaiting those who mention it. In scenes as different as the juxtaposed accounts of Clerk's death and Usk's faux pas, the striking symmetry is that each says something about the legitimacy of a prince and each is silenced; the more drastic form Clerk's silencing took shrouds the story of Usk's with the danger to which such opinions might lead. Even the single asymmetry enforces the connection rather than otherwise. Yes, Usk only speaks his opinion (in the story) while Clerk writes his, but this of course only calls to mind that *now*, in the chronicle, Usk is writing just as Clerk did. In this case, then, may we judge that Usk's air of secrecy indicates a self-protective caution, a desire to steer that narrow course as precisely as possible, maintaining some "deniability" about the facts of view he reports?

Such theoretical deniability does play a role in Clerk's story, in the one phrase still undiscussed, "haec aliis imponendo": *haec*, these accusations against Henry, Clerk is reported as having "put on others." So he acknowledged producing the treasonable utterance but denied that it was his own. He was a professional *scriptor*, so in "putting these things on others" he must have said that he had only copied, as a scribe and in the line of work, the treasonable words. Now this defense as inferred sounds largely formal; I cannot manage to believe that Clerk—at least in the case that Henry was presenting—had merely the bad luck to be hired for the wrong job, or that serious agitators would hire an unaffiliated scribe to copy material they knew could betray and destroy them.[30]

But the formalism is this gambit's point. Given-Wilson suggests of Usk, and literary criticism has routinely assumed of many, that state repression caused writers to employ coding, evasion, and indirection, what in a different milieu Annabel Patterson called "functional ambiguity."[31] Criticism of fourteenth-century poetry often assumes that censorship went without saying,[32] and then argues, or assumes, that evasion and indirection may be cited to confirm that it did; so that these strategies are taken to allow the author at once to voice and to disavow an opinion, saying, in effect, "I did not say it; I only repeated it."[33] The Prologue to Chaucer's *Legend of Good Women* enacts an instance of the device. Cupid has charged Chaucer with the *Troilus* and the English *Rose*; Alceste intervenes with several excuses, incompatible with each other but all amounting to the claim that the words Chaucer put on paper were not *his* words: that he was copying a source without noticing what it said ("for he useth thynges for to make, / Hym rekketh noght of what matere he take," 364-65) or obeying a patron ("Or him was boden maken thilke tweye / Of some persone, and durste yt nat withseye," 366-67).[34] With such she seeks pardon on the grounds that the author was only the material agent of production, that the offending matter was stumbled across inadvertently or performed at another's command. But neither is offered as grounds for acquittal; they are two of several improvised grounds for mercy.[35] Indeed, Alceste seems unable to bear the thought that Chaucer might be innocent and her mercy otiose: when he objects that the works just are not guilty of the faults alleged, she snaps, "lat be thyn arguinge," "Thou hast thy grace, and hold thee right ther-to" (475, 478). Her advocacy demonstrates the *copia* of royal power and royal pardon precisely because it is unconstrained by fact or law. Innocence would spoil the effect. But this is a poet's conceit. When William Clerk brings it forward, whether as defense or as grounds for mercy, it does him no good at all. In the event it hardly mattered what legal defense Clerk introduced, since the point of trying the case in Chivalry was to override legality. The formal defense is either unnecessary or inefficacious.

This aspect of Clerk's story shows what is obvious in any case, that a winking "reticence," implying without saying, is no reticence at all: merely formal defenses ("You'll notice that I didn't actually say that") work, at best, in merely formal circumstances. The author concerned to protect himself needs more than this. A work that successfully communicates criticisms thereby communicates the author's endorsement of them. So it is hard to believe Usk's suggestions, themselves only hinted at, that he censors himself from fear of retaliation, if to "believe" him means to accept the motives his gestures seem to signal. His story of William Clerk shows how little the fig-leaf of performed self-censorship would cover, did he truly fear what he seems to fear. His utterances do not act as though they really are exposed to the dangers they pretend to ward off.

~

Once the story of William Clerk is precipitated into fact, it leaves itself open to investigation. What is on first impression the mark of Henry's tyrannical power shows to closer inspection the constraints on it: the insolent and peremptory violence in this case illustrates the impoverished choices he faced. Henry found his attempts to govern, and to secure his governance, dogged both by the recalcitrance of legal procedure and by their own self-refuting logic. We saw that in 1405 his justices refused to sit in judgment on a prelate: in Scrope's case, Henry could not shortcut the pertinent legal principle even though the accused had allied himself with armed rebellion. In 1402, Frisby and his fellow friars admitted to organizing resistance against Henry, but the *Eulogium* continuator reports that the first jury declined to return a verdict.[36] While showing that the king could secure the execution of a dissident by extraordinary means, Clerk's case shows also how helpless he was to secure it by ordinary ones. Henry had cornered himself by his criticisms of Richard: in 1401 he could not force the judgment at common law of a commercial scribe of no public importance (that Usk alone preserves the story suggests that Clerk was not a figure to inspire curiosity) or did not think it worth trying. Ecclesiastical powers had a freer hand in creating legislation, like Arundel's constitutions,[37] in part because they did not have to answer directly to any constituency other than the king (and one measure of constraint on Henry's actions was Arundel's freedom to create such legislation), and in part because the stakes were so small.

This logic had its effect in the aftermath of Clerk's case, which seems to have spent Henry's ability to use the Court of Chivalry: he found himself granting the common petition, mentioned above, against such use.[38] Perhaps it was a strategic expenditure, and what Henry bought so expensively was a public example meant to intimidate others whose thoughts were unfriendly toward himself? After all, the heretic William Sawtry, at almost exactly the same moment, was made by his well publicized burning into a "terrifying example."[39] Strohm calls Clerk's punishment similarly "theatrical," purchasing public acquiescence with public violence.[40] But there is the difference: Sawtry was denounced publicly, and burned publicly at Smithfield; the royal instruction for his execution was registered in parliament and widely reported,[41] while Usk's forty-seven words constitute our sole notice of Clerk. Vernacular poets did not celebrate the event. This is not monitory publicity; it is hugger-mugger; if so, then Henry was trying to avoid the consequences of having it known. None of this could cheer William Clerk through his torture and death. But his story shows with a particular clarity the political logic of persecution. On the one hand, Henry had little capital to spend, and his political position in these years, far from producing a regime of terror, forced him into a persistent state of self-consciousness and reprised negotiation. In circumstances so carefully watched and so tightly constrained, political terror meant to secure legitimacy could quickly turn delegitimating. An author like Usk would have little cause to fear retaliation; and Clerk's case shows more than anything how little Henry could afford to do.

~

My discussion has (I think) shown good reason to think that the execution of William Clerk did happen, that what seems in Usk's narration a diffuse air of looming violence, where sharp detail is diffused into unspecificity, proves on investigation to be real violence, but more contained, shrunk back into Clerk's body; the date of Mardi Gras 1401 is not invented as a parody of specificity or a bitter comment on Henry's bloody "carnival," but is the actual date of the event; it was not a threat to Usk and those like him; it was not a menace hatched by Lancastrian fantasy, or an atmosphere of the political world. It was not Usk's fantasy, either, and does not seem to be a symptom. It was just one of those transient acts the world is made of.

Chapter 3

Fear

The previous chapter showed that Usk did not seem to fear his thoughts' being heard. Perhaps he was afraid to hear them himself. The office and perquisites that assure us that he probably would know and probably would not bungle the report of Clerk's execution—his longstanding service to the Court of Chivalry and his more recent service to Henry's regime—might seem to make him uncomfortably complicit with it; in just such a way, we are told, Thomas Hoccleve was sometimes so busy trying not to know what he knew that he induced in himself the thoughts he wanted most to avoid.[1] On this guess, Usk's stammers and stumbles could be discursive oddments, "incommensurates" that resist assimilation and mark the fascination of he wants to forget;[2] and the reason his nervous disavowals can give no adequate reasons for themselves could be that their job is to distract him from the adequate ones. As the servant of a régime that (as we also have been told) substituted brutality for legitimacy, Usk might have compulsively enacted a secrecy meant to keep him from seeing blood on his hands. This guess would lead us to seek out a secret whose workings are subtler, less neatly defined, and more fully symptomatic; to look for unexplained ripples on the surface of discourse and trace them back to the impact that produced them.

~

The violence that befalls Clerk befalls others also in this book; and its insolence and caprice discompose the world, puncture it and drain its substance, just when that world seems fullest and most assured. Narrating Henry's coronation, Usk gives us a unique moment of captivating serenity, all awash in colored fabric ("all the great men of the realm, trimly dressed in red, scarlet, and ermine"[3]), laid out in ceremonial symbolism (four swords are carried before the king representing his virtue, his "double mercy," and his "justice executed without rancor"), and underlined by promises heard with his own ears ("I heard the king swear to my lord of Canterbury, before receiving the crown, that he would carefully rule his people wholly in mercy and truth").[4] In this flicker of beauty, Usk sets off the detail from the coronation oath with the rubric "In mercy, in truth," *In misericordia, ueritate*. These two virtues, pulling together the joy of the great messianic Psalm 84 (85), whose verses—"Mercy and truth have met one another; justice and peace have embraced," *Misericordia et veritas obviaverunt sibi; iustitia et pax osculatae sunt*—lovingly laid out in exegesis and homiletics and art, bespoke throughout the Middle Ages the reconciliation of justice and mercy in the Incarnation of Christ.[5] Henry, chivalrous and unafraid, offers himself to perform the office of his ceremonial champion; Usk explains the five insignia conferred on Henry's son Henry as prince of Wales ("the rod of gold, the kiss, the crown, the ring, and the letters conferring the office"); and he tells of other acts of beneficence and of justice.

Then, with not even an adverb to mark the shift, Usk introduces the settling of scores:

> John Hall, of the Duke of Norfolk's household, condemned by parliament because he was present at the duke of Gloucester's death and gave his consent to it, is drawn, hanged, and—once his entrails have been removed and burned before him while he is still alive—is beheaded and quartered; and the quarter of his body containing his right hand is displayed on a pole, across London Bridge.[6]

Gloucester's murder was among the most notorious of Richard II's crimes, so there was no obvious injustice in what happened to Hall. But the passage gazes not on the justice of torture but on its experience. No division or rubric prepares for it, which only sharpens its intrusive edge; it matches agony with immediacy in a jarring recourse to the historical present. By two devices Usk evokes sensation that overwhelms and flattens the celebratory perspective of the paragraphs that precede. It is not merely the suddenness with which this violence enters the story, and not merely the clash of its tone against the coronation's high cheerfulness, that causes the shock; it is not even just the details that spell out this gory procedure, though this last comes close to it. The words describing his execution are drawn almost verbatim from his sentence. Parliament had ordered that

> the said John Hall should be drawn from Tower Hill as far as Tyburn Forks, and there disembowelled, and his entrails burnt before him, and then he should be hanged, beheaded and quartered; and his head should be sent to Calais where the murder took place, and the quarters sent to other places, as the king pleased.[7]

By a single detail Usk shifts the scale and focus of judicial formula and resolves familiar details into an unwelcome concreteness. The laconic specifications of the sentence (a sentence that Usk would have heard more than once in his life) mention the burning of the criminal's entrails as a detail of location ("... burnt before him ..."). The two words Usk has added to this sentence (*adhuc uiuus*, "... while he is still alive ...") make that detail a shift of perspective: since Hall still lives, the viscera roasted "before him" form a scene he looks on. The reader looks as if through his eyes. This technique, imagining one seeing his own spilled innards, is one of Dante's methods of pathos;[8] Usk gains horror, not merely jarring against the larger perspective on Henry's coronation in this passage but voiding that perspective altogether in the intimacy of torture imagined from within. When the scene pulls away from this unhappy closeness, the more spacious view "across London Bridge" highlights the butchered quarter of Hall's body, and sees it closely enough to make out the *right* hand—an optical impossibility that emphasizes how plastic and unreal this scene has left the empirical world.

In Hall's execution, that "formlessness" (*Ungestalt*) that the medieval historian typically "locates beyond his 'own' ordered, regulated realm in a savage 'outside,'"[9] is pulled right to the center of English political life. The horrors do not abate. Again without transition, break, or rubrication (Thompson and Given-Wilson insert paragraph breaks), two unconnected events follow. First, two valets of the king, at their dinner in London,

> found in five eggs, which were served up to them, the exact likeness of men's faces in every detail, the white having congealed and separated from the faces above the forehead in place of hair before passing down the jowls to the chin. One of these I saw.[10]

Then, again without transition, we see King Richard transported down the Thames,

> in the silence of darkest midnight . . . , wailing and shouting that it pained him to have been born. One knight there present said to him, "Think how in all things you treated the earl of Arundel in just this malicious way."[11]

The visual realization of the eggs calls forth the auditory realization of Richard's cries.[12]

Henry's coronation has skidded without warning into violence, eeriness, and inarticulate pain. The cutaway from the happy wash of color to Hall's spilled entrails and quartered body; then to the bizarre triviality of the eggs; then to the sound of Richard's wordless wails in the night, makes the ornate furniture of rule seem less a decorative scrim meant to hide political violence than an imbecile indifference to it. The brief moments of sensation—violence, freakishness, grief—call attention away from spacious festivity to claustrophobically close focus: on the severed parts of John Hall's body, on the configuration of yolk and albumen. But when the focus moves back *out* again for a moment, the festive scene of the *heroes regni* in their red and scarlet and ermine has been replaced by London Bridge overgazed by a hunk of Hall's body, arm dangling, and by the sound of Richard's cries. The absence of transition into and between these episodes suggests that violence in this world may come from at any time and from anywhere. The unexplained intrusion of eggs that look like heads detached suggests that within the story such fears have already propagated themselves even as the king celebrates.

The violence itself, as I have said, is no secret. But that is what makes it look like a symptom of some other secret: though public events publicly recorded, these moments are connected by a freakishness and a close focus that disarranges, evacuates, Henry's coronation and the coherence of the political world.

And in their narration, they leave the world itself derealized. The concreteness of detail in these episodes does not extend to the historical world into which they intrude: suffering banishes rather than reveals the world around the body. In these stories, torture seizes the visual field of narration and disperses the solidity of the everyday. The Epiphany rebels, after their failure, fled to Cirencester,

> where, on the day after Epiphany, they were beheaded by a crowd of folk from the countryside; and many who were found with them, led to Oxford, were there hanged or beheaded; and their corpses, divided up like the flesh of wild animals taken in the hunt, some in little sacks, some on staves between two

> men's shoulders, I saw carried to London and then pickled with brine.[13]

These deaths, he says, the archbishop, using the text "'I bring you good tidings of great joy,' announced to the clergy and people of London"; with the *Te Deum* sung in gratitude, "he passed through the city in a festive procession."[14] Another such story immediately precedes the execution of William Clerk; this is the execution (in this case historically uncontroversial) of William Sawtry, chaplain, "convicted and condemned for heresy" and burned in anticipation of the statute *De heretico comburendo*, while the parliament that forwarded the statute to the king was still in session.[15] After telling how Sawtry spoke "with great force" a threatening prophecy—a passage we will consider later—Usk disposes of him:

> And once he had been thus condemned, first being solemnly degraded, afterwards in Smithfield in London, chained to a post standing straight up in a barrel surrounded by red-hot faggots, he is reduced to ashes.[16]

That is the end of the episode.

In each case, the percussion of violent detail establishes the solidity of the human body as felt fact and then violates or dissolves it, leaving a world unmade.[17] The effect depends on imagining a bodily member so solidly, so suddenly, and at a range so close that all the rest of the scene and all the rest of the body, even, are blocked from view at the moment of agony. The instances seen so far illustrate the quick shift in scale and focus. John Hall's possession of his own body is seen and felt by the reader just when he no longer possesses it, when the reader is looking through his eyes at the entrails burned in front of him. William Clerk's right hand and tongue alone are visualized, as they are removed from him. Word that the Epiphany conspirators were "hanged or beheaded" is, in the disjunction, no more than information; what seems the merely conventional comparison to the slaughter of hunted animals shunts the corpses into visibility when it proves unexpectedly to convey the literal truth, the members stuffed into sacks, slung across poles, and seasoned in salt. The vividness of the narration here is only marked, not caused, by Usk's claim to have seen these things happen.[18]

A. D. Nuttall coined the brilliant phrase "snuff tragedy" to describe a certain kind of violent representation;[19] it describes neatly Usk's portrayal of destruction and dismemberment without distance—both in the sense that carnage is closely observed and precisely described and in the sense that it is rendered with a facticity that precludes the emotional cushion of fiction. The technique paradoxically and imperiously excludes meaning and understanding: the hyperrealization of violence effaces the working-day world, depletes its consistency. "Nothing is more certain than death, and nothing more uncertain than its hour." The moments of abrupt and uncensored mayhem enact the proverb with grim comedy: you know that Usk is going to make you watch these scenes but you never expect them when they arrive. And when they do they absorb the foreground to the point that the rest of the world is evacuated. The sharp focus on severed limbs and carved bodies elicits readerly engagement and bats it about: the perceptual density of the details fixes attention while their gore repels it, makes it want to turn elsewhere.

But—and this is the wicked brilliance of it—the book offers no "elsewhere." Historical narrative discourse, previously unmarked, comes by contrast to be marked as empty, vacated. The sudden and gory concretions that drive the mind to seek a different object leave materiality itself rarefied like an apparition; they strand the public world in the attenuation of mere scenery. The effect is a kind of derealization. This we also see sometimes in episodes that do not narrate official terror and torture, but displace it into metaphor. One instance has been mentioned in the introduction, when Usk wakes during the 1401 parliament sensing still the sonic impress of a voice heard in sleep.[20] Fear of the consequences of legal violence names itself twice as the substance of the experience—"fearing" (*timens*) some evil to himself he "fearfully" (*timidus*) committed himself to the guidance of the Holy Ghost—but what is arresting about this episode is its evocation of the disoriented state of one just waked (*expergefactus*), when dream remnants make the waking world seem briefly strange and unreal. (That Usk seems to be describing a portent does not affect the case. In the next chapter, it becomes the case.) The mind lingering in a dream is as isolated as waking subjectivity can well be, and in that isolation it is confronted with a world nightmarishly insubstantial. This passage does not portray but recalls the anticipation of violence: earlier on the same page, he reports that it was "ordained in this parliament that men of the March could take reprisals against those Welsh in debt to them or injuring them."[21] But the voice still "sounding in the ears" begins with an image that is absurd when it is assembled—"upon my back they wrought"—until it calls up the recollection of the psalm that makes the metaphor clearer: "Upon my back have the wicked wrought; they have lengthened their iniquity." But once recalled, the psalm moves in its next verse to claim another victim: *Dominus iustus concidit cervices peccatorum*, "The Lord who is just slices through the necks of sinners."[22]

~

So the scene of bodies unpieced by state action, rendered into prose with unnatural vividness, draining solidity from a world left unreal by incursions of unexpected violence, is a kind of type-scene for Usk. What could be its secret? The executions do not call into question the justice or integrity of the Lancastrian régime: John Hall's death punished a crime emblematic of Richard's tyranny, and Usk tacitly endorses the scorn of the unnamed knight who rebukes Richard's self-pity. It is rather the quality of attention they wring from the reader, in the affect conveyed around and through the facts reported, in the sense of a world derealized through state terror and the expression of vulnerability before it. These passages that cast up images of members too brightly and finely focused—a tongue, a right hand, another right hand, a head—are what convey the sense that Adam Usk has a secret glinting in the fear at these scenes' edges. But this does not go without saying: other chronicles report acts of violence frequently enough, without making their world toxic and eerie; it is not by the matter of these episodes, not by the mere report of violence, that Usk gives his chronicle this effect.

It is by the technique. The story of a different kind of violation demonstrates it. In early 1401, about the time Sawtry and Clerk were executed, Usk and Archbishop Arundel investigated Robert Bowlond. The story he tells there begins by closely echoing Bowlond's own confession[23]: Bowlond, Usk reports, committed "diverse crimes, heresies, and errors," committed them "wickedly" (compare Bowlond's confession: "nequiter"), "as if by a serpent under a pretended appearance of holiness" (compare Bowlond's confession: "sub quadam specie fictae sanctitatis"). But unlike the recorded confession, which has by this point specified that Bowlond "knew carnally and made pregnant" the nun Alice Wodelow, Usk still withholds any details of the transgression.[24] That emerges belatedly and alarmingly at the end of the episode, when he reports that Alice, through Robert's "disordered lust," had "in a sodomitical manner, through the dripping of his seed and not through the entry of his organ . . . been impregnated."[25] The unwelcome magnification of precisely visualized detail places readers in a repellent intimacy with the event's bodily apparatus before they can prepare for or decline it.[26] Given-Wilson calls this moment "almost photographic,"[27] but this is not quite right: it achieves its effect by withholding, not displaying, details, herding the mind to create a picture that will explain the event: one who has not previously wondered how conception might occur by these means must, to make sense of the passage, imaginatively assemble the parts and set the semen in motion, must visualize the sequence of events and the topography across which it transpires.

It is a device that coordinates two separate choices: engineering a surprise by engaging suddenly a degree of precision that the register has not prepared for, and simultaneously introducing into the narrative a close focus on a violated human body. We have seen this pattern in the episodes already discussed: John Hall's execution is given in judicial terms until the *adhuc uiuus* reminds us that he is looking at his viscera just as we are, and then again a scene across the river is interrupted by his right hand seen with disproportionate exactness. In the execution of the Epiphany insurgents, what sounds as it passes like the most routine simile (they were slaughtered "like animals") leads to descriptions of the bags in which their cuts were carried and the brine in which they were pickled—with the sentence converging on its concluding word, the main verb *uidi*, "I saw," which floats the visualizability of these details to the thematized surface of the discourse. This verb-final pattern is the syntactic analogue, and in these episodes a means, of sudden hyperrealized detail. To that pattern are added other techniques, like a deliberately angular use of the historical present. The single sentence that tells William Clerk's story gives his name, origin, and final destination in participial phrases ("born in the county of Chester, and condemned in the Court of Chivalry"), then begins naming body parts as they are removed, attaching each not to a body but to a crime ("first his tongue, because he had spoken against the king—he put these things on others—and then his right hand with which he had written"); that severance is accomplished not (as the explicit numeration along with the syntactic suspense has led us to expect) on the third instance by a finite main verb, but on the second by another participle (*priuatus*, "deprived"), before the third element does arrive, not merely introducing the historical present but suddenly hauling the whole sentence unceremoniously from secondary to primary sequence: the former in the pluperfect of *protulerat* and *scripserat*, the latter in the perfect of *non probauit* and the present of the main verb, the last of these (*decapitatur*, "is beheaded") ending Clerk's life and the only sentence that records it simultaneously. The tortuously verb-final construction is not a tic or compulsion, but the syntactic emblem of sudden discontinuity.

To achieve such discontinuity, Usk designs his narrative episodically, and makes the episode a unit of felt incompletion. This requires his skill. Episodic construction almost by definition characterizes chronicles, but the serial arrangement of events without connection is in most chronicles as ubiquitous as air and therefore as invisible. The simplest chronicles, of course, do not even try to fill the gaps of sequence in their annalistic records; these therefore are not even marked as gaps. At the opposite extreme of historiographical skill and ambition, Higden's *Polychronicon*, the work Usk's chronicle continues, so finely calculates the chronological location of events that the sequence of episodes forms an array of juxtapositions rather than a narrative. What earned the *Polychronicon* its success was not conceptual originality or exhaustiveness but its ability to dispose history as a thing known and subjected to discernment. Temporal precision is its proudest boast: "to compile, not merely the series of times from the beginning of the universe down to our own age, but as far as possible a finely grained computation [*supputationem*] extending even to single years."[28] Higden interrupts the compilation in his own voice (as *R.*, *Ranulphus*) to police temporal boundaries and resolve history's copia into chronological consistency: "*Ranulphus.* Note here that unless three years of Aeneas' reign are counted under those of King Latinus, calculation of the history that says that Latinus reigned for thirty-two years will be impugned, especially since according to all historians Aeneas came to Italy, after the taking of Troy, in the twenty-fifth year of King Latinus."[29] He stacks the separate stories of separate peoples and then evens the edge of the stack. Watching stories one knows from Livy and from the book of Kings intercalated with each other, their temporal relations adjusted, the reader experiences historiography as an achievement not of narration, but of prospect, viewing synoptically histories that could not view each other. But for this very reason meaning is evacuated from the discursive organization: synchrony alone, not cause or analogy, dictates sequence.

Indeed, continuity is not native to the chronicle form, which means that in order to create these sudden shifts of focus and untimely terminations Usk must create the expectations of continuity before he can violate them.[30] He devises several means of hinting at continuity and meaning between episodes. Outlandish wordplay is one. The episode of Robert Bowlond—the man he investigated for impregnating a nun—concludes by reporting that the nun gave birth to a daughter ("who looked like the aforementioned Robert") *in festo sancte Petronille iam ultimo lapso*,"on the feast of St. Petronilla just past" (120). The participle (*lapsum*) that dates the feast is identical to the noun that describes the dripping (*lapsum*) of Bowlond's semen. William Clerk's trial takes place on Mardi Gras, which contrasts the extravagant violence to Clerk's body with, or brutally embodies it in, the carnival abandon that enlivens that day. Usk of course does not say "on Mardi Gras," but *in festo carniprivii*—"on the feast of (the eve of) the depriving [*-privium*] of meat"—which creates a grotesque lexical rhyme with the detail, thirty words later, that Clerk was "deprived"—*privatus*—of his hand and tongue. After the Oldcastle rebellion, Roger Acton, a former intimate of the Lancastrians, invested with golden spurs (*calcaribus aureis*) by Prince Henry and the duke of Clarence, "was not ashamed to kick against them [*recalcitrari*]";[31] the brief episode that ends with such verbal wit is a flashback, dominated by the picture that precedes it, the body of the executed Acton hanging from the gallows for a full month.[32]

Such lexical rhymes connect episodes as well, creating the sense that events are woven together just in time to reveal that they are not. I have mentioned that the story of William Sawtry's execution immediately precedes that of William Clerk's, and that the first detail of the latter dates it to Mardi Gras. The words that end the episode immediately preceding say that Sawtry was burned "to ashes," *in cineres*.[33] Mardi Gras is so celebrated because the next day is Ash Wednesday, *dies cinerum*: the quick suggestive crossing of conceptual echoes briefly suggests a counterhistorical movement, in which the metaphorical resonances of the language run "backward" against the sequence of events, implying connections that are not explained and are not even rationally explicable. Such narrative slant-rhymes adumbrate meaningful connection without supplying it. Techniques of narrative in themselves more familiar, but no more explicable by the logic of either the historiographical enterprise or the symptomatic betrayal, do similar work. The quarter of John Hall's body seen across London Bridge calls up the scene of the Thames, across which, sixty words later, Richard's wails echo. There is no causal connection between these scenes, and no conceptual importance to the Thames itself; but together they create a scene (the butchered body looming over the river that moves King Richard from one prison to another) that seems somehow the unacknowledged obverse of Henry's festive coronation. By these devices Usk gives his chronicle an air of continuity and connection on which he can, at will, inflict an abruptness that seems a skittish changing of the subject.

What feels like symptom is constructed as art. The suddenness that characterizes these scenes is the kind that also creates the sensation of Usk's surprised disorientation in those moments which got this inquiry under way—moments when he seems to stop himself in the very act of saying something improper: the normal flow of discursive or syntactic continuity is hijacked by something unlooked for. Neither the design nor its self-consciousness proves that the symptoms are no symptoms; but if they are, they are symptoms that Usk has designed as such, placed there, deployed as teasers for a reader to grab at. The question then is not what the symptoms mean, but what Usk means by devising them. Discontinuity, as Burke noticed, generates fear.[34] Created artistically, it conveys the illusion that the artist has been overtaken by the unexpected, but that is, precisely, an illusion, and a component of the device. Making such observations does not, of course, dismiss the possibility of diagnosing moments like this, of moving back along their clues to motives concealed. But it does mean that the concealment and the revelation look different: affect evoked by passages like this is not a quantum of uncensored experience; it is the product of deliberated artistry. If anything will lead us to Adam Usk's secret, it will be his advertent choices, not his inadvertent betrayals. What gives rise to this desire for these devices and effects, in this author and at this moment? The book's unnerving atmosphere points to the secret concealed as an instrument points to its purpose, not as a symptom points to its disease.

The aesthetics of derealization and destruction, of a world blotted out by pain, is summed up in the "badge" Usk says he adopted: "a naked man digging on a black field," fallen Adam condemned to labor in a world that has faded to black.[35] Taken on its own, the brooding violence in Usk's chronicle exposes him to the judgment Auerbach passed in his withering characterization of the Goncourts as less concerned with the injuries of class than with "the sensory fascination of the ugly, the repulsive, and the morbid."[36] Tracing back along the path that leads to those explosions, we find no practical motive for fear, but the artistry expended in making us feel it. But enigmatic echoes between events, riddles of half-perceived connection, suggest something less futile and indulgent: the possibility that the secret belongs, not to Usk, but to history. The direction in which these passages point seems to imply that what needs explaining is not why Usk's prose jerks and surprises, but what leads him to refine a technique of jerk and surprise. If this is indeed concealing a secret, it is not artlessness, but the imitation of a more terrible art.

Chapter 4

Prophecy

Anent that, think again about those freakish eggs, shaped like heads and served up to the royal valets in London.[1] Their juxtaposition with the gruesome story of Hall's execution effects a "tincture" that dyes the minor curiosity with the suggestion of violent death.[2] What the real valets (if there were real valets) thought is irrecoverable, but the report implies that a weird portentousness afflicts the characters in Usk's chronicle as much as it afflicts the chronicle itself: if Usk saw only one of the eggs, he was not present when they were served, but if he saw that one, then a valet carried it away—an untidy operation that bespeaks a sense of their significance. The previous chapter suggested that the conscious artistry of such uncanny moments means that they are not unconscious symptoms; but artistry on an imposing scale is precisely what we might suspect if Adam Usk's secret is not his secret but history's: the idea that future events are portentously foreshadowed by present ones implies they are designed.

The portent is a unit of enigmatic meaning, extensible into prophecy, and England saw a glut of both in Richard's and Henry's reigns.[3] Portent is a common, though not an inevitable, component of chronicling; some scholars have incautiously suggested that its occasional appearance tells us about the task historiography expected itself to do; and it has been suggested that Usk's use of portent and prophecy shows him shouldering this task with relish.[4]

Such descriptions of Usk do seem likely on their face. He knew some of the most lurid prophecies, and his chronicle, even before it quite gets under way, shows vatic energies barely controlled. At this point it seems haunted not by the past but by the future. On the blank pages between the (C) continuation of the *Polychronicon* and Usk's own, there are memoranda that play a florid and unrestrained fantasia on historical and prophetic resonances of Usk's names. He jumbles quotations from Bible and canon law and satirical verse with keening stridency, and, precisely at the moment he makes prophecy clang together an impossible combination of affects, he creates a true authorial signature from matter in the Merlin prophecies:

> Behold, throwing away the spade of all wretchedness, how glorious in his virtues becomes Adam. Usk—of this name the prophet Merlin sang, "The River Usk through seven months will seethe, and by its boiling heat the fish will die and serpents will burden the land"—interpreting "serpents" in their good signification, as I take it, according to that gospel passage, "Be wise as serpents." Of whom does Merlin sing this? I believe it to be the earl of March.[5]

He goes on to identify Edward III with Merlin's "boar," but these opening lines overwhelm all that subsequent detail.

There is not just prophetic material here, but a louring prophetic air. The straining Merlinian style usually drops into banality, through unskillful devices too frequently and obviously repeated. Usk revives their capacity for horror by the paradoxical device of taking the most menacing details *in bono*: by insisting that transparently nasty things—the river afflicted and boiling, the fish massacred, the land heavy with serpents—really mean nice things, he reinvigorates their nastiness, inflicting the scene on readers and then asking them to like it. The details, though drawn from Geoffrey of Monmouth, clearly are chosen to replicate images of the terrifying central section of John's Apocalypse, when the angel casts the fire to earth from the censer and the seven angels sound their trumps; at the second of these, "a great star fell from heaven, burning as it were a torch, and it fell on the third part of the rivers," so that "the third part of the waters became wormwood; and many men died of the waters, because they were made bitter" (Rev 8:10-11), when the woman clothed with the sun—who herself has a crucial cameo in Usk[6]—is persecuted by "the dragon . . . that old serpent, who is called the devil and Satan" (12:9), and concludes when the "vials of God's ire" are poured out on the earth, the third vial "upon the rivers and the fountains of waters; and there was made blood," and the sixth "upon that great river Euphrates; and dried up the water thereof" (16:4, 12).

As apocalyptic languages will, this folds the beginning of history onto its catastrophic end. The "spade" that "Adam" throws away in the first lines is certainly, as Given-Wilson says, an allusion to Adam's "delving"[7] (which we have just seen Usk adopted as his emblem). The historical sweep of these lines, from history's beginning in Adam up to its end in apocalypse, places Usk himself as the very joint where they meet, in the signature that juxtaposes "Adam" at the end of one sentence with "Usk" at the beginning of the next. These scribblings play variations on the same theme. He quotes God's words from Genesis, immediately after the fall ("Adam is become as one of us," Gen 3.22), notes the tunic of skins that Genesis says Adam wore, and recalls the "happy fall" (*felix culpa*) celebrated in the *Exultet*; but then, without acknowledging the change of direction and disproportion of scale, he speaks of the "fortunate approvals of transfer" (*felicibus translacionis assencibus*) that Adam enjoyed. After puzzling for a moment we conclude, amazed, that he is speaking no longer of Adam the first man, but of Adam Orleton, about whom he quotes verses: "Adam is a trigamist" (they read) because he "neglected Thomas" (Hereford, in 1317 Orleton's first episcopal see, once ruled by St. Thomas Cantilupe) and "poorly ruled Wulfstan" (Worcester, his next see, once ruled by St. Wulfstan), and "preferred Swithun" (Winchester, his third see, once ruled by St. Swithun) "because it was richer." These verses Usk attributes to "a certain envious man."[8] In the passage following,

"Adam" is again the first man—although "envy obstructed" him when he had been "free of every misery," so that he was "expelled from paradise by the envy of the devil" but then "restored to heaven by the blood of the Son of God"—but immediately becomes Usk himself:

> although by the envy of a certain knight he was deprived of his benefice, behold how majestic was his restitution, forced by the testimony on behalf of Adam. And although he was expelled from the counsel and favor of his lord through the envy of his hunters, behold how glorious likewise is his reparation, forced by the laws: Adam coming according to the nature of April, in which he was created, first undergoing the changing and bitter storms of winds and whirlwinds, but finally bringing the flowers and delights of May, and of summer itself.[9]

This extraordinary sequence of prefatory sketches makes Usk himself both prophecy and fulfillment, recalling creation and anticipating restoration; his career is an epitome of the world's history, laden with auguries of disaster and hope. And so it sounds like the picture of Usk as the late medieval Englishman driven by the instability of his age (while none too stable himself) to an obsession with prophecy.

~

But what he does in these prefatory scribblings is just what he avoids in the chronicle proper. A single detail suggests the difference: the name "Adam" appears on this two-page opening ten times, while in the entire chronicle that follows, it appears precisely once.[10] In his narrative he is sometimes "I," but more often and more notably *compilator* or *notator presencium*.[11] These phrases not only withhold his name but point to its withholding, even though he supplies details of his biography—the author is Welsh, born in Usk, held the chair of civil law at Oxford, served Arundel and Henry IV, and, mentioned once, of Christian name

"Adam"—which would make identification of him a simple matter. That the prophetic memoranda appear with his chronicle shows that the difference between them is one of style, not outlook or purpose or imagined readership; it also shows that his style in the chronicle is a choice, not a reflex. These little passages that preface his chronicle audition prophecy as a mode of writing, try out varieties of expression; the chronicle accepts some and declines others. Their style and their inclusion show that he is not averse to displays of premeditation, a disability (as we will see later) that he turns to advantage. His presentation of self within the narration is neither unconscious nor unselfconscious, but an apparatus of composition achieved through experimentation. In these "prophecy trials," he makes himself the object of disclosure, while in the chronicle, he makes himself the subject of concealment. There he abandons the style of prophecy and portent found in them. These prefatory passages are fantastical versions of the most explicitly theorized and extensively practiced understanding of the providential "plotting" of history available to the Christian west, the typological coordination of events by which God's meaningful and creative recapitulation traced out a pattern of anticipation and fulfillment in human history: he gives it a sensational and disorienting specificity, a shrill lyricism that tries to convey the affecting power of prophecy by an affecting expression.

In the chronicle, as I said, he works differently. He uses his name only at one dramatic moment; he makes a show of choosing to vanish from rather than to star in his book; and "Merlin" and its like, when they appear, do not guess the future, but gloss the past, and they are inert, sounding neither the strained intensity of the scribblings nor the eerier understatement of the five facieform eggs. Looking back at Richard's coronation in 1377, he says that the accidents which befell "three of the royal insignia were omens of three misfortunes that would befall him":

> *first*, during the procession he lost one of the coronation slippers (and so, *first*, the people, rising against him, hated him afterwards through his whole life); *second*, one of the golden

> spurs fell from him (and so also the knights, *second*, rising up in rebellion opposed him); and *third*, during the dinner a sudden gust of wind threw the crown down from his head (and so, *third and finally*, thrown down from the kingship, he was supplanted by King Henry).[12]

Nothing could be less uncanny than this. My translation needs typography and punctuation to convey the static order Usk achieves through syntax and diction alone. These portents are determinate, and they are dead, unenlivened by sensation or menace: the details do not spring from their narrative context hyperrealized. They are not realized at all. They are announced as formal analepsis, categorized as omen in advance of their relation, and are marshalled into fussy coordination: numbered, named, and dissolved into tabulated significance. Other fulfilled prophecies, like his citations of "John of Bridlington," and "Merlin" and the "prophecy of the three kings," are similarly bland.[13] Like the "rehearsals" on the opening pages of his chronicle, these connect events determinately across time; but they lack the elevated rhetoric of those "rehearsals," and the riddling sensational intensity the rhetoric tries to create.

~

But the chronicle has another kind of omen that sounds another tone. Here is one extended passage. We have encountered part of it already:

> *The Duke of Bavaria becomes Emperor*. The Duke of Bavaria, brother to the queen of France, who—because the King of Bohemia who had long occupied the imperial seat had been rejected for being useless and for being still uncrowned by the pope—had been elevated to the empire with the help of the French, was with many French defeated on the field of battle [*campestri bello*] by this same King.[14]

Bells ring of themselves. The four little bells [*Quatuor campanelle*] affixed to the four [*quatuor*] corners of the tomb of St. Edward at Westminster, by their own motion, much more than if set moving by human powers, to the great terror and wonder of the monastery, four times in one day [*quater in uno die*] miraculously rang.[15]

A fountain flows with blood. The spring near Builth—the one in which the head of Llewelyn ap Griffith, the last prince of the Welsh, had been washed after its amputation—for a whole day ran with the purest blood.[16]

Two popes through .xxii. years. One thing there is in these days which I relate with pain: that two popes, like a monster in nature, which for for twenty-two years now have most impiously torn the seamless tunic of Christ (contrary to that passage in Solomon: "One is my dove") have stirred up the world, with error of souls and various terrors of torment. And alas, if it is true what I now bring back to my memory, that passage of the Gospel, "You are the salt of the earth. But if the salt lose its savour, wherewith shall it be salted? It is good for nothing any more but to be cast out, and to be trodden on by men."[17]

Venality in the priesthood. And so because of a priesthood grown venal, did not Christ, making a whip, cast out those buying and selling in the temple? And therefore I fear that, punished and ground down, we will be cast out from the priesthood, as I regard that in the old covenant, after such venality had dishonored the priesthood, the cloud of smoke, the unquenchable fire, and the sweet savor ceased in the temple. But why draw it out? The Virgin Mother herself, according to Apocalypse, fled with her son to the desert from before the beast sitting on the throne. But here Plato orders me to be silent, since nothing is more certain than death, and nothing more uncertain than its hour.[18]

The paragraphs are thick with vague and weighty promises of coherence lodged in sidelong glances to past and future. The little episodes of the bells and the spring are suspended between the great contests over empire and papacy, and imagined in abruptly close focus. Each implies a question (ringing for what? whose blood?) that bears the promise of secret meaning, and that trespasses on a delicacy of scene (a flowing spring, the tinkle of "little bells") and so suggests by the contrast their fragility and that of the public world on which they seem to comment. Usk laments this fragility at the end of this passage, and he will go on, in the sentences immediately following its close, to connect it with the fragility of the individual life and the plans that can be made for it.[19]

The episodes seem bound in slant rhyme, promising significance but defeating the promise. Given-Wilson think that it is "far from difficult" to supply the meanings that Usk expects his reader to discover in them: the bells referred to either Richard's deposition or his death and signaled either the saint's approval or his disapproval of same, the blood signaled either the good or the bad fortune that Glendower's rebellion would encounter. These are "obvious," because of Richard's devotion to St. Edward and Glendower's claim to Llewelyn's line.[20] But no mention of either Richard or Glendower prompts, or even sits near, these two entries. If the bells meant miraculously to toll Richard's fall or his death, they are behindhand: by the time of this passage, Richard has already been deposed in the chronicle's narrative (six manuscript leaves before it), and is already dead (two leaves before).[21] If Richard is in even a broad sense the referent of this portent, it seems improbably like an afterthought.

More to the point, it does not act like a form of knowledge, which Given-Wilson says medieval chroniclers took omens to be. True, the whole passage seems confident that it knows things we do not. But (so I will say) its gaze is turned inward, on its own workings. Let us attend for a moment to what Usk actually wrote, to the connections the passages actually establish, the forms of prolepsis and analepsis that can be found there rather than those we expect to find. The bells and the blood are both described with a stylized shape meant to convey the shock of the prodigies. I have mimicked that shape as far as I could in English: each, a single sentence sweating to achieve the verb-final construction we have already seen as his emblem of surprise, delays as far as possible anything that would betray prematurely the substance of the report. This is more effectively the case in the latter instance, where the substance of the prodigy appears only in the final two words, *sanguine manauit.*[22] The phrase *propriis motibus* in the former does give away that the bells were ringing; and it is hard to imagine what other trick bells might perform. But that episode places its formal exertions elsewhere anyway. It too is an episode of a single sentence. Four times it uses numerals as it narrates the bells four times ringing themselves; the numeral "four" (*quatuor*) is its first word, its forms appearing a second and a third time (*quatuor . . . quater*), and when the rhythm of the repetition and the closing of the sentence seems to promise neat symmetrical resolution in a fourth "four," the fourth number proves to be "one": *in uno die.*[23] This initiates a play with numbers that informs the whole sequence. "One thing [*Vnum*] there is which . . . I relate with pain," he says a few lines down, and this "one thing" is the schism that has (as the rubric says) produced "two [*duo*] popes," where Scripture says that the church should be "one [*Vna*]," the two instances of "one" already anticipated by the *in uno die* of the bells at the Confessor's tomb and fulfilled by the division of the papacy, properly unitary itself and cause of unity to the Church. Now this sequence already has broached the topic of singular authority unnaturally divided, reporting the election of Rupert of Bavaria to supplant Wenzel IV of Bohemia. Writing years later, Usk would lump together the disputed papal see and the disputed imperial throne as comparably disastrous instances of schism.[24] The mention of Edward the Confessor, a ruler who disastrously left a disputed succession, fills out the pattern: the imperial throne, the English royal throne, the papal see all, in this passage, suggest each other. But they do do it by a compositional device, a set of conceptual "rhymes," not by any program of prophetic knowledge. And they teach no lesson, suggest no conclusion about history; they suggest each merely other through the play of pattern.

Instead of knowledge, they conjure sensations with no function but the beauties and terrors they can inflict on their audience.

In these terms, the spring at Builth stands apart: it does not concern a disputed crown as directly as the others do. But the image of the head (*caput*) wraps a still tighter and more elegant package. For Usk's description of the papal schism as "a monster [*monstrum*] in nature" was one he encountered in canon law. It had a determinate content. A learned proverb had it that a diocese with two bishops is like a body with two heads.[25] He has already used this image to characterize Richard's intrusion of Roger Walden into the see of Canterbury still held by the exiled Arundel: "two archbishops in one church, like two heads on one body."[26] The image of the *monstrum biceps*, the "two-headed monster," appeared constantly after 1378 in writings about the papal schism.[27] Usk used it that way.[28] So the very word "monster" used, as here, in relation to the papal schism bespeaks the idea of two heads, and the mention of the emperor Wenzel's deposition does the same. But the only *single* head that the imagery of this passage proffers is the severed one of Llewelyn ap Griffith, over which the spring once washed.

The heads in this passage condense into metaphor the "headship" of political and churchly rule and the norm of unity, but only by reprising a conventional image for them. It does no conceptual work; rather, it sets up more abstract patterns, which proliferate as Usk rebukes the schism. The "two-headedness" is monstrous, Usk says, for scripture says that "one is my dove." The pertinence of the verse is obvious—"My dove," the beloved of the Song of Songs, the Church beloved of Christ, "is but one," not double or divided.[29] This commonplace citation for the unity of the church was used throughout the schism. But the passage in the Song, the lover's praise of the *amica*, sweeps into itself a little repertory of images that have just appeared in Usk's sequence. Twice—once shortly before the verses already cited and once immediately after—the Song compares the beloved to an army drawn up for battle, "terrible as an army arrayed in the field" (*terribilis ut castrorum acies ordinata*, 6:3), "beautiful as the moon, choice as the sun, terrible as an army arrayed" (*pulchra ut luna, electa ut sol, terribilis ut acies ordinata*, 6:9). (This also is the passage that praises the beloved's teeth as "a flock of sheep which go up from the washing," which, in its turn, recalls Llewelyn's head "washed" [*lotum*] in the spring at Builth.) The army "terrible with banners," in the Song figuring the solemn power of undomesticated beauty, in Usk recalls the army arrayed for battle against Rupert of Bavaria in the *campestre bellum* mentioned just before. And the Song's *amica* is not only "terrible as an army," but "choice as the sun" and "beautiful as the moon"; a few lines further on, reflecting on the schism and clerical corruption, Usk recalls the woman delivered of a son and driven into the desert: "the Virgin Mother, according to Revelation [Rev 12:6], fled with her son from before the face of the beast sitting on the throne" (118)—the woman who, in that passage of Revelation, is the *mulier amicta sole, et luna sub pedibus eius*: the woman clothed with the sun, the moon under her feet: the collation of "woman" with "sun" in the passage from the Song seems to have suggested, or at the least is emphatically echoed by, the same collation in the passage from Revelation. (And in that passage from Revelation, the "beast" from before whose face the woman flees has, not two heads, but seven; Rev 12:3.)

In this performance, the prophetic diapason sounding through these paragraphs gives way finally to full-throated biblical apocalypse. But though her appearance creates the panic of the passage's tone, it in fact prophesies nothing that was not already known, that was not already a chestnut of orthodox and conventional expectations about the last age. More, it touches on the most resonantly apocalyptic elements from that passage—the sun, the seven-headed monster—without engaging their apocalyptic force. More still, this image, like those around it, takes its most important bearings as part of a pattern of prolepsis and analepsis *wholly divorced from any chronology* of plot or story, effective only in the before and after of sheer verbal order, and involved in nothing more than the creation of pleasing symmetries. Usk allows that he could have mentioned the schism (which began in 1378) anywhere in the chronicle (which begins with 1377)—it has afflicted the Church "for twenty-two years now"[30]—and so instructs us to wonder why, then, it has been mentioned here and not elsewhere. The answer seems to be the devices of composition: the image of the head and the numerical patterns have summoned it by sheer formal attraction. The same principle obtains even on the smallest scale: Wenzel's defeat of Rupert calls up the marvelous ringing of Westminster bells (and not some other story associated with Richard) simply by rhyme: *campestri bello*, "on the field of battle," suggests *campanelle*, "little bells."[31]

The portent, as I said above, is a unit of enigma. It assumes prophetic promise by offering a moment of sensation that creates a deficit of understanding (nothing in the *past* of this story explains what this means . . .), and thereby signals a prolepsis (. . . and so the meaning must come from its *future*). But Usk's portents sever these components: the sensation has no epistemic function, and the prolepsis is merely formal. The sensational effect of narration produces the prophetic expectation that the future will echo the past, but expends this promise on the patterns and echoes of the verbal surface he creates. His portents convey no knowledge, or none that counts. Conversely, those that could convey knowledge fail to do so because they are unrecognized. The omens that befell Richard's coronation (the dropped slipper, the tumbled crown) betokened his fall, but not in a usable form: they were understood as omens only in retrospect. Indeed, he suggests that Richard's accession seemed at the time simply propitious: the first sentence of his chronicle reports that "many glorious things were circulated hopefully about his rule" when he became king.[32] So the omens were seen (since Usk's narrative reports them), but not seen *as omens*: their meaning emerged only once it was otiose. The "fiery ball" that crashed against St. Mary's Church in Bruges was "a very great presage of the ruin" of Bardolf and Northumberland,[33] but only "as it later appeared," *ut apparuit postea*. But this is odd: a celestial event landing actually at their doors does not make them think again about their undertaking or the promises on which it relies. Portents grab the attention when they befall (they are noted and eventually remembered), but to no purpose. Their meaning uncovers itself only when it no longer matters, swamped by the sensation of their vehicle. What Brandt and Given-Wilson describe as a virtually prereflective habit of perception in medieval chroniclers—the expectation that events are woven into providential patterns that narration can make visible, and that writing history reveals those patterns—proves in Usk's chronicle to be a pointless and autistic byproduct of episodic design. Their power promises meaning and then overwhelms it. The only patterns that emerge are traced on the verbal surface, and what looked like an escape from the formalism of the book's affective life is another formalism. What cannot be symptoms of Usk's unconscious awareness cannot be symptoms of history's meaning, either. It provokes hope for such meaning only to provoke immediately thereafter the recognition that such hope asks more than history can deliver. And asking for it (so the next chapter suggests) is an alibi for not thinking.

Chapter 5

Utility

For knowing the future does not require prophecy; it requires at most history. What has happened already in Usk's world—the rhythm of actions and of their worldly consequences—tells all anyone needs to know about what will happen henceforth. A disillusioned gnomic wisdom widely diffused during the Middle Ages claimed that the possible patterns of habitual action and habitual consequence in the world were finite in number and stylized in form. Another person's story is a "life tried out."[1] What has happened to others warns what may happen to us: "another's life is our teacher."[2] A "life" is a bundle of normative commitments,[3] and to enjoin readers to observe what has befallen others reminds them that their lives are bound to pattern as others' are bound. Similarly but on its larger scale, universal history promoted historical knowledge as an expertise in possibility: the conception of history as the "keye of remembraunce" opening the history "Of holiness, of regnes, of victories," celebrated by Chaucer's narrator, is a conventional idea. Chroniclers said so habitually. History is the "witness of ages, the memory of life," laying out for observation all that the acts of the past offer to knowledge: these words Usk saw before him when he opened his copy of the *Polychronicon*.[4] History showed how things would likely go, where choices would likely lead, and "utility" had for centuries been, and for centuries would remain, its purpose.[5] Those who have it know the future better than those who do not. Before such claims, an appetite for prophecy seems to seek ignoble shortcuts through the hard work of just knowing the past. Chronicles know that worldly acts are worldly acts, and that there are not many of them. The disenchanted recognition that history is secular process open to observation and inference offers the only promise of mature and reliable prognostication; ostentatious portent can offer no more than rhymes and feelings. Usk's prophecies, leading nowhere, humiliate the desire to bypass historiography's work of compilation and comparison. Historiography, though, will suffer a different humiliation.

In a central scene, he presents an exemplary instance of historical education successfully completed and knowledge of the future thereby achieved. The successful student is Richard II. On 21 September 1399 Usk was sent to join the imprisoned king for dinner. Elsewhere in the chronicle Richard is a creature of mere impulse and mere sensation, innocent of discourse: we hear his wails across the Thames, and at the end of his story we witness him "grieving himself to death," but we do not hear what he says while doing either.[6] This dinner-time interview is the only speech Usk assigns him,[7] and it is a historiographical miniature:

> This king during his dinner related stories with pain, speaking thus: "Oh God, this is a wondrously faithless land: so many kings, so many prelates, so many magnates it has exiled, killed, destroyed, and plundered, always corrupted and oppressed by dissension and mutual hatred." And he told the names and the histories of those thus tormented, from the realm's first age.[8]

Richard infers from what has happened to his forebears what will happen to him. The cry he begins with and his speaking painfully (*dolenter*) show what conclusion he draws. The temporary dispassion of Usk's account underlines the pathos. Because Richard knows what England has done to its kings, he knows what it will do to him.

Usk himself does the same thing: he routinely infers the future from the past and experiences it as fear:

> the followers of Master John [Wyclif], like those of Mohammed . . . have most treacherously sown slaughters, traps, contentions, and dissensions and seditions lasting even until now, and, as I fear [*timeo*], will last long enough to cause the fall of the realm.[9]
>
> I fear [*timeo*] that in the end it will happen as it did before, when many of those loyal to London rose up against the Duke of Lancaster.[10]
>
> I fear [*timeo*] that since possession of the sword is permitted them this time, against the prescriptions of order, they will in future be caused to use it against the lords.[11]
>
> I fear [*timeo*] that, just as when venality corrupted the priesthood in the Old Covenant, the three miracles ceased . . . , so it will happen in the new.[12]

At the same time, fear was a part of the political vocabulary of Richard's and Henry's reigns, the language in which the subject could explain action and assert rights against the crown.[13] In each of these cases, Usk's apprehension derives from seeing in the past a narrative arc that the present might recapitulate. He sees eerie and terrible things as he looks forward, but through natural inference, not prophetic illumination. The last lines of his chronicle fearfully anticipate a future: "May my highest lord not prove subject to the sword of the anger of the Lord, along with Julius, with Ahasuerus, with Alexander, with Hector, with Cyrus, with Darius, with Maccabeus."[14]

His expressions of fear seem cold, formulaic, unlike Richard's little speech. But the sound of emotion frigidly expressed is the sound of his chronicle straining to make history useful, just as Richard's anguish shows that his historiographical clarity has not been useful to him. Utility is a problem, something that the chronicle weaves around, hints at, and then shrinks from, where it is something that other chronicles are unabashed to claim.

~

Utility was, in fact, the decisive term in the greatest action Usk played a part in, Richard's deposition. He reports that in the autumn of 1399 the victorious Henry summoned him, "the writer of these presents," along with other "doctors, bishops, and others" to consider the causes in law that should be alleged for deposing Richard and crowning Henry.[15] Usk's brief memoir of the proceedings preserves one detail, otherwise unattested, about the reasoning behind Henry's challenge: its legal grounds were to be found, he says, in the decretal *Ad apostolice dignitatis apicem* and its glosses.[16] Usk's comment alone tells us that this, Innocent IV's sentence of deposition against Frederick II, was the source for both Richard's renunciation and the sentence deposing him.[17] Those documents do not themselves trouble to record this debt; their casualness on that score suggests that they were chiefly meant for an international audience: quotations of *Ad apostolice*, and echoes of Hostiensis and Johannes Andreae, would have been recognized at the papal court, or on the continent, but not by any sizable or influential English constituency. That is why the committee was staffed with doctors of the learned laws: they spoke to acquire international legitimacy.

And when they spoke, they therefore said that Richard was useless, *inutilis*. It was inevitable that they should. "Inutility" was the ground canon law prescribed for deposing an unfit king. It was illocutionary, announcing his deposition for cause, not so much specifying a reason as confirming the existence of reasons.[18] Thus Richard's "inutility" concludes and summarizes Usk's catalogue of reasons he was deposed: "the perjuries, acts of sacrilege, acts of sodomy, fleecing of his subjects, reduction of the people to slavery, madness, *and inutility in ruling*, with which King Richard was notoriously corrupted."[19] Richard was made to describe himself thus in his renunciation (" . . . meque ad regimen et gubernacionem . . . fateor, recognosco, reputo . . . fuisse et esse insufficientem penitus et *inutilem*"), and parliament to affirm in its sentence of deposition ("se fuisse et esse insufficientem penitus et *inutilem* ad regimen et gubernacionem regnorum").[20] Following the pope's formal sentence, Usk applies it as well to Richard's brother-in-law Wenzel IV, who was deposed as emperor.[21]

Inutilitas implied an anatomy of political power and efficacy.[22] From it emerged the popular image of the *fainéant*, the king unable to summon himself to action, so familiar that it became a kind of self-deprecating joke.[23] The vices of sadness and depressive sloth were associated with a failure of usefulness, and a picture of vitality defeated can be found wherever a king is deposed:[24] Boniface says that he acts against the emperor-elect Wenzel to avert the threat posed by the his "indolence" (*desidia*) and "inertia" (*segnicia*). Usk copied Boniface's bull into his chronicle; it illustrates the political imaginary that informs discussions of the useless king:

> Finally the electors themselves, seeing that his delay [in pursuing coronation] was becoming the source of infinite loss, and that the exhortations aforementioned were pointless and empty . . . , and that the same W[enzel] was altogether useless for the rule of the said empire; and lest its goods through his indolence veer irreparably toward collapse, they took care to signify to us that, the inertia of the aforementioned W. thoroughly considered, through which crises were springing up in the world, that they had decided, once he had been removed, to proceed to elect another who would run to meet them with power.[25]

The *fainéant* is deaf to events' call for decisive response and to the voice of those begging him to produce one. In the face of such need and such opportunity, his "uselessness" seems compulsive or willful.

This is what deposing someone made you say, and torpid unresponsiveness is what saying it made you picture. Events are imagined as summoning response from the prince who would be "useful," as being themselves responsive to his efficacious handling, while the depressive sloth of the "useless" king allows events their head.[26] And so the imperial electors impute to Rupert of Bavaria (the man they have met to elect) a vigor of response, and to the world a malleability he can work on: Rupert's ability to "run and meet" present crises "with power" implies a faith that they will prove tame before vigorous initiative. The theme of Archbishop Arundel's first parliamentary sermon under Henry IV, with its theme *Vir dominabitur populo*, sounds a note of relief that real power had at last acceded to the throne.[27]

~

Vir dominabitur populo: it is a man who shall hold sway. That verse bespeaks the expectation that virile dominance is what hastens out to confront danger. A useful king is therefore also a threatening one; the king this language wants is a king you must fear. To the subject, then, feeling fear is the beginning of public maturity. In the passage with which we began this book, Usk encounters adult political reality as the violent disenchantment of youthful exuberance. During the 1388-89 Oxford riots ("brawls, encounters, and frequent killings of men"), he led the southerners in the disturbance, defeated the northerners ("their expulsion many attributed to the compiler of these present matters"), and

> Why draw it out? We could not be pacified until many of
> us had been indicted for treasonable insurrection; among
> them, the compiler of these present matters was charged
> as commander and patron of the Welshmen, perhaps not
> unworthily; and once indicted, we barely secured our freedom
> through a jury, before a royal justice. The king, however,
> unknown to me before this in his power, and his laws—from
> here on I feared him [*timui ipsum*], taking the bit in my jaws.[28]

This story shows the bravado of Usk's political youth abruptly contracting before a world more complex and refractory than it had looked for. Maturity comes with the ability to recognize the danger of action and the danger of rulers. Historiography inspires dread, not because events conceal menace, but because their menace is unconcealed, unapologetically integral to what kings do and what others do to them.

This is what history teaches. No prophecy is needed to break the code of the future and fear it: there is no code. The only way not to know something as obvious as the tyranny of Richard II and the matching tyranny of Henry IV is to choose not to know, and one way to indulge that choice is to convince yourself that you must still search for the knowledge. The hope for prophetic foresight, the hope that history knows and plays a script, is just a pusillanimity that cannot bear to look the facts of historical life in their face.

There is more than one way to offend a king. William Clerk found one. If history becomes useful by revealing the patterns of consequence, laboring to infer meanings instead of hoping for prophecy, and if kings become useful by "dominating their people" and must first of all be feared, then whoever records the history must be afraid of recording it too plainly. Stick your head up to speak, and it may get sliced off.

~

Usk's chronicle seems habitually to discover, just a moment too late, that it has said more than it ought. Sometimes it is others who silence him: the king in his youth, Trefnant with the Bavarian ambassadors.[29] But much more often he silences himself. "Concerning [Richard's] birth, much unfriendly comment was bandied about in public—that he was born not from a father of royal stock, but from a mother given to slippery ways of life—as also concerning many other things I heard I remain silent."[30] Given-Wilson says aptly enough that this illustrates how Usk "enjoys giving the impression that he knows more than he tells" (lxxxiii). But it is more than that. The sentence is brilliantly constructed to insinuate meaning through syntactical disturbance, and also to imply to the attentive reader how the disturbance has come about. The sentence makes tolerably clear sense; but it makes too much sense and can be construed in two different and irreconcilable ways, either of which is possible only by suppressing part of it. Without the last five words, it works: "At his birth . . . , much unfriendly comment was made." Similarly, without the five words that precede them ("multum sinistri predicabatur in uulgo"), it works: "Concerning his birth . . . , as concerning many things that I heard, I shall remain silent." Taken in sequence, the sentence seems to show an emergency switch of tactic: he starts to speak of Richard's alleged bastardy, realizes in mid-clause that he should not, and jerks the utterance around as if all along he had only meant to say that he would not say anything about it. By then the syntax is deranged and the "secret" is out.

It is an accident to which he is suspiciously prone. Twice when speaking of the clergy's deficiencies—once of unspecified corruption, once of papal luxury—he aborts discussion before it concludes, explaining, "But here Plato enjoins silence."[31] In the passage above describing how he had learned to "fear the king and his laws," he gums up the syntax with an extra object, as if the very mention of royal power puts grammar beyond reach.[32] In these cases, as in that of Richard II's parentage, circumspection arrives late, after the beans are spilled. The implication is that as he narrates the violence of the past he exposes himself to that of the present; he learns that he does not control history and is not exempt from it, and so comes to speak with a reticence born of powerlessness and fear. On this reading, Usk's moments of self-censorship—Plato "bidding me fall silent," the brisk "Why draw it out?" just as things become interesting, the sudden abortion of stories unmatured—portray a historian disabused of enthusiasm and carelessness, awake to the need for prudence in the mature conduct of worldly life. Historical narration as the evasion rather than as the medium of disclosure is acted out in Richard's improvised historiography at dinner in the Tower: Usk after all is there to spy on him (*explorando*),[33] and more important than what Richard says is what he does not say: he does not seem in this episode to have given Usk and his masters what they were looking for. Usk, walking away, thinks the very substance of Richard's pain that "it was not those whom he had chosen to serve him and grown used to, but others, strangers laying traps for him, who had been assigned to his service"; he reflects on "the glory to which he had long been accustomed and on the deceptive fortune of this world."[34] But he does not seem to have secured signs that Richard would resign his crown, as Bennett sensibly suggests Usk was sent to do:[35] Richard's historiographical speech here works not only to describe dangers but to elude them.

Usk's panicky dramas of self-censorship, however, are in fact dramas; they mime a nervousness their very presence refutes. His scribes copied from written drafts, not from dictation;[36] indiscretions or flustered second thoughts could have been buried in revision. He has composed these stutters and reversals and self-silencings and then passed them on to his scribes. By them, he portrays himself as an imperfectly self-monitoring narrator, alert to threats of detection and shame but repeatedly overcome by impulses he tries belatedly to contain. These are not evidence of authorship looking nervously over its shoulder; they are artful evocations of it. He pretends to be anxious about banal revelations—nothing was duller or more commonplace than criticism of clerical or papal misdoings, and slanders of Richard II were hardly unwelcome in 1401 and 1402 when Usk wrote—and then pretends to bungle their suppression.

This sense of danger only just evaded, of self-surveillance cultivated but inadequate to the threats on every hand, does not arise from any worry about what he writes or any realistic fear of surveillance like Richard's. Instead, it embodies a literary idea. The protagonist and the antagonist of this first section of the chronicle, Usk and Richard, seem both to achieve a belated maturity. Richard's allies all suspect that he is oblivious to his approaching fall: his mother, who had "rejoiced" that her son was king, eventually can "see ruin hanging over you, because of those cursed flatterers of yours."[37] During his reign and after, Richard remained to sources both friendly and hostile a *young* man: he sponsored youthful images of himself (notably the Wilton diptych), but also provoked the lament, "Woe to you, O land, where the king is a child."[38] This, too, was surely meant to be recalled by that sermon of Arundel's for Henry's accession, on *vir dominabitur populo*.[39] Once he no longer reigned, these impulses could be viewed in an affective suspension: Richard could be a king "at once innocent and alienated."[40] Pictures both verbal and visual overlay the memory of his promise with the knowledge of its waste, of his chronic immaturity seen through the lens of disenchantment. In the Bedford Psalter, John Gower stares across an opening at Richard II, young and beardless but looking as though he "has lost everything and is praying for the salvation of his soul."[41] And thus, in other ways, Usk recalls the beginning and end of Richard's reign—and especially, here, the moment of Richard's disillusionment. Usk uses, as everyone used, the thought that Richard never quite grew up; did not grow up as Usk himself claims to have done, when at Oxford he learned "to fear the king and his laws." An excellent gloss on that story is the explanation that a truly useful knowledge of the laws "does not mean knowing their words, but knowing their violence and their power."[42]

~

That quotation comes from a comment on Cato's *Distichs*, the "My First Book" for aspiring literates throughout the period; this line glosses Cato's injunction to attend and learn, to reread and "remember" the precepts in his book. The study of grammar, beginning in childhood after the abc and construing, included the collection of aphorisms known by Cato's name: the *breves sententiae* (sententious imperatives of two or three words) and the epigrammatic distichs. Along with them traveled a collection of other texts, easy to scan, easy to read, all painting an easy and lurid portrait of life's adult negotiations.[43] The *Distichs* and their progeny instilled in generations of students a wary notion of utility. This important part of their early schooling told boys the world was full of traps, betrayals, and humiliations, and that maturity means scanning for them. These were learned early, stuck in the memory, and were easily retrieved: the frequency with which Cato's phrases suggest themselves to poets shows how easily they became a second nature.[44]

Cato's voice conveyed a garish fantasy of disillusioned worldly wisdom in chirpy epigrams that were stylistically unmistakable,[45] in mode and occasion ostentatiously paternal. Most medieval readers encountered on Cato's first page a prologue in which the author informs his "dearest son" that the maxims will teach "how to construct the character of your mind."[46] The self-regarding means of doing so, and the hostility of the world that requires it, both become visible almost instantly: "The first virtue is to curb your tongue," says the third distich. Though "He is closest to God who knows how to keep quiet when required,"[47] this is not a monastic or penitential silence: "When you have been injured, dissemble: the one who knows how to hide his hatred can later harm whom he wishes."[48] In this world, safety requires silence; even in jubilation or intimacy, you must hold back a piece of yourself. Drawn by the allure of friendly ease into incautious reciprocity, you stumble into an insidious enjoyment. "Staying silent has never harmed anyone, but having spoken has."[49] The infectious promise of talk can induce imprudent trust: "good faith is rare; so many people say so many things."[50] Speech is an easy seduction; a stealthy diffidence may miss some enjoyment, but it holds off danger and dishonor. "What shames you, remember to hide from your fellows"; "what you wish to keep silent, do not say"; "whatever anyone says, stay silent and anticipate [*perspicito*] everything, since men's speech both hides and reveals their characters."[51] Conversation is tactical, and the only defense while listening to others is to "look through" it, *perspicere*, to track its drift and purpose. But silence is tactical too, an instrument of caution and indirection: "To act stupid at the right time is the highest prudence."[52] The most dramatic reason for your own silence is what you should fear in another's: "Remember to avoid those who are silent or retiring; the river that seems calm may be troubled deeper down."[53] In other words, the silence of other people is dangerous because it conceals the same vigilance and calculation that yours should. "Much talk is stupid talk," one commentary says.[54]

The *Distichs*' means can look like ascetic Christian discipline, but their end is avowedly a contented selfishness. We are told that by interpretation medieval pedagogy sanitized, Christianized, their disenchanted and selfish advice,[55] but the evidence of commentaries and poems alike shows that the self-serving character of Cato's moral stance was perfectly visible.[56] The *Distichs* do not worry that concupiscence arising from original sin desires the infinite and gorges on the finite; they take their addressee's compulsions as less elastic and redeemable, not the misconstrued hunger for God but unskillful self-management. Those who fail the book's measure are not malign or perverse, but foolish, undisciplined, and forgetful: "It is foolish to ask for what can be rightly refused"; "it is foolish always to lose the joys of life through fear of death."[57]

Cato's most frequent injunction is *memento*, "remember." Its neat fit at the end of a hexameter line creates some of its allure, but the effect is dramatic: "Remember to beware words that lisp and fawn"; "What you suffer rightly, remember to bear patiently"; "When someone praises you, remember to remain judge of yourself."[58] The *Distichs* do not imagine themselves to offer new information: the first warns less against flattering speech than against forgetting to test for it; disasters spring not from failing to know the world, which they think easily known, but from failing to use the knowledge. The problem against which they contend is *absorption* in anything. Absorption leaves you exposed, open to others' inspection when you are not attending to the presentation of what they will see: lechery and greed are not evil but incommodious, "contrary to reputation."[59] To be carried away by celebration, pleasure, arrogance, or avoidance is to pawn yourself. Even successful self-indulgence requires taut self-restraint: "Between Venus and Bacchus there is both contention and common pleasure; embrace in your mind what is beautiful in it, but flee from the contention";[60] discipline in drink and sex is required to enjoy either.

We can see one source of the *Distichs*' appeal to Usk in their warning to the impatient heir, "Doubtful and fragile is the life given us, so do not rest your hopes for yourself on the death of another."[61] Since Cato does not direct the filial reader to eternal rather than temporal goods or warn him from greed as from a moral failing, it is hard at first to see why the heir should not wait eagerly for the testator's death. The distich speaks of the shortness of life, but another one advises, "It is foolish to lose the joys of life while you are busy fearing death."[62] Indeed, Cato's one good reason to think about death is to stop worrying about it.[63] But that cannot explain his advice that because life is fragile, one should not hope for the death of another. The line of thought is this. You will be tempted to hope for someone's death—a legator whose property you want, an enemy whose presence inconveniences you. But in imagining his death you forget your similarity to him, forget that what you wish on him will come to you also; you will have been *caught out* forgetting your own mortality, will shame yourself by blundering on unconscious of life's most obvious fact. The *Distichs* sees in its reader's future, in everyone's future, the permanent prospect of a shameful and clumsy comedy of inadvertency. Seeing how Abbot Samson foiled the plans of a bishop of Ely that he could not directly refuse, Jocelin of Brakelond thinks immediately of Cato—*Sic ars deluditur arte*—and "laughs to himself" as he recalls the words.[64]

That repeated injunction "remember" implies that the "son" will usually forget: though the maxims' principles are known, they have not become second nature. Against the mechanical force of undisciplined habit, disciplined habit must be cultivated. He must be reminded to remember. The subject of pedagogy in the *Distichs* does not yet possess his deliberate actions as character, is chronically outrun by his impulses, and must therefore haul himself into sallies of belated self-correction. The picture is implicit throughout. "Remember to bear your wife's tongue," *ferre memento*:[65] impatient reaction must be checked by the maxim of discipline recalled. Though another praise you, "remember to remain your own judge."[66] Midcourse correction implies that action will unroll in a staccato of interruption and emergency self-restraint. "Flee gossip, lest you begin to be thought the source of it; having been silent harms no one, having spoken does the harm."[67] The epigrammatic form recalls how casually rumors are traded, how thoughtlessly one can speak, and how consequential and beyond recall are words once spoken; the silence the *Distichs* commends is one that usually will be imposed only at the last minute, only when he has already begun to speak, with the strange hiccup of self-silencing.

Late medieval literature, which felt the imaginative appeal of Cato's pedagogy, habitually inflected it as the thought of youth, paternal words as heard by the child. With the apostle James's observation that no one can tame the human tongue,[68] Albertano of Brescia begins his popular advice-book *De arte loquendi et tacendi*—on the art of speaking and of being silent.[69] Like Cato, Albertano addresses his son, warning him that the press of speech is the nearly untameable object of necessary and extravagant discipline: "You, therefore, my dearest son, when you wish to speak, begin with yourself, like the cock who thrice strikes himself with his wings before beginning to sing."[70] The work discusses how and when not to speak, how easily offense and humiliation and loss can follow from a tongue incautiously loosed. Whether to speak is, quite literally, a question of circumstance: his son should consider the "circumstances" of classical rhetoric (who? what? why? to whom? how? when?) in deciding whether, how far, and in what voice speech should be allowed. He concludes by saying that this is all one needs to consider: "As all writing is formed about the abc, whatever should be spoken or kept silent can be inflected on this verse."[71] Albertano shares with Cato his fierce concentration on what is *useful*: "See whether what you want to say is useful, weighty, and profitable, or idle and empty. Useful, virtuous, profitable words we must always speak, but must silence altogether those that are worthless."[72]

The Bodleian Cato commentary notes that Cato not only addresses a child, but thereby figures the reader as one: "Cato instructs his son, and everyone else in the person of his son";[73] later, Caxton would call it "the beste book for to be taught to yonge children in scole, and also to peple of every age it is ful convenient if it be wel understanden."[74] Albertano enacts this recognition with a straight face; Chaucer does so as farce. One distich quoted above—"Rumores fuge, ne incipias novus auctor haberi"—is better known in its Middle English form: "My sone, be war, and be noon auctour newe / Of tidynges."[75] The end of the Manciple's Tale is a manic fantasia on this literary mode; the insistent repetition of "My sone," instanced here,[76] enacts the mere formality of wisdom literature's filial address. (At the same time, it pretends to take that address seriously, claiming at one point that this is not book-learning but maternal empiricism.)[77] And it wittily embodies the prolixity with which silence is commended. Something, indeed, of the extravagance that the recollection of Cato could call forth in Chaucer had to do precisely with the recognition of how these schoolroom passages, as they press on the memory, push the mind back into chronic immaturity, and offer possibilities of bleak comedy and lurid paranoia. Usk translated the same possibilities into a different kind of virtuosity. From the anticipation of shame and exposure Cato teaches his son to cultivate, Usk devises an immature picture of mature public life, mixing the ambient and unpredictable threat that childhood fears with the humiliation that adolescence dreads. The self-censorship he keeps imposing on his chronicle suggests a disenchanted maturity as imagined by a child precociously straining after it; the civil lawyer portrays his experience through schoolboy anticipations of it, as if he himself is still learning his lessons. Learning them, the figure he most resembles is the perpetually, disastrously, but also (we will see) alluringly boyish Richard II. The disenchantment is not the reward of grownups, but the ambivalent desire of youth. The utility kings should manifest and historians confer proves for both of them to be Cato's idea of utility.

And it does neither of them much good. For most of the chronicle Richard looks like the only person who has failed to see his fall coming, but then he shows that he has, and that his seeing it was the problem all along. Under 1396, Usk reports how Richard had taken Isabelle of France as "wife, though a useless one [*licet inutilis*], since she was not yet seven"; despite other opportunities more fitting and politic, Richard married her "with the greatest expense and the greatest worldly pomp" to secure French support against his domestic enemies.[78] This attempt shows that Richard did see the threat he faced and sought to forestall it. So Usk eventually humiliates him not for ignoring the threat but for trying to avert it. What twists the knife of *inutilitas* is the contrast between the hopes with which Richard prodigally sought her and what he accomplished thereby:

his enemies still won, and with a wife only eleven years old, he left no heir to block Bolingbroke's succession to the throne.[79] The measures taken by royal power to protect itself, and the measures taken under its sponsorship and protection, end in degrading reverses: this marriage to Isabella contracts "infinite expense" and brings no gain; John Hall's service in murdering Gloucester is finally rewarded by watching his intestines burn during his last painful moments of life. But if Usk's chronicle thinks that Richard saw the trap and acted to avoid it, then the tone of self-reproach in his historiographical aria cannot be his regret for ignoring it. And because it shows his shifts at avoiding danger, it cannot blame him either for a torpid laziness in securing his throne.

Characters in Usk's chronicle, and the chronicle itself, sometimes speak as though Richard alone was misled about the dangers to him. But the chronicle then makes it clear that he was not misled, that he anticipated his fall. That is the strangest thing about him. Archbishop Scrope, summoning England to indignation in 1405, urged its amazement that a king could be killed ("Who, I say, ever heard such a deed? or who has seen anything like it? Be astounded, Englishman").[80] Richard, dining with Usk in the Tower, shows no confidence that this is amazing, or that it is anything but routine. But if his shame does not concern a luxuriating confidence, an obliviousness to dangers only too obvious, then what does it concern? The answer to that question has everything to do with the identity of Adam Usk's secret. The next two chapters will offer it. They start at the grief in which the shame voices itself, and the shape of the history that levies grief as the tax on experience.

Chapter 6

Grief

In Usk, then, you don't need prophecy, because history tells you all the future's secrets you need to know. But then (this is the next turn) it does the job so easily that you don't need history either: the future, like the present, is so brutal and obvious that it can have no secrets. What is coming is more of the same, plus more hopeful and pointless efforts to avoid it.

The world in Usk's chronicle does not have a narrative so much as an invariant drive toward ruin. The image of a world tottering, physically unbalanced, is commonplace: Bishop Despenser, after the 1400 Epiphany Rising, determines to stay on his estate "until the world is better steadied," and Chaucer complains that the world, once "stedfast and stable" is now "turned up-so-doun."[1] But the former makes its perturbations sound temporary, the latter makes its permanence sound settled. Usk imagines the instability both chronic and violent: the world *pitches forward* (as the etymon of "ruin" implies), and everything goes with it. Joan of Kent grieves for Richard's "ruin"; Richard's plan for the Shrewsbury parliament, "like the statue of Nebuchadnezzar, at the highest point of its vainglory, toppled [*ruit*] with all its helpers"; Richard was moving "straight on to his ruin" as he gathered his Cheshire bodyguards, who anyhow proved to be "the greatest cause of that ruin"; Richard raised men from the dust "who were later dragged down in ruin because of their inordinate leap upward"; a plague came "suddenly" in 1400, "falling upon [*irruens*] souls and carrying them away"; Glendower's cruelty to churches led eventually to his "ruin"; as it is written that "before ruin, the heart of man is exalted," the Percies "collapsed into ruin [*occasum*]."[2] "All things press toward their end," Usk observes at a moment of personal application.[3]

Such is not a world in which the idea that rulers should be useful can expect to last. The hope that kingly action, vigorous and purposeful, could master the world must ignore its clearest message, that every enterprise ends vainly. The shipwreck of Sir John Arundel's expedition to France brought a brilliant beginning to sodden anticlimax, destroying "the flower of our country's youth."[4] This leads Usk to tell how the earl of Pembroke was captured making for the continent with the profits of a war tax; and then how Edward III, invading France, assembled a "great army" ready to sail, waited six months for winds to favor a Channel crossing, and finally gave up, "returning with his army uselessly [*inutiliter*]."[5] The action was a pointless and crushing contrast to the history it was meant to crown: the king taxed the people, assembled his army, prepared an invasion to repeat the glory of Crécy, and returned with nothing to show but the bustle and loss.[6] Arundel's expedition occurs to the chronicler's mind because he has already mentioned Bishop Despenser's failed 1383 crusade to Flanders. That expedition also failed, and the failure was a shuttlecock of faction.[7] Usk's brief, grim account neither accuses nor defends, but merely humiliates. The mission begins as a success—"about nine thousand Flemings, because they supported the schismatic French, he killed in a military assault"—but ends in ironic disaster: "but from those parts he was forced to retire and return home by the power of the French king and his army, once very many of the English had died of diarrhea."[8] In substance the story accords with Despenser's defense that he was deprived of victory "par l'aventure de Dieux";[9] the facts of Usk's account draw closer to the bishop's apologia than most others, but the reversal from the "warlike assault" his army launched to the bowel-flux that disabled it turns accident to abjection.

The story of Arundel's shipwreck speaks of the "sadness" of these pointless deaths. Uselessness is the chronic upshot of action; grief is its affective remainder, punctuating the narrative with its most familiar formula: *pro dolor*, "Oh, the pain of it!" The appellants' reforms angered the king, so that "alas" (*pro dolor*), only "irritations" followed, and years later (*pro dolor*), "griefs [*dolores*] and troubles" afflicted them. Sir John Arundel "alas" (*pro dolor*), died at sea; tax has grown to plague the English nation, "and so, *pro dolor*, things go awry"; the accomplished and promising Edmund Mortimer, Usk's patron, "alas [*pro dolor*] . . . left this life," "long before I would have wished," as did Archbishop Arundel, "alas [*pro dolor*]."[10] The phrase is banal, ubiquitous, and baroquely formulaic,[11] a rhetorical convenience that assumes the pose of powerful feeling. It gives no sense that we have touched Usk's heart, nor does it pretend to. It is a pain, indeed, that seems to avoid the touching of hearts. Usk cries out, *O Deus!* recalling how Michael II Paleologus, the Greek emperor, who visited the English royal court during his tour of western Europe, desperately seeking aid in his empire's defense.[12] Of the many reports of this visit, Usk's alone funnels it into a personal grief: he recalls that he "thought within himself" how mournful was the decline the empire had suffered, and then exclaims "O God, what are you doing, former glory of Rome?", now so beggared as to afford no defense of the faithful.[13] So too, "O God, how painfully [*dolenter*] now the Church (with two rulers) and the Empire (with three) attack each other and lay each other waste in mutual destruction"; "O God—the glory of Caesar and Augustus, of Solomon and Alexander, of Ahasuerus, Darius, and the great Constantine, where has it gone?"[14]

History stores up pain and releases it in the telling. It is felt by historical agents: "A great grief [*luctus*] flashed forth in the realm" during the 1381 revolt; the Jews "lamented" (*doluerunt*) their lost kin after the golden calf, and the English likely will have to do the same; Gloucester's son was murdered "to the great sorrow [*luctum*] of all the realm"; Giangaleazzo Visconti died, "to the great grief [*dolorem*] of the pilgrims" whose routes he secured.[15] It is felt by the historian, narrating: one sees "painfully" (*dolenter*) how Church and Empire tear themselves apart; Henry Hotspur, sadly (*dolenter*), died in battle, and Henry IV, sadly (*dolenter*), was infected and died; the papal schism had "monstrously and sadly" (*monstruose et dolenter*) disturbed christendom.[16] And feeling it is a duty of readers: the spectacle of the Greek emperors begging aid from the English king was "something to be grieved" (*dolendum*); Richard ordered Lord Cobham sentenced to the grievous (*lugendam*) life of perpetual imprisonment; Rome's decline must be grieved (*dolenda*).[17]

In assuming this pose, Usk's book displays an affect that, like fear, presented itself in public discourse as the claim of subjects and of rulers alike against delinquencies. Setting out the rights of one's position and contemplating the wrongs of one's opponent's, one claimed sorrow: the shipowners ("your poor lieges") petition Richard II for remedy lest "the fleet of the realm . . . be destroyed . . . and the owners of the fleet forever ruined, a sorrow and a great pity";[18] the commons in the notorious parliament of 1397, forced to beg pardon, "made great sorrow . . . that the king had come to have such thoughts of them";[19] of that same parliament, it was complained against Richard two years later that he had instituted acts "wrongly and grievously [*tresdolorousement*]" to his subjects' loss;[20] the papal schism, grieved a common petition of 1401, had persisted "to the great sorrow and desolation of Holy Church."[21] Obviously the work done by the public performance of grief over others' failings of others can be seen in many other contexts, before and after late-medieval England parliamentary language: Pope St. Gregory I in the sixth century habitually presents himself as grieved by the pressures of an office he did not want.[22] Grieving in this language is a partisan act, presented as a decent nature's instinctive reaction to history's indecencies, and a tic of chroniclers who register the force of disapproval in their sorrow.[23]

~

Usk's cold and formulaic expressions of pain recall such strategic avowals, but without strategic purpose; his feints of feeling mainly call attention to its absence. He thus makes himself the isolate and mercenary self that Cato's *Distichs* advised, which cultivates mistrust even in the maintenance of intimacies. The profit of friendship must be looked to, and profitless friends cut off: "Get rid at once of an ungrateful friend," Cato advises; "give regularly to the good, and know that your gift is a good investment."[24] Your friends will lie to you, so "Do the same to them; thus fraud is confounded by fraud."[25] Because life is "doubtful and fragile,"[26] the proximities that matter must remain always clear: by all means be bountiful to your acquaintances and loving to your friends, "but always remain closest to yourself."[27] Friendship is a risky good, tempting to unguarded attachment. Like pleasure and passion, it induces carelessness about reputation and opportunity and rivalrous friends waiting their own profit. Cato counsels isolation, but isolation dissembled with shows of fellow-feeling; he does not say that you should avoid being a friend, but that you should be a friend without revealing confidences. This isolation shapes the self Usk wears in his book. Autobiographical episodes must sometimes presuppose social exchange, but they rarely narrate it and usually obscure it. He renders his self-portraits in settings where the self is a detached and lonely thing: crepuscular return to consciousness; a midnight ramble;[28] saying masses for food, a refugee shunned by former connections.[29] In social exchanges he is the butt of embarrassment (reproached by Trefnant, guyed by the pope) or the favorite of superiors, or both; but he is never attached to confreres. Just past the lowest point of his fortunes, impoverished and denuded of office, he recalls the proverb, " 'Not for myself, but for my goods did others love me,' and so," he comments, "when misfortune befell, they neglected me."[30] It comes as a shock to hear him claim that others loved him for anything, that others even knew him. His dissembling, by contrast, appears in the narrating. Usk's sorrow, like the reported sorrow of subjects in parliament, is designed to be marked to the speaker's account, though too insistent and too rhetorical to be believed, or to expect belief. The greater the insistence, the greater the skepticism it provokes.[31] Like parliamentary petitioners', his sympathies are self-regarding. But unlike them, his sympathies seek no obvious goal.

The chronicle's one moment of shared feeling oddly underlines the point. After he has heard Richard's historiographical aria—"O God, this is a faithless nation"—Usk, "saw his agitation of mind [*animi sui turbacionem*]" and "departed thinking about the glory to which he had been accustomed and about the deceptive fortune of the world, agitated in my mind [*animo meo . . . turbatus*]."[32] The feeling passed on does not bring them closer; Richard's disturbance (*turbatio*) is a personal response that installs itself impersonally in Usk.

I want to show that this is consistent with the coldness of his avowed affects, and that all of them together demonstrate a consistent notion of human interiority. His notion is eccentric, not because it ignores conventional representations of thought and speech, but because it takes them more literally than they can seriously be taken. Albertano of Brescia's advice on speaking and remaining silent urges his son to give thought "before the breath brings the word forward to your mouth."[33] This figure, which he obviously does not consider remarkable, imagines speech as a material thing that carries meaning from one soul to another. Aristotle (in the *De interpretatione*, part of the organon of logical works available throughout the Middle Ages) defines the word as that which conveys the "conception" of the soul, a conception that itself entered the ideational demotic of medieval Europe. Augustine explains the distinction between *vox* and *verbum*: "The word pertains to the heart, the voice to the ear."[34] The heart conceives something (an idea, an impulse) that the voice carries to others.[35] There is nothing we say or do "which we do not anticipate with a word brought forth within."[36] The "word uttered" internally may remain unarticulated even in the mind, and certainly need not be intellectual: even impulsive voluntary acts are described this way. His point is that movement or action can only be considered voluntary, not adventitious, if something precedes and generates it. So this "word" that remains in the heart and initiates the act of speech is the originary impulse, whatever form it takes in the mind. The act of speaking is generated as a mental act, conveyed as a bodily impulse, and received in a mental act. The idea of understanding, including mutual understanding, was built around this picture for centuries.[37]

In Augustine, the burial of the intention deep in the self paradoxically enables engagement and friendship: the obscurity of other selves, because it makes one infer their intentions and thoughts, is a vehicle of curiosity and thereby of attachment. You cannot see your friend's will, but you can infer it from the material evidence of act and voice, and respond, "so that your life will not be without friendship": "from your heart, you believe a heart that is not yours, and to that heart, unseen by the body's eye or the mind's, you measure your faith."[38] The soul is veiled; one veiled self recognizes another, and grants it attention.

~

Usk takes this picture of the internal word with brutal literalness: feeling lands as a physical impact, is "communicated" more like a virus than like a thought, and becomes a wedge driven between selves rather than the way of their free mutual approach.

Usk's wooden formulas of a passion are not so much deficient as uncanny, because they give back the psychic immediacy they pretend to refuse. Just because they are so inadequate both to the material and to the feelings they bespeak, they look like screens for something obscurer happening behind them. The suspicion seems confirmed when Usk's most mercenary friendship erupts into a briefly vivid evocation of feeling. This comes during his last dealings with his friend the earl of Northumberland, who tries to persuade Usk to join a plot against Henry IV. Usk declines; hearing later that his friends have failed and been "decapitated, and their heads, eventually placed on the far side of London Bridge, . . . sent on to King Henry," his response is gratitude: "When this was heard of, the compiler of these presents gave thanks to God for his remaining behind, to the one who probes the future."[39] That their torture and death can wring from him only relief at his own escape suggests how Cato's self-guarding seems to leave him a self without feeling or character. But at the heart of that scene, Usk reveals a motion of the soul that comes as a surprise as much to himself as to the reader. Here is how he describes refusing Northumberland's invitation:

> To convince me to go with him, he promised me great advancement. God visited my heart, and I thought, "You, Adam, placed in a labyrinth, make your settlement with God. God has sent a malign spirit, and rightly, between the king and this earl, in the manner of Abimelech, as is read in the book of Judges." And I turned my coat, and to my lord of Powys, to await the grace of the king and of the kingdom, I disposed my steps to return. And thus it happened.[40]

This is the only time in his chronicle Usk uses his own name, and it is the unanticipated crisis of his story: he turns from revolt and begins his rehabilitation. But he does not know why. In the episode from Judges he cites here, the statement "Misit Dominum spiritum pessimum" names an event it cannot explain, the sudden hostility of the men of Shechem to Abimelech, whom they had made king. Usk's formula (*misit Deus spiritum*) for this event exactly echoes the structure of agency in the description of his own thoughts: *Visitauit Deus cor meum*, "God visited my heart." The sounding of a voice, not quite God's, but not quite his own—"*God* visited my heart" but "*I* thought"—and the twitching of a metaphorical cloak, turning from a man already departed, emphasize his isolation in a stylized figurative gesture. The account separates Usk from himself as much as from others: his own thoughts waylay him. Augustine says that perception of ourselves allows us to identify the motions of others' souls, but Usk's perception cannot extend past the actions and words to perceive its origins; so the self does not understand even its own motions, cannot resolve the impulses of action back into the internal "words" that originate them. He is external even to himself.

His story of William Sawtry's execution shows what this impulse from within looks like from without. We have seen how Sawtry died; here is the whole episode:

> *A heretic is burned.* In convocation a certain William Sawtry, chaplain, convicted of heresy and condemned, once

> the sentence was pronounced against him by my lord of Canterbury, with a great force spoke these words: "Sent by God, I tell you that you and your whole clergy, even the king, are to die in a short space; that the tongue of a foreign nation will conquer and reign in this kingdom; that this is waiting even at the door." And once he had been condemned, first being solemnly degraded, afterwards in Smithfield in London, chained to a post standing straight up in a barrel surrounded by red-hot faggots, he is reduced to ashes.[41]

Usk alone relates this dying prophecy.[42] He may have been present (he was in London then), but whether he reports or invents, he devises a narration of a hauntingly distant clarity. It is clear because Sawtry evidently knows what he is prophesying; it is distant because we cannot get near enough to make it out: Will clergy, prelates, and kings die *in* the conquest he mentions, or *as the occasion of* it? What foreign tongue—French, Welsh, Arabic? We have seen Usk's chronicle molested by adumbrations of unspecific disaster, and here, for once, someone offers to specify it. Sawtry's words pick up dismal echoes from other portents scattered about the chronicle, including those in its immediate neighborhood: the same page begins Usk's discussion of the legislation against the Welsh bruited in Parliament, which he seems to say included what he later calls a "decree of destruction of the Welsh language."[43] But though Sawtry's speech obviously has a distinct idea of the disaster, it does not convey the idea distinctly. Sawtry means it to arrest and teach and terrify into reform; but it only arrests, and the stark statement of its urgency—"waiting even at the door"—cannot disclose what it threatens as imminent. That failure is the frustration of the scene. It is also its pathos: the imminence proves a backfire. Sawtry predicts England's instant collapse but instantly suffers his own: the barrel and faggots are no sooner assembled for burning than he is *already* burned, "reduced to ashes." The suddenness with which his prophecy speaks is mocked by the suddenness of his demise; the prophecy is snatched away before it can be discerned, and the glimpse into his mind is pulled away the instant it is offered in the mocking irony of his prophecy turned back on himself.

His speech comes "with a great force," *magno impetu*: not something Sawtry marshals but something that marshals him, raises utterance within.[44] Speech originates not in a meaning conceived but in an impact felt, pushing speech out of the speaker, its blast narratively realized by the flame that consumes him instantaneously. Sensation explodes, propels itself outward as speech, and annihilates the speaker.

Sensation as a sudden material force pierces the narrative during the cameo appearance of Isabelle of France, Richard's second queen and a collateral victim of his deposition. Under 1401, Usk describes how she was escorted from London and returned to her father, the king of France. He renders her unforgettably: she "left London to return to her father—many discussions about this had meanwhile been held—dressed in black, scowling with deep hatred at King Henry but saying scarcely a word."[45] The bitter intensity of reserve (*uix os apperiens*) joined with display (*exhibendo uultum*) invites interest but repels connection. That same division greets the reader's experience of her: the scene summons a response to Isabelle but refuses access to her. One does not know the source or content of the hatred so vividly expressed: that a girl married at six and widowed at eleven has suffered losses is certain, but what loss afflicts her here? What does she hate Henry for? She provokes a reaction she does not welcome, a curiosity she will not satisfy.

The more obviously the mind is found to hide within its material expressions, the more urgently it asks to be uncovered. Isabella's picture hits the narrative like Usk's thoughts or Sawtry's prophecies; palpable but underexplained, her grief provokes a curiosity, and thereby implies the presence of thoughts that can be the object of that curiosity.[46] To take this one step further, Richard himself experiences in history the grief that Usk unconvincingly declares he feels in historiography. Richard is placed to feel the pressure of history as pain as the substance of his own emotional life: his voice echoes on the Thames when, "weeping and screaming, he grieved [*doluit*] that he had been born"; when his greyhound deserts him for Bolingbroke, Richard "bore it painfully" (*dolenter*). Grief is the disease of which he dies: "sorrowing, he mourned [*condoluit*] himself to death."[47] He is its connoisseur, its prime exhibit, and its provocation; more than that, he is the only character whose passions are easy to imagine and to understand. They show themselves plainly; and they turn out to be precisely the passions that Usk so coldly avows in his formulaic cries of *pro dolor!*

Usk's sudden reversal and Sawtre's cry show what the rest of the book more quietly assumes, that intentional acts—of feeling, thought, will—*befall* the subject formally intending them with the same disruptive surprise any other event might bring; affect or thought or choice is a precipitancy that overtakes the person who then feels or thinks or chooses, stirring actions and utterances unforeseen. Speech bursts out with the unoriginated suddenness of violence or its portents. The quick, vivid concretion of detail unprepared by the narrative is a device for generating sensation, I suggested, but that kind of sensation, the *impetus* that blasts through the mind, is Usk's model for events both external and internal: abruptions surprise the person who watches events, whether in the world or in historical narration; but they also surprise those who create events with the events they create, surprise those who speak with the words they pronounce. History happens when the world hits bodies, and when it does, it slaps out an utterance charged with feeling. That utterance typically takes the form of narrative: a narrative of the present ("Adam, you are in a labyrinth"), or of the future ("the tongue of a foreign nation will conquer to reign in this kingdom"), or of the past: "Oh God, this is a marvelously faithless land! so many kings, so many prelates, so many magnates has it exiled, killed, destroyed, and plundered."

Augustine, we saw, says that such intentional movements, because half hidden, invite curiosity and fellow-feeling. The imperfection with which external words convey the "internal word" they want to express is the very motive of friendship, because their brittle materiality sets off the richness of soul they express but brokenly; piecing the fragments of another man's meaning, you are pulled into attending to him. The "intention" of speech is conventionally described as the attempt to turn the mind out so that it may disclose itself: "If we consider closely what we intend when we speak, clearly it is nothing but to enucleate the mind's concept for others."[48] The depth of that mystery is symbolized precisely by the fact that we ourselves, knowing that the voice proceeds from the internal words, cannot know where those words emerge from: that is *just me*.

Usk takes this model with a deadpan seriousness that confounds the promise of intimacy, or even of self-knowledge: the unknowability makes that internal word itself act like a material sign that comes from somewhere unknown, and makes the self simply that which is afflicted by the force of such words that make themselves within. For Augustine, the will is the most secret place the self resides, and its unknowability is the sign of its ultimacy. In Usk, that unknowability does not contain the self, for the simple fact that it is not content at all, is not a cause but an effect. Its unknowability does not make intention a secret; it makes it a clue.

~

In other words, beneath Usk's cold and unpersuasive avowals of grief (*pro dolor*) must lie something, some impulse unavowed that is concealed, but evidenced, by them. What is that?

After concluding his account of Sir John Oldcastle's rebellion, Usk turns to the next episode. The mad, heartbroken sentence that begins it must be quoted in full—

> On the nineteenth day of February, in the year of our Lord one thousand four hundred and thirteen, my most brilliant lord, uncle of our king and his brothers (as well as of the earls of March, Arundel, Nottingham and Stafford, and of Abergavenney and Despenser); son of the late earl of Arundel, lord Thomas of Arundel; archbishop of Canterbury, primate of all England and legate of the apostolic see; the power, lantern, and wisdom of the people; the lamp and delight of the clergy

> and the church; the firm pillar of the Christian faith; he who conferred on me the good churches of Kemsing in Kent and Mersham in Surrey, along with the prebend of Llandogy in Wales; through whom, as he had promised, I hoped to be advanced to things greater still; he, overtaken—through that contingency by which all things press toward their ruin, by a sudden change, and long before the end I hoped for—

(here we pause for breath, still awaiting a main verb)—

> alas [*pro dolor*], ended his days at Canterbury, certain to receive that voice of sweetness from the heavenly king, "Good and faithful servant, enter into the joy of your lord," along with life eternal.[49]

Here is the same stiff, formal declaration of grief (*pro dolor*), the same declaration of an attachment apparently mercenary (*per quem me ad maiorem . . . promoueri sperabam*), and the same knowing resignation that all things pitch to their fall (*omnia tendunt in occasum*). But despite that bored, bloodless knowingness, the mortal change still comes as a surprise (*subita)*: his knowingness does not cause him actually to know that Arundel will die, because he has been baffled by hope (*longe ante michi optatum terminum*). We have seen many events Usk complains happened *dolenter*; but this one happens *quam dolenter*. The picture of Christ advancing the faithful soul into blessedness softens and resolves even Usk's craving for reward and advancement with a fleeting suggestion less grasping and mercenary, for once, than his own formulations like to suggest.

Usk seems to let the veil drift aside for a moment, to display what hides behind that formal grief he usually portrays, whose stiffness now seems to show that it is the mask of something else; and what it seems to mask is a grief not stiff or formal, but ingenuously felt. Whether it was so we cannot say: the rendering of grief as something authentically experienced here could be as deliberately performed, as premeditated, as the rendering of it elsewhere as a gesture mechanically made. That is not the issue. The issue is that Usk's chronicle makes expressions of grief look like a screen, *but also makes grief the secret that hides behind that screen.* The apparently mechanical formality of those expressions makes them seem all the colder and less ingenuous; their apparent concealment of grief makes that grief concealed seem the "real." Its reality is certified by the gesture of hiding it; grief is certified by shame.

What is the point of that?

Chapter 7

Theory of History

At the end of the previous chapter I quoted Usk's account of Arundel's death. This painful passage follows it:

> His death I saw, while in London that very night, in a vision: leaving his whole household behind and wearing short garments, as if to travel far, he was running very quickly, and alone. As I labored with all my might to follow him, he handed me a wax candle and said, "Break this in the middle between the two of us," and, so saying, disappeared from my sight. As I woke from that, I realized that we had been separated from each other, and, very sadly indeed, I offered Mass for his soul. Later I was apprised of his death.[1]

Usk is of course one of the retainers "left behind," and the breaking of the candle signals the rupture. But the focus is on the vain effort to go with him, who, "alone" (*solus*), leaves Usk alone. The dream-paralysis ("I labored with all my might to follow him") evokes the push to do something useful where there is nothing useful to be done. But it is literally a failure *to follow* (*insequi*), which amounts almost to a bad joke. For to this crucial and affecting episode there succeeds another, gossipy and trivial—the story of the greedy Bishop Burghill—which seems, in fact, *not to follow*.

~

"Friar John Burghill, a most greedy Dominican and the bishop of Lichfield," it begins after Arundel's death, without transition, "hid a great sum of gold in a certain niche opened in his chamber." Unknown to him, the niche also opened to the outdoors, and two jackdaws, cleaning it for a nest, dumped the gold outside where lucky passersby carried it off. This brought him "a scandalous reputation throughout the realm."[2] The vice that brings him scandal is not desiring wealth—Usk admires the sumptuousness of Arundel's furnishings[3]—but neglecting the duty of magnificence exacted by wealth and rank: the vice of "tenacity," he calls it elsewhere.[4] The story gets the laugh it is told for: among the magnates at Arundel's table, Usk relates, it provided "great entertainment."[5] But what makes Burghill scandalous is not what makes him funny. He becomes a joke because tries to thwart the normal course of things—bishops with money should spend it—and is himself thwarted in the attempt: his secret becomes a byword, and his hoarded wealth is lost by the effort he makes to keep it. This irony is by now familiar to us: had Burghill read Usk's chronicle, he would have seen disaster coming. That is how the world goes: the man who thinks he can be confident in his wealth loses it pointlessly. But then Burghill *did* see disaster coming to his wealth: that is why he hid it, and what makes him comic is not the disaster but the crude irony by which his evasive maneuvers bring it about, the perennial irony of the *distraits* whose foolish optimism makes them trip on their own plans.[6]

Ruin so ubiquitous and uselessness so inescapable should not surprise; the shame is that they do, that people ignore evidence that does not even try to conceal itself. Burghill becomes a dinner-table joke not because his undignified device backfires, but because he plows ahead with the indignity against the vulgar fact that devices like it backfire. I could turn to any of this chronicle's defeated hopes to illustrate this pattern, for it informs them all—especially, of course, Richard II, who grieves and is mocked as if he did nothing to save his realm, and then grieves and is mocked when it proves he did. I turned to this one because it shows how confidence in one's disillusioned savvy leads straight to exposure of one's naive illusion. Usk finds this pattern in Richard's story, and Bishop Despenser's, and his own, in the stories of all those who despite their experience of the world try to work on the world.

In his baselessly cheerful thought that prudence could defeat the ironic accidents of history, Burghill is shamed because he is *caught hoping*. Shame in this sense makes you want to cover not your deed, but yourself,[7] and the comedy of Burghill's exposure is coextensive not with his loss, but with the humiliation of naivety exposed.

The same pattern appears spectacularly, and closer to home, in what immediately follows. Among those who laughed at Burghill is Usk himself: "One day, at my lord's table," this episode concludes, "I heard this story told as a great recreation by the several magnates of the realm who were my table companions."[8] The mention of his table companions suggests an expansive enjoyment indulged after his years of exile, relaxation in the easy amusement of those above hoarding money or worrying about it. This in fact explains the apparent non sequitur, the connection of Burghill's humiliation with Arundel's death. As Usk laughs with the *regni magnates* at Burghill's mishap, he does not see his own approach. At Arundel's table, he does not know how little time is left to Arundel and therefore to his own ascendancy. Immediately—without leaving that table, so to speak—he shifts the temporal frame, surveying how Arundel's death then moved everyone but himself one step up the episcopal ladder. After the archbishop's death,

> to the see of Canterbury was translated Master Henry Chichele, Ll.D., then bishop of St. David's, for whom Master John Catterick was named as successor at St. David's. (To that same Archbishop of Canterbury, at my departure from Oxford, I left my chair in civil law.) Eventually, within half a year from this, when Friar John Burghill, aforementioned, was withdrawn from his life, he [that is, Catterick] was named

as his successor to his see, and N. [*recte* Stephen] Patrington, O.Carm., to his.[9]

Arundel's death strands Usk but advances Chichele, Catterick, and Patrington: these men, his age and younger, have all passed through the see of St. David's, which he had received from Pope Innocent but had never been able to occupy,[10] and one of them, his successor at Oxford, is now primate of all England. Usk's place at that table expires when Arundel does, and has expired by the time he writes. Relishing a *schadenfreudlich* amusement at Burghill and luxuriating in hopes of advancement, Usk precisely mirrors Burghill squirreling away his cash. This obvious and mirthless comedy is borrowed from the imaginative world of Cato's childhood imagination of adulthood. *Neminem riseris*, Cato says in the very first lines of his work, "Do not laugh at anyone," not because such laughter makes you cruel but because it sets you up.

This bitter coda to the tale of the archbishop's death will help answer the question put at the end of the last chapter: what is the point of using an obviously artificial grief to hide a genuine grief from view? Let me show it in three steps. First, Usk's recollection of relaxing at his lord's table, laughing at Bishop Burghill, recalls a happiness now lost, an easy confidence snatched away at his lord's demise; but once snatched away, the confidence and optimism look desperate and even deranged. "Through [him], as he had promised, I hoped to be advanced to things greater still":[11] these words can only mean that after the king's disfavor, his adherence to schism, and his treason against his king, he still thought he could hope for a bishopric. The enjoyment of another's discomfiture leaves him oblivious of his exposure to the accidents and wounds of history, to his zany optimism and its shaky foundation, to the near approach of disaster. But laughter and insane hope beat grief: they at least feel venal and therefore detached. To own a real grief over such a wound is to acknowledge that one has allowed oneself to grow attached enough, and to grow absorbed enough in the attachment, to be caught off guard and vulnerable by its disappearance. Such absorption tempts fate and invites the laughter of those who have seen the desperation coming and seen oneself not see it.

But then so has his laughter, and this leads to the second step. For, in Usk's chronicle, no matter what affect you display, you set yourself up for ironic reversal; and so the smart strategy is to display affects you do not even pretend to feel. Formulaic expressions of grief acknowledge the reality of loss and disappointment while implicitly claiming by their very coldness a detachment from the object: a routine "pro dolor" always ready to hand sounds wearily familiar both with the occasions it fits and with their banality and predictability. Such a spirit can acknowledge the misfortune, but cannot let itself seem surprised at it.

But (the third step), Usk is surprised anyhow. This pattern we have seen already (Richard looks foolish first because he did not anticipate his fall and then because he anticipated and tried to avert it), but we have not noted its most interesting feature. It is not just that Arundel's death comes as a shock despite Usk's knowingness, but that it is his very knowingness that leaves him vulnerable to the shock. The sentence in which he acknowledges the inevitability of Arundel's death follows the formulaic phrase of inevitability "through that contingency by which all things press toward their ruin" (and it is in fact a formula; he has already used it to speak of Mortimer's death)[12] immediately with the phrase *subita mutacione*, "by a *sudden* change"; he is surprised *as*, not just *although*, he remembers that all things rush to ruin. His attempts to learn the disenchanting lessons of history enchant him into stupidity.

~

Examining these passages and untangling their logic, we find a "theory of history," a generalized doctrine of experience and narration conceptually so clean that it can be abstracted from the chronicle's patterns and formulated in its habitual vocabulary.

What we have seen so far perhaps does not seem to have the quality of theory. This is what we have seen: The world is nothing but pratfalls;

Cato told us this as children. Despite daily confirmation of that bleak truth, we will forget it; this also Cato told us. Humiliation awaits those who forget it, and the danger of forgetting requires a continuing effort to bring it before the eyes. But by watching for the dangers that are coming, one wishes to dodge them, which is precisely what it means to forget the ruin toward which the world pitches. We chronically ignore what we knew even as children, and chronically humiliate ourselves with the accidents we cannot keep ourselves from trying to avert. Teaching this lesson is the function of history. Its import is that evasive maneuver is useless and humiliating. But it provokes the desire to avoid at least *that* humiliation, which itself proves another compulsion to avert what cannot be averted. Like kings, historiographers snare themselves in this paradox and this failure. It is not so much that you can't really learn history's lessons, but that those lessons, once learned, inspire the hope that they warn against.

This is not the theory; it is a mechanism—crude, jejune, and static. But the theory includes it, a theory that is also crude and jejune, but not static: it is mobile and it produces mobility, explains the sensations that the chronicle evokes and sets the mind to working on them, gives these sensations an intellectual intricacy (though not a depth) that prolongs the narrative's shocks and even helps them to keep functioning as such, though the reader should learn what they do. It is genuinely a theory, an intentionally elaborated structure of thought that choreographs what is made to look impulsive, unwilling, and unwitting.

Let's look one last time at a passage discussed in the first chapter and again in the fifth. Usk worries that for their venality,

> we [priests] shall be ejected from the glory of the priesthood, with great whipping and trampling. . . . Why draw this out [*quid mora*]? The Virgin Mother herself, according to

> Revelation, fled into the desert from before the beast sitting on the throne. But here Plato orders me to fall silent, since nothing is more certain than death, or more uncertain than the hour of death.

And he continues with this story about his benefactions to his parish church:

> And so (blessed be God) to the church of my origin, the church of Usk, now that I am learning to die, my memorial—a suitable missal, gradual, tropary, sequentiary, and antiphonal (newly composed, with the new additions and notes), and a full set of vestments with three copes, all elegantly worked with my badge (of a naked man digging on a black field) commending me to the prayers of worshipers there—; this I leave. Further on, if God grants it, proposing to elaborate this same church with a more decorous reconstruction in honor of the Blessed Virgin to whose nativity it is dedicated;—but not thinking that this latter redounds to my praise, because I pray that this writing of my present foolishness not be seen during my lifetime.[13]

We have seen this passage earlier, and we have seen Andrew Galloway's brilliant description of how his panicky self-silencing in the person of Plato (pointless as we saw it is) resolves itself immediately into an art of dying. But this is not the most bizarre thing about the passage; for he does it again, standing on the brakes in mid-benefaction and staggering away from the wreck that results. The awkwardness of the final lines (which my translation labors to capture) derives from deranged expectations of both syntax and sense. Usk (1) announces that he *has already made* some benefactions and (2) lists them; then he (3) announces the he *will make* other benefactions, making as if he will (4) list them; in this structure the participial phrase of (3) expects a main clause. Instead he breaks away into a qualification of what he has just said, in the form of *another* participial phrase, so that neither expectation—that he will list his coming benefactions and that he will complete what seems a new sentence—is fulfilled. Instead he turns away, deflecting an apparent boast and blushing at his foolishness. Were it not for the second of these, the first would seem clear enough: he pretends modestly to disavow what he has now avowed. But what "present foolishness" (*presentis fatuitatis*) is in question? The otherwise otiose pronoun in "not thinking that *this* [*hoc*] redounds to my praise" implies the contrast: *this*, the more recent of two things in contrast with *that* earlier one [*illud*], in the familiar usage. *This* refers specifically to future benefactions, which is why Usk speaks of his *present* foolishness: the phrase refers by definition not to what he *has done* in the past but to what he *is now doing*. He is now producing writing, *scriptura*, about an intention still unfulfilled. And talk of this foolishness cannot be merely a pretended modesty about the source of the benefactions, since their very point is to identify him as an object of prayers. So, again, what foolishness could attach to what he is writing *now*?

It is the foolishness of describing something he means to do as if he can confidently assume he will do it. Notice the tightness of the paradox he pulls around himself. *Iam mori adiscens*, learning to die, he focuses on the clearest instance of guaranteed failure, the mortality that mocks all hopes. Learning the lesson, he acts in accord with it, enacting disillusionment with the future by investing in his death, planning for the prayers his soul will need. But the act of trying to surrender the future leads witlessly and almost instantaneously to another attempt to control the future. His expensive remembrance of death leads before the sentence's end to a forgetting "how certain is death and how uncertain its hour."

Now this, so far, is simply the pattern we saw before: the mechanical habit that makes men who recognize their hopeful illusions try to remedy those illusions, the disillusionment that designs new illusions. But this passage lets us note two things. First, it is an exercise in a literary technique Marshall Leicester brilliantly described: the representation in narrative of a speaker hearing his own speech and responding, sometimes in surprise, to what he hears.[14] Both moments of stammering self-censorship are in response to something at that moment: "*now* learning to die," he has made his donations, his description of which proves to be his "*present* foolishness." The first silencing of the passage, Plato's intervention, comes in response not to something that has happened, but to something Usk has heard himself say: wandering onto what it pleases him to fancy is dangerous ground, he recognizes it as such only on hearing his own speech. Likewise the second: as he hears himself speaking about the future, he recognizes the trap of counting on it, and sputters to a halt. It is what Leicester calls impersonated artistry, the representation of a verisimilar voice rather than the transcript of an actual one. This is a property of all such passages. The very conditions of authorship mean that Usk is not stuck with any passages he discovers, on composing, he would prefer to delete: the manuscript we have is a fair copy made from his own (presumably wax-tablet) copies, meaning that no pentimento need ever show. Their inclusion is therefore his decision, and his stammering surprise a part of the premeditated design.

The second thing this passage shows fills out what is missing in the first, in the mechanical recidivism of a mind whose recognition of uselessness spurs again the hope of being useful. Fear, we see, is induced and performed as the solvent of hope: remember your death. But the remembrance of death can induce a new complacency that he must try to remedy by reminding himself that death might interrupt his preparations for death. But what keeps the mind returning to hopes of which it works to disabuse itself? What blurs the sharp focus of disillusionment; causes it to luxuriate in the thought that, now disillusioned, it may consider itself indemnified against further disillusionment; interrupts the antinomy of knowledge that the world admits no efficacy and its impulse to use that knowledge efficaciously?

It is all over this passage, but shows most clearly in the adverb *ornanter*. Lingering over his benefactions, he pauses over their pleasing artfulness: the look of the liturgical books' pages, newly written and notated. Both the writing and the vestments are *composita*, well worked, and the latter done *ornanter*, elegantly. We see up close the design of his badge placed on the vestments, and we see the whole set of the vestments gathered together, recalling that moment at Henry's coronation when the flutter of colored fabric announces a brightening abruptly dismembered with the execution of John Hall. In the larger passage in which it appears, and leading directly to this climax, there is the image of the smoke he calls *impressibilis*, an allusion, if it is an allusion, that I have had no better luck tracking than Usk's editors and other commentators, but that describes something rarefied and shapeless made plastic, given persistent shape; and of course the magnificent vision of the woman clothed with the sun; the beloved of the Song of Songs; the flowing of a stream, the ringing of little bells, the rhyme and design of a passage itself elegantly composed.

The thing that keeps bringing minds back to the hope that they are trying to suppress is the beauty that emerges as the upshot of trying to suppress it.

~

How it does that is clarified in the central person and the central episode of Usk's story: Richard and his deposition. We saw that Usk began writing after Richard's deposition and death.[15] The first words of his chronicle, introducing his reign, do not immediately mention his fall, about which Usk and any conceivable reader already know. It does not pretend not to know about it, either. Instead it alienates the knowledge in absorption and then recalls it as surprise:

> When the aforesaid Edward [III] had, on the vigil of the Nativity of St. John the Baptist in the fifty-second year of his

> reign, been removed from this life, his grandson Richard—the son of Edward, Prince of Wales and firstborn of this king; a child eleven years old and among all men, like a second Absalom, the most beautiful—succeeded him, crowned at Westminster on the feast of St. Kenelm. Of this Richard, at the time he began his reign, many glorious things were said with satisfaction. And because he was of tender age, others who had responsibility for him and for the realm did not desist from inflicting acts of licentiousness, extortion, and other unbearable wounds on the kingdom.[16]

We know about that coronation from later in the chronicle: three omens occurred (the accidents that befell the coronation slipper, spur, and crown), but there is no sign of them here, no sign that anyone saw them or thought them omens.[17] The attention is on Richard's beauty and the hopes it seems to encourage, and then on their ambush by the realities of his early reign. The beauty itself is an omen unregarded: the comparison with Absalom should suggest dangers rather than glorious expectations. But it prompts instead the celebration of Richard, the glorious things said *uotiue*—"with satisfaction, according to desire."

In the clearest evidence of deliberate design in his chronicle's large structure, Richard's beauty is again recalled, and again by analogy with Absalom's, at the moment his death is narrated. It is an amazing passage. First we are told that Richard, "sorrowing, grieved himself to death on the last day of February."[18] Then those three unregarded omens are recalled.[19] And then the chronicle, remembering its opening lines, bids Richard farewell:

> Now Richard, farewell [*uale*]—or rather the one who should have fared superlatively well [*ualentissime*], if I may put it that way, since after death it is permitted to praise anyone; and, if you had disposed your affairs according to God and the relief of your people, one who would have been praiseworthy.

> But although you were bountiful like Solomon, beautiful like Absalom, renowned like Ahasuerus, a surpassing builder like the Belinus the great, still, just as Chosroes king of the Persians fell into Heraclius's hands, you in the midst of your glory, with the wheel of fortune turning, into the hands of duke Henry, along with curses your people bore within them, most wretchedly fell.[20]

Here again Absalom appears, as the measure of Richard's beauty, and is accompanied by other exemplars of kingly good fortune, but the effect of all of them is the same: idolatrous Solomon cursing his kingdom with division, rebellious Absalom, boastful Xerxes, and clever Belinus—all of them fallen, killed in battle, deposed, or otherwise unfortunate at their ends—are presented as if models of good fortune whose resemblance proved ironic to Richard. Unlike those first sentences of his chronicle, this one is not presenting the views of others; it is manifestly Usk's own voice giving his farewell, and he falls to the same bemusing absorption in Richard's beauty and the magnificence of his reign, ignoring the grim certainties they enclose. At the beginning of his reign, what everyone ought to know about kingship and beauty did not suffice to suppress hope; now, at the report of its end, they do not suffice to ward off attachment and desire.

For that is what we see. Of all the labored verb-final sentences in his chronicle, this is the most pointlessly labored and artificial, stretching out the statement of an end already known in a *de casibus* frame that is already hackneyed.[21] It lingers over its series of similitudes, a qualifying temporal and circumstances phrase ("in the midst of your glory"), a trite image ("the wheel of fortune turning"), the specification of a destination already known ("into the hands of duke Henry") and of a circumstance retailed ("along with curses your people bore within them") and one trite adverb ("most wretchedly") before reaching the verb that everyone knows will come, as if it were in suspense. And it is not the only evidence of lingering, for the sentence before it ("Now Richard, farewell . . .")

tangles itself in precious wordplay that manages to suggest an unintended authenticity surfacing through deliberately bland convention. It is impossible to reproduce in translation what he does with the word *Vale*, farewell. The dead metaphor hidden inside the utterance is revived and disclosed as the promise of "faring (superlatively) well" that his birth and beauty and coronation conferred.[22] The emotional logic is clear, especially in the setting given by its baffled syntax. Like so many sentences begun that we have already seen, this one, of such different tone, never reaches completion: after the imperative that "farewell" formally comprises, it never lands on a main verb: the parallelism would require a second imperative form in place of the subordinate clause. It stalls on the vocative of pathetic address to the dead man, and as it sits there his breathtaking image appears just as it was when he was crowned.

Beauty does the deed here, beauty that inflicts itself precisely as a drag on the effort to dismiss Richard. The sentence mimes a mind lingering over the dead man's memory, luxuriating in it, experiencing him as again present, and again feeling the hopes that his person could inspire, brought vividly and crushingly back to mind by the explicitness of its final defeat: grief at Richard's death induces the revival of a hope that his very grief recognizes is irrational. The whole procedure therefore suggests the dementedly perseverant character of hope as such: it always conceals the treachery of convincing you to ignore what you know. Wishful thinking turns beauty into a promise that Usk should know better than to trust, when the world he portrays, unrolling its events, so clearly announces its character. In a world of mechanical "ruin," those who have hopes of themselves or others can have them only by refusing to know what they know. But this refusal emerges in the effort to know it. Usk's repertory of monitory comparisons transforms itself before our eyes into gallery of magnificence. The image of Absalom that sits at its center and returns us to the chronicle's first lines is, in medieval iconography, conventionally the image of a beardless youth, just as Richard's typically is. At the moment of his death Usk gives Richard's image an immediacy it never has before. This youthful beauty is also the image of youthful heedlessness, the heedlessness that Cato's *Distichs* make their young charge know while insisting that he will not succeed in using the knowledge.

Cato warns that the young man should not forget to remember, should not let slip from his mind those clichés of experience that the author passes on to him. Usk's farewell to Richard shows that trying to detach himself from the past by seeing how mechanical and inevitable it was brings it back with such arresting vividness that he desires it afresh. Beauty ascribes to the object the properties that explain its desire. It is the key that aligns the tumblers of Usk's chronicle, that explains its effects and its thought. He disenchants prophecy and historiography; but he thereby leaves his chronicle nothing to do but to recall him and his readers to the elemental and adolescent suspicion that Cato teaches, to learn the lesson that utility is a snare for the wary, a temptation to believe that there is something that might usefully be done. The adolescent's shame is to be caught in an unposed moment, and hope is the most vulnerable and unposed of stances. The chronicle teaches you to avoid it by inflicting grief and fear, calling them up to enact the surprises with which history ambushes the unwary, to make defeats felt: the defeats of the past that you mourn and those of the future that you fear. This exercise aims to produce a rehearsal of affect rather than its experience: what you want is to register grief and fear without feeling them, to register them the way formal expressions register them; for if you were to feel them, you would already been the victim of the trap and would be shamed as you were caught hoping. But there, in the deepest logic of the chronicle, is an impossibility, because the grief and fear, if unfelt, are unregistered as well. Thus the proof of detachment carries the virus of attachment; and thus the palpable reminders of the uselessness and hopelessness of action revivify the hope for utility, and the conviction that there is some way one might escape. The book locates that desire that holds every enterprise hostage; it portrays itself as hostage to that same desire; and its account of it is the theory of history that constructs the book.

~

I claim that this is Usk's "theory," an intentionally elaborated conceptual structure of thought that organizes his chronicle's effects. Theory is a discursive form, and he did not articulate this one discursively; but he contrived it. It would be easier, and certainly more conventional, to describe it as the unexamined or disavowed workings of his imagination. But the very manuscript shows him using the opportunity for supervision and second thoughts that drafting and scribal copying allow him: the passage about the omens at Richard's coronation, omitted in error or belatedly composed, is inserted (by the same scribe) at the top of the page. I am describing not what he did without realizing, but what he did without saying. Usk does not stutter and clutch in the grip of his memories; he designs a stuttering, clutching way of evoking that grip, and the logic that catches one in it.

To say that it is a theory is not to say that Usk actually believed it, any more than previous chapters said that Usk held particular convictions about the inutility of events or the vanity of worldly action, or that he felt shame or detachment. It would be interesting to know whether he did, but would not bear on the present inquiry. Believing it, if he did, would hardly redound to his credit: as an attempt to account for the shape of events in time or for the exigencies that attach to recording them, this "theory of history" is so willfully nugatory as to be parodic. It is scaffolding that holds up his narrative and its stylistic and sentimental effects, offers a setting without which those effects could not matter, imagines for them a relation to the empirical world, fills them with the activity of the thinking mind, and stretches them into history. His theory does all it needs to do: it makes a facsimile of explanation for Usk's facsimile of a world. It does not need to explain the real one, nor does Usk need to have thought it did. Then again he might have: his almost systematic self-subversion might imply that he had a systematic but inadequate program of action that, acted upon, produced a lurid and piecemeal apprehension of history and constrained his actions by constraining his understanding of the scenes in which he acted. But what difference? In either case we have a program; we do not have a secret.

Chapter 8

Adam Usk's Secret

At this point, the attempt to track down what thoughts or expectations or knowledge are hidden in Usk's secret reaches a dead end of sorts: its trail leads to no more than unverifiable guesses about what might have been in his mind. But then this is what a secret by definition is. More to the point, this failure points to its own solution: track the secret all the way to its end, to the intellectual structure that is built around it, reduce it to the trivial alternatives we reached at the end of the last chapter, choose to believe one and then the other, and you realize that Usk's secret has not been disposed of, but still remains. Say (as we said) that the bogus theory of history devised for the purposes of this chronicle either is his self-destructive view of the world or is a mere game assembled in language; then commit yourself to believing one of those. Whichever you choose, you realize that what the book has been hiding is not *that*: whatever was unexplained is unexplained still. But this tells us something. Pulling the net of investigation tighter and tighter, we have found that no matter how intimately we enter into what lies outside the work's own expression—its political and legal contexts, the intellectual structure it embodies, the feelings it seems to charge by seeming to hide—none answers the question. Which suggests that it is in its expression that the secret is held. The secret is something built into the structure of the writing itself, as the rhetorical tradition had advised that no art is as artful as the one that dissembles itself: "the device [*ars*] is successful if it is invisible; if it is noticed, it provokes shame and ruins your credibility for good."[1]

As it happens, there is an art that Usk acknowledges; that was curled together with his professional ambitions and his academic training; that (we will see) he made use of; that thought programmatically about its own hiddenness; and that has everything to do with the sense that his work keeps a secret and with the secret that it keeps. And it is the commonest and most obvious of arts: the dictamen, the vocational training in the rhetoric of the letter that was second nature to lawyers, diplomats, and bureaucrats. The dictamen brought the sources and thought of classical rhetoric into the mainstream of medieval writing.[2] Usk's inflated vision of his career—the one that made him seek commission as a notary while he was an Oxford student, that made him dream of the curia and the bishop's pallium—steered him toward both the pragmatic use and the self-idealizations of this ubiquitous and overweening art. It was an art associated with the culture of notaries, of the Roman law, of international relations.[3] Above all, it was an art associated, indeed nearly identified, with the Roman curia, which teachers of the art called both the origin and destination of all eloquence; and it was a means by which the ambitious hunted papal favor.[4] The most widely read author of the dictamen, Thomas of Capua, was an auditor of the papal palace, as Usk himself would be.[5] One good measure of an art's clientele is the drift of its most routine jokes, and Guido Faba gives, as an example of the bathetic incongruity of banal matter with high style, an eloquent celebration of "safe return from the Roman curia."[6] The relevant skills were taught both formally and informally at Oxford,[7] and the materials of them remained in the possession of just the circles Usk rejoiced at moving in.[8]

~

On the other hand, one thing I have just roundly asserted is roundly and routinely denied. One of the few confident judgments about Usk has been that he does *not* use or know the most distinctive and most evidentially salient aspect of the dictamen: the repertory of rhythmical periods for concluding clauses, systematized and taught as the cursus. The tradition that periods formally composed should come to a recognizably patterned conclusion lay deep in the muscle-memory of Latin prose.[9] Among the cadences the language most commonly sorts itself into, the cursus names some, in specific relation to word-boundaries, appropriate for enacting the conclusion of a sentence.[10] The conventional patterns are so familiar that anyone who reads a large selection of medieval Latin prose will recognize them instinctively,[11] as apparently did speakers and auditors of Latin in classical Rome: a famous passage in Cicero suggests that Roman crowds might cheer a neat clausule.[12] Prescriptive, regularized, and explicit medieval formulations originated in the medieval Roman curia, and passed from there into documentary practice on the continent.[13] The cursus entered England, as a distinctly Italian import, only at the end of the thirteenth century; but mastery of it, and instruction in it, were required for licensing as a regent master in grammar at Oxford, which places this skill in the course of ordinary university instruction there.[14] The old notion that it was meant to be authenticating is obviously wrong (why devise a method of authentication any schoolboy could reproduce?) and long since discredited. Its practical textual function, if it had one, probably lay with making mistakes in copying or pointing easier to detect. It may also have had the different practical function of performing distinction.[15]

Whatever practical work the cursus did, it did it by embodying a coherent aesthetic, and the aesthetic is the clearest and most important thing about it. Thomas of Capua defines the dictamen as "a worthy and artful collection of words, with a weight of meaning and order of utterance, allowing nothing to be truncated, conceiving nothing unnecessary." He defines the "order of utterance" in that sentence simply by saying that "utterance must be ordered":[16] he can rest content with redundancy because the "order" involved is immediately evident in the experience of reading: the clarity of line that comes from units of thought and diction that signal their conclusion precisely as they conclude. Ends sound like ends, which is another way of saying that abruptness and surprise are unworthy. The *venustas*—the charm—of such writing is a matter of grace, an art that shows the genius of naturalness by knowing when to stop.[17] This is polish, a kind of beauty specific to law and its practitioners[18]—precisely the kind of beauty Usk can exclaim over, referring as he can to a document made "sub gloriosa forma."[19]

But, as I say, it is usual to deny that Usk bothered with this aesthetic. Noël Denholm-Young cited him as evidence that "all did not avail themselves of the opportunities which we may suppose they had at the papal court"; indeed, he says, Usk "is almost deliberately unrhythmical."[20] Denholm-Young knew a cursus when he saw one (he spent many years editing the letter-collection of Richard de Bury); you do not want to brush his judgment aside on a question like this, and I can satisfy myself that I adhere to it more closely than he meant anyone to: Denholm-Young is both wrong and right. But first the evidence.

The opening pages of the chronicle conform almost perfectly to the cursus's prescriptions. Assuming that most readers will not care to examine the evidence, I drop it into a footnote.[21] On the first two leaves of the chronicle, the first seven pages in Given-Wilson's edition, the cursus is very regularly observed: in a relatively conservative view, excluding all in which a case for exclusion can be made, over 85 percent of the periods close according to the rhythms of the cursus. Usk had learned rhythmical prose, as anyone would conclude he must have done, and its flag waves proudly in these first paragraphs. Abruptly—the change is audible to any reader—it drops to less than 50 percent of the periods (and this on a relatively liberal view, *including* all that I exclude in the earlier calculation). That is, Usk dramatically controverts Denholm-Young's judgment before more dramatically confirming it. This fact is not fated to be interesting, since two related objections might concede the evidence but explain it away: one might object that he began with the resolve of observing the cursus but grew hasty or indifferent, or that he cared to polish only those apples at the front of the cart.

These explanations are inefficient, for several reasons, the first being that Usk assures us that he can practice it if he wants to and that his audience will expect him to. Under the year 1399, he copies into his chronicle a petition he composed for Sir Thomas Dymmok, but concludes with a remark that translators have found a little baffling: "Translatio ex gallico in latinum hic non patitur modum endictandi, ideo lector parcere dignatur"[22] ("The translation from French to Latin here does not permit the style of composing [*endictandi*], and so may the reader deign to forgive it"). The document was French; he reproduces it here in Latin; the act of translation has caused some failure the reader is asked to forgive. What failure? The phrase he uses (*modum endictandi*) suggests the formal rules of composition, and in fact the periods here do not close rhythmically. The purpose of this concessive sentence is to recall that since what he includes is not a Latin document of his composition but the Latin translation of a French document, it cannot be expected to hold to those rules. Usk knows that many readers will know the cursus and note its absence, and declares that the cause of that absence is not incapacity. Such reassurance would do more harm than good unless he could assume that the rest of his chronicle would confirm his claim here: there would be no point making it if he knew that no *other* sentence of his conforms to the rhythmical prescriptions of the cursus. So he expects his hypothetical reader to recognize both its presence in and its exit from his book, and his concession here implies the distinction between capacity and choice needed to establish that what he does he chooses to do.

~

A second warrant that this is a change Usk chooses and not one he drops into by accident or default follows a few lines later, on the same opening of the manuscript, and it helps suggest his reasons for thinking about cursus and the rhetorical tradition. After telling of how he took the bit in his jaws, he tells the story of Sir John Arundel's disaster at sea, briefly quotes and moralizes upon two verses of Bridlington's prophecy of taxation, and then addresses the reader: "May the reader be gentle on the order of years for those deeds related thus far, because the things which I saw and heard, more powerfully from the truth of the deed than from the order of occurrence, only thus did I entrust to my memory."[23]

Here he claims (the language is odd, but this seems to be its force) that it is because his own mind responds to the vividness of events, as he works to make readers respond to the vividness of his narrations, that he scrambles the order of events; but more important than the reason he gives is simply the fact that he announces having scrambled it. In doing so and saying so, he declares himself in violation of the first canon of dictamen, and of rhetoric itself. "Narration is called faulty . . . when the order of the action performed is disregarded," says Guido Faba's hugely popular *Summa dictaminis*. A narrative must be lucid, he says later, that is, must preserve the "order of matters," without wandering.[24] He is talking about the brief *narratio* that got the work of letters under way, but what he says is universal in rhetorical training, and in the rhetorical texts most commonly read, in the Middle Ages. His instruction that narrations must be "brevis, dilucida, et probabilis" is derived from the precept of the *De inventione* that narrations must be "brevis . . . aperta . . . probabilis," which defines an narration that is "open" (*aperta*) as one in which "the order of matters and times is preserved," as when what was done first is told first.[25] Isidore of Seville, in a discussion unconnected but to the same effect, defined prose as discourse "prolonged and direct." That is, not "bent" (*perflexa*) by verse, it can stretch itself "straight" (*recta*) to its goal, arrange an efficient route to its end.[26]

~

The cursus's exit from Usk's book is sudden, timed for effect. The place where it changes is the passage with which this book began, Usk's recollection of the time at Oxford when he stepped into public life and nearly found himself executed for treason:

> But why draw it out? We could not be calmed before many of our number had been indicted for treasonable insurrection, and among them the compiler of these presents as the chief leader and maintainer of the Welsh—perhaps not undeservedly—was indicted; and thus indicted, we barely managed to gain our liberty from a jury before one of the king's justices. But the king, unknown to me before this in his power, and his laws—from here on I feared him, and took the bit through my jaws.[27]

Ignoring the unrhythmical expletive that begins this passage, there seems little to make it stand out from Usk's practice until this point: there is one unrhythmical period ("indictátus fúerat") and then two rhythmical ones ("iusticiário liberári" [velox] and "frénum imponéndo" [trispondaicus]). But the syntactical malfunctions seem to display a speaker who is rattled by what he says to the point of forgetting it. The sentence forgets that it has already supplied the main verb (*timui*, "I feared") with a direct object—"the king and his laws" (*regem . . . et eius leges*)—even though the predicate has just completed, and so lamely concludes with an *ipsum*, "him," for the king. The preposition *per* is introduced redundantly, since the prepositional work is already done by the participle's prefix (*imponendo*, "placing in"), and introduced disastrously, governing the wrong case (*per* would require *maxillas meas*).[28] Here, too, an unstated effect is conveyed: while trying to say that he has, like a good domestic animal, taken *between* his jaws the bit that is naturally suited to them, the passage through suggested by *per* communicates a violent piercing that nowhere is plainly stated and plainly could not transpire (after all, it is a metaphor), but that suggests real pain squeaking out through the crack of the language. And the change in the book's style, its abandonment of rhythmical clausules, happens just here. The lines systematically violate the most common stylistic canons of medieval written rhetoric. Rhyme is regularly denounced in manuals, and we here have *iusticiario liberari*; hiatus, the juxtaposition of vowels is still more regularly denounced, and there are six of those in these lines.[29] The "ugly resonance" (*turpis sonoritas*) of clustered sibilants is a vice,[30] and we find in this passage, remarkably, four instances of the letter *x* and sequences like "michi prius in ipsius potencia ignotum et eius leges timui ipsum, per maxillis meis frenum imponendo." As its parts go flying, the sentence makes as if to end on a spectacularly unrhythmical period—"eius leges timui ipsum"—not only failing to create a cursus but creating the worst kind of hiatus with the juxtaposed instances of *i* (one that could still offend Rousseau),[31] before the imposition of silence allows him to slide briefly into correctness with the concluding rhythmical phrase.

~

These failures are not inadvertencies. Usk has seen carefully to correcting the scribe's work in this paragraph, righting errors through interlinear additions: and one of those is the addition of the *ipsum*, the unnecessary and ungrammatical "him," initially omitted (the scribe perhaps recognized and charitably corrected the solecism) but restored in correction. These failures are choices, not lapses, and throughout the book we can see him choosing emphatically rhythmical or emphatically arhythmical cadences for dramatic purposes easily recognized. Recreating a brief address in convocation by John Trevor, a fellow practitioner of the learned laws conspicuously more successful than himself, he packs the short discourse with rhythmical clausules, even in mid-sentence;[32] representing an urgent and private conversation, by contrast, he catches the feel of talk with short sentences abruptly and arhythmically concluded.[33]

That this *is* a style, a literary effect deliberately cultivated, is a conclusion hard to avoid. As Denholm-Young's remark suggests ("almost deliberately unrhythmical"), Usk conjures a distinct literary self from deliberately artful ugliness (Croce called the baroque "una sorta di brutto artistico").[34] But describing his style and discovering that he has chosen and refined it only poses the interesting questions; it does not answer them, and it does not give us his secret. That comes only when we work out why he starts by laying down the smooth nap of the cursus and then brushes roughly against it.

~

This question can be treated swiftly. The dictamen's resources, like those of any craft, bespeak intentional design; the craft's visible operation warrants the confidence that whatever may be visited on the reader unforeseen is nevertheless visited in the operation of that design. Unlike some other systems of literary norms, rhetoric usually tried to make design function as if naturally, as something mutually recognized and acknowledged, by allowing its audience not only to spot it but to recognize it as a contract the skilled orator fulfills. Practical rhetoric of the middle ages deployed this feeling that its norms were *mutually* constituted even more than that of antiquity. The cursus moves this a step along. Each sentence, as it ends, palpably signals that it is doing so, and the informed reader can take pleasure feeling the familiar beat of the clause-endings cooperate with the sense and slot together into place. For precisely unlike poetic meter, the cursus's rhythm is prescriptively bound to syntactic and sentential closure.[35] This pleasure is a specialized one, catering to expectations fulfilled loyally and locally, and so offering the satisfaction of beholding the proficiency one shares with the author. It is also a pleasure that, being artful, is not in fact found in nature, even in the conventional "nature" of unmarked discourse; only when trained in or trained by the cursus do you learn to expect that periods will conclude on a schedule they continually publish. The cursus's appeal is that it displays premeditation not as a substantive ruse of argument but as a formal design in which speaker and audience, writer and reader participate in a rhythm of surmise shared and fulfilled; this is one reason for its durability in rhetoric oral and written, classical and medieval. A skillful and elegant clausule, even if you have never encountered quite that formulation, arrives like a familiar tune.

That is, the cursus performs design in real time and fits it to the resolution of meaning and structure; it makes the fact of design part of the experience of reading. And the work involved in performing thus makes two things visible to the author who learns its recipes. First, it raises to immediate and practical awareness what rhetoric's norms aim at, encourages the author to see them as ideas expressed and epitomized in the agreement that he pursues continually with his reader. And second, binding these norms together and laying them out for thought, it suggests what local effects might follow, sentence to sentence and episode to episode, from violating them. I suspect that these things are clearest to those authors in whom the habits of dictaminal practice have not become second nature, who must still make those choices consciously. I suspect also that Usk was such an author.

~

Of these broad norms of rhetoric, one of the deepest and commonest is the injunction against discontinuity and surprise. An abrupt shift requiring readers to catch up and take their bearings, a shift in subject or tone or style, is a "vice of thought"—*vitium sententiae*, which in this context seems to mean "a vice in the composition's very conception."[36] This vice is reprehended in the design of letters (when the parts do not fit), and also in the relation of its parts (when the style drops abruptly from the high to the low.)[37] These are vices because they make the reader work for what should come effortlessly and remark what should go unremarked. Such failures include those that make the reader labor to discover a plain sense, and as well to discern where to puctuate sentences: "a faulty delivery, when the points do not fall where they should fall," as Geoffrey of Vinsauf has it in his *Summa de arte dictaminis*.[38] The "delivery" of which he is speaking evidently is not that of a speaker; it is the delivery (*prolatio*) built into composition itself, and the words that follow explicitly remark the unmistakable connection of this expectation with the use of rhythmical cursus, precisely because this shows where sentences end. This passage shines a beam on what the cursus was thought to *do*:

> And so let the attentive *dictator* take care that he discipline the course of his delivery through each unit of its composition, that he provide the distinctions germane to the ordering of that composition, and with periods that are now long, now short, now in an elevated voice and now in one falling somewhat quiet and now in one with a sound still more subdued, let him distribute or disjoin the undiscriminated masses of his composition.[39]

It is not the noun *cursus* (which in this passage means just the discourse's itinerary), but the assumptions encoded in the whole passage, that instruct us, and the most instructive are the assumptions that style is most importantly a means of displaying the distinction of sentential units, and that even the "voice" conveyed by style—the protraction and contraction, the raising and lowering of the tone—is directed to that end.

This injunction, that works should not make their readers labor through trial and error to discern the tone, subject, drift, or even scale and pointing of the composition, amounts to the injunction that they should not *surprise* their readers, that every shift and distinction should be signaled in advance, not least that most basic distinction that comes with the ending of any sentence.

Chapter 4 showed how Usk devises the juxtapositions of sudden and deidealizing contrast to suggest the banal predictability of a world that people still deceive themselves is complex and uninterpretable: he invites readers to relax into the detailed, merry, and ornate account of Henry's coronation to whiplash them with the sudden picture of John Hall watching his entrails burn.[40] He also registers that suddenness stylistically, closing the scene of Hall's execution with an especial dissonance: in *ultra pontem London' in palo ponitur* the arhythmical construction is emphasized by the quick alliteration, which, continued from *pontem* three words earlier, makes gaudy overuse of an ornament proscribed anyhow. This stylistic punchline to a quick gruesome narration continues a pattern Usk has already established: the sudden effects of violence on lives and livelihoods are brusquely narrated and ended arhythmically. When Henry, advancing across England against the king, works summary justice on Perkyn de Lye, keeper of the forest at Delamere—another case in which we are presented an amputated extremity across an urban landmark—we see it: "the head of the notoriously great malefactor Perkyn de Lye he [Bolingbroke] caused to be cut off and placed beyond the eastern gate [*affígi fécit* (**irregular**)]."[41] Then we learn that many of the nobles who defected from Richard to Henry got nothing but imprisonment for their pains (*plures non bene sibi credulos custodiis trádidit divérsis* [**irregular**]); then that Sir William Bagot, who trusted in the king's favor, found himself "led chained" by Bolingbroke's son (*secum inuinculáto dúcto* [**irregular**]). The pattern continues itself thereafter as well. The story of the traitors of the Epiphany rising, seen by Usk to be executed, dismembered, returned to London, and pickled, ends arhythmically (*postea sale condíri, uídi* [**irregular**]);[42] So too those of Ricardian sympathizers lynched, whose severed heads are displayed and, arhythmically, "remained displayed for some time across London Bridge" (*públice patébant* [**irregular with alliteration**]); so too that of the justice who tried the bishop of Ely on criminal charges, and who, dying unexpectedly and excommunicate, was dumped into a pit (*próici obtínuit* [**irregular with hiatus**]).[43] It becomes habitual not only for violence proper, but for the bitter reversals history forces on those who think they can control it. The Cheshire archers Richard kept to secure his reign were the greatest cause of his fall (*fuit causa ipsius ruíne máxima* [**irregular**]); an outbreak of the plague in 1400 arrived "suddenly" (*subito*), "as if it were falling upon them and carrying off their souls" (*ánimas tóllens* [**irregular**]).[44]

Subito in the last instance sums up the connection between the scenes of violence and sudden ruin, the narrative effect Usk labors to give them, and the stylistic device that reprises them. The rhythmical habits of the cursus, I said, instruct readers what is coming, imply that the discourse has contracted not to surprise them. These deliberate failures of rhythm catch in the cadence of prose the refusal to keep such a contract. The violence and disappointment, the ruin and the pain that afflict historical actors, afflict them because they scheme to sway the course of events that are too crude to be swayed; the tough stupidity of events leaves agents self-deceived and thus surprised by what happens.Usk deranges at the moment that they are narrated the patterns that try to believe in such control: his prose cadences itself just enough to engage the expectation of continuity and regularity so that it may, time and again, mock it. The promise of continuity sets off the spasms. Geoffrey of Vinsauf had instructed that the composer should make no sudden moves: "it is not beautiful to begin with a forceful thrust or to end with one."[45] This cadencing is a device for ending that way and for making it clear that one is ending that way.

This marked irregularity is a device Usk uses both to model and to effect his moments of bleak or lurid suddenness. He uses it simply and directly to convey the sense that William Sawtry, burning in his barrel, is cut off anticlimactically in mid-prophecy: declaiming at his last moments, its cola rhyme densely and impressively but the period as a whole hiccups: "Sent by God, I tell you that you and your whole clergy, even the king, are to die an evil death in a short space [*mala mórte moritúri* (trispondaicus, though with alliteration)]; that the tongue of a foreign nation will conquer to reign in this kingdom [*superáuerit regnatúra* (velox); that this is waiting even at the door [*próxime expéctans* (**irregular with hiatus**)]."[46] He uses it clearly and simply in creating his portents, with their suggestion of significance abruptly and anxiously signaled. The spring at Builth, which bubbles along peacefully enough until the last two words specify that it is the blood that is bubbling, contrives the abruptness with an irregular clausule (*sánguine manáuit* [**irregular**]);[47] he inflicts a trite warning to the priesthood of its corruptions with the reminder that Christ threw the money-changers out of the temple (*eiécit fóras* [**irregular**]); describing the "terrifying coat of arms" of the duke of Milan, Usk specifies only at the end of the sentence that these were seen, not displayed on pennons, but "in the sky were often seen [*túnc uísa* (**irregular**)].[48]

Of course deliberate faults of rhythm cannot work such effects alone or mechanically; they require other devices and other techniques. But they govern and focus those techniques. A good example is that unhappily vivid career of Robert Bowlond's semen.[49] The remarkable sentence repeatedly obscures what precisely has happened with an almost precious rhyming of every colon and several commata—

> Where and at which time we found a nun [*únam moniálem* (trispondaicus)], who by the disordered lust of the said Robert had in a sodomitical manner [*móre sodómico* (**irregular**)], through the dripping of his seed and not through the entry of his organ [*instruménti ingréssum* (planus, though with hiatus)]—found both through the confession of this same nun [*eiúsdem moniális* (trispondaicus)] and the letters of the said Robert [*dícti Robérti* (planus)] and also through the inspection of the body of the pregnant woman done by older women [*per matrónas fácta* (**irregular**)]—was impregnated [*fuísse impregnátum* (trispondaicus, though with hiatus)], and a daughter much like the said Robert, on the feast of St. Petronilla just past brought forth [*ultimo lápso peperísse* (trispondaicus)]; and this crime the same Robert himself in full convocation confessed [*éxtitit conféssus* (**irregular**)].

The sentence retards construing at every point, but its grammar, fastidiously correct, is never so tangled that its construction cannot be discerned. One problem is the overabundant provision of cursus, which cries wolf, signaling conclusion too often without actually concluding; but when the sentence does conclude, it neglects to signal itself rhythmically. The whole bad joke of this episode formally regarded is backformed from the contract of completion that the cursus professes.[50]

~

But this describes only part of the effect. Notice this passage in the account of Henry's advance against Richard. As Bolingbroke passes through Coddington in Cheshire, his army wastes the place ("sparing neither fields nor crops, devastating the whole countryside"), and Usk, visiting its church the next day "nothing—except everything carried off, and doors and chests broken into—did I find," *hostiisque et cistis fráctis répperi* [**irregular**]). Here the aggressively irregular rhythm, combined with the ugly sibillation of *cistis fractis*, does embody the derangement of order, but more to the point, it conveys Usk's experience of expectation defeated in a clause curtailed without stylistic announcement. As in passages already cited, the rhythmical derangement in this case is both an analogy for rhythms of historical experience disrupted and a way of programming that disruption into the experience of reading; but it is also the specific expression of suddenness subjectively experienced.

And so the haunting, unanticipated glimpses of Usk's mind in denuded moments rely overwhelmingly on these mechanisms. Waking from the psalm-laced nightmare during the 1401 parliament, "I fearfully committed myself especially to the guidance of the Holy Ghost [*tímidus commísi* (**irregular**)]";[51] of the portentous eggs the valets of the king were served "I saw one [*únum uídi* (**irregular**)]";[52] struck by witnessing Pope Boniface's sudden death, "I had two visions [*uisiónes hábui* (**irregular**)]," and in the second of them saw a fox threatened by dogs disappear into a pit (*de cétero dispáruit* [**irregular**])"[53]; he grew suddenly and rightly apprehensive for his patron Archbishop Arundel during another nightmare in which he could not catch up with the archbishop who "was running alone [*currébat sólus* (**irregular**)], and waked to celebrate a Mass for his soul and to be told that he is truly dead (*certiorátus fúi* [**irregular**]).[54] His nighttime wanderings through Rome have a structure similar to the Bowlond incident just discussed, though without the syntactic maze: cola and commata alike rhyme overinsistently,[55] until the reason for his insomniac brooding—resentment at the snubs of other Englishmen—is revealed in this expressively clumsy sentence: *sic cogitaui quod consimilis liga inter fortes patrie et exules silue in partibus dinóscitur ésse* [**irregular**]," "I reflected that just that sort of league between the strong ones of the country and exiles in foreign woods is known to obtain." The role the chipped periods and angular constructions play in these passages is the one they play in the others just discussed—they orchestrate rhythms, invite expectations they then disappoint—but here they simultaneously *portray* the disappointment of expectations in the author's own recollected experiences: the surprise of a nightmare, or the embarrassing motives, only half-avowed, for wretched wakefulness. These passages snap a shot of the mind surprising itself as it works; what the failed cursus adds to the picture is a taste of what this feels like to the mind itself: in full career and heading toward a well-formed period something happens that cuts it off.

And that suggests a closer relation and a more interesting possibility. A failed cursus can do more than *evoke the feeling* of a mind surprised at what it hears itself saying; it can *seem to provide evidence* of a mind so surprised, can seem to witness a belated anxiety that forestalls the utterance intended and aborts the final cadence it was heading for. In a passage we have already encountered, an abrupt and arhythmical period conveys what it is like to be shut down impatiently at a faux pas one was not aware of committing: "Then the bishop of Hereford told me to be quiet [*siléncium indíxit* (**irregular**)]." My point here is that the cursus and selective drastic avoidance of it are as if designed to portray the writer *himself* shutting himself down upon the belated recognition that his sentence is pushing toward revealing a secret better kept. And indeed, we see those moments of most explicit self-censorship concluding with failed rhythms that sound as though things have been cut off before the end envisaged for them. We have seen some of these already. The most explicit passages include all the major moments of self-censorship: when he nervously curtails rumors about Richard's rumored bastardy (*ut de audítis táceam* [**irregular**]); when he stops himself speaking about clerical corruption (*nil incercius hóra mórtis* [**irregular**]) and about papal wealth (*hic me Plato quiéscere iúbe*t [**irregular**]); and when he abruptly realizes the power of the king and his laws (*tímui ípsum* [**irregular, with hiatus**]), which he smooths over with the lame addition of a gerund clause that simultaneously smoothes the period into a trispondaicus.[56]

~

We can go further. Working back from the chronicle's suggestion of secrets imperfectly withheld to this rhetorical device, which seems to be the only thing left once those secrets are traced, takes some complex inference. But once the inferences have been made, the route going the other direction—from instruction in the cursus to a chronicle that teases its readers with shudders and flinches—is startlingly direct. Of course I can hardly call the route inevitable, since I do not know of anyone else who took it, over the many centuries of Latin rhythmical conventions or the fewer centuries of the codified cursus. But given the desire to create a certain kind of effect, to explore the stylistic resources of this elementary form of composition, and to create effects in the mind of a reader, the conventions of the cursus can almost write their own ticket. Failed rhythm caused by dramatized self-censorship, by enacting the interruption of speech by the thought working to produce it, though arrived at in my analysis through discussion of other kinds of surprise, is in fact the kind that is most obviously suggested by the very stylistic ideal of the cursus. It answers to what is most distinctive about its stylistic ambitions and to the conditions imposed on the *dictator* by those ambitions and the training that instilled them. Crucial to the conception of such formal prose is that cadence punctuates discourse instead of governing it; like graphic punctuation, and unlike poetic meter, it is coordinated with the period, the completed utterance. I have mentioned already the effect it has of communicating a continued assent to a kind of contract, the text's agreement that the readers will feel their construction of the syntax and sense confirmed by the smooth landing of the cursus.

Along with this comes a feature at once more obvious and more profound, a feature tackled willy-nilly by every author executing the cursus and conveyed to every reader who grows familiar with its ways: that is, the realization that the period itself is the unit of conception and composition, a unit that must be shaped and forecast to allow rhythm and sense to tally at its close. Each sentence bespeaks its foreconceit. The training of the *dictator* involved teaching him to know where each sentence aims and how to slip a rhythm under it when it arrives there. It is usual to warn the student in dictamen that he must keep his mind on the sense that he is conveying and subordinate the individual devices of rhetoric to that; Alberic of Monte Cassino tellingly speaks of "keeping a tight rein" on a device like repetition "lest it wrest control of your writing,"[57] which thinks of the style as a precipitant animal prone to destroy the order of what it should convey. The mastery that the quiet grace of the dictamen is supposed to express is the constraint of the thought to the period so that they fit with an easy appearance of naturalness. A neatly executed series of periods presents thoughts whose clarity seems to speak for itself and to demonstrate its orderliness with familiar cadences. Both the organization and the cadence are brought to mind when they fail to appear; the use of failure in producing these fruits is Usk's discovery—and, I suggest, his secret.

The precipitancy of undisciplined prose, the self-discipline needed to resist it, the rein by which that discipline is imagined: these recall for us the moment when Usk first deploys his device of abruptly failed rhythm and first portrays himself as a problem to himself: "But the king, unknown to me before this in his power, and his laws—from here on I feared him, and took the bit in my jaws."[58] And this picture of bold self-assertion that cravenly submits to the laws, taking the rein to itself and filling its mouth with the bit, recalls and puts a paradoxical point to the most familiar way of describing what prose itself is: prose is discourse "freed from law of meter." The idea is of long standing—Jerome says that Hebrew poetry is not "bound to meter" (rather, it was written "like Demosthenes or Cicero" "per cola et commata," that is, in rhythmical prose).[59] Isidore of Seville made the definition "freed from the law of meter" usual for the Middle Ages,[60] and it was freely taken up by grammarians and by writers on the dictamen.[61] Even Boncompagno's reason for resisting the cursus—"prose is discourse composed after the will of the composer, and freed from the laws of meter"—assumed the normative force of the definition.[62] Boncompagno had a point, which was that the language of freedom sorted oddly with the normative patterns of the cursus. It hardly required a Boncompagno to make the point; everyone is aware of it, and the need to make the requisite distinctions, of understanding *how* prose was "free of law" but trammeled in rules, led to a striking vocabulary. Geoffrey of Vinsauf elaborated Isidore's definition this way: "Dictamen is a series of complete utterances severed neatly [*intercisa*] at distinct intervals, bound by no laws of meter."[63] Justifying prose as free, in this formulation, requires pre-empting the "laws" with a cut.

Intercisa detonates a surprising suggestion of bodily violence, coolly regarded, in the discourse of prose composition. But it was always there. The divisions of a period, of the syntax marked by the cursus's rhythm, were *kommata* ("stampings") and *kōla* ("members"). Cicero, translating to Latin, makes these *incisa* (or *incisiones*) and *membra*. (Even the relatively innocent *periodos* is Latined as *comprehensio*, "capture.") The *kōlon* subdivided a *periodos*, and was subdivided further by the *komma*; the components of a *comprehensio* therefore were *membra* divided by *incisiones*, members sliced by incisions.

The jargon of prose composition sounds like a butcher's art, its sentences made of severed limbs. That is of course precisely not how the art was supposed to seem: as I said, the results aimed at were those of measure, order, and limpid grace. This, indeed, is part of what is implied by the definition of prose freed from verse's laws. In verse, especially quantitative verse, rhythm enforces itself persistently and in regular measures (one line or two lines usually), and shapes everything: syntax is marked as artificial, and the effective disposition of sense against the rhythm's counterpoint, fitting itself variously to the inescapable unit of the line, is its goal; its characteristic pleasure, the constant small surprises of utterance elegantly achieved as words slot into the rhythmical pattern. The requirements of verse-rhythm are inexorable, experienced as law; and prose accordingly defined itself precisely in that contrast. But the prerequisite for its air of naturalness is the composer's gimlet eye: sizing up thoughts and narrations, measuring them out, hacking them down, and sewing them up. Sounding free of law is a labored and messy business; and doing it well even imposes its own laws of rhythm on the period. The impression built into the language is of a bloody-mindedness constantly marking the labor of the writer but sublimated before presentation to the reader. Usk's fits of arhythmical period are so many moments of desublimation, and the many severed limbs of Usk's chronicle—Clerk's hand, tongue, and head; the bodies of the Epiphany conspirators bagged and carried; John Hall's right hand displayed across London Bridge, and Perkyn de Lye's head displayed across the city gate; Llewelyn's head washed in the spring—so many embodiments of sentences composed together from lifeless organic parts.

Those skilled in the cursus tended always to use it.[64] Usk seems not to have been especially skilled: too many hiatus, too many clausules kept rhythmic only awkwardly, suggest that he was drumming out beats with his fingers. Why bother with it, then? Because it was a token authenticating a professional identity ("Translation from French to Latin does not permit the style of composing, and so may the reader deign to forgive it"); and because it was the *stilus curiae romanae*. Even those who had mastered it warned that one needed to stay alert: John of Limoges's *De dictamine* describes an unskilled writer working by the mechanical force of "habit, which is a second nature."[65] All manuals warn against *vitia*, faults of style so easily committed that only by chronic watchfulness could one detect and evade them. The implication is that even for the skilled *dictator*, and a fortiori for the unskilled, the art was a matter of continuing awareness and adjustment, an object of attention (and therefore potentially of thought) as well as a means of expression. Like any skill imperfectly mastered, it must be an object of thought even when used as a tool of composition, just as languages can show some of their deep semantic structures most clearly to those who are not natively fluent. Thought *about*, its very components and the vocabulary used to describe them suggest regularity, disruption, and surprise as techniques of expression and of narration; members and dismemberment as defining images; constraint and freedom, design and naturalness, as incipient ironies of expression. The effects of Adam Usk's history are not simply matched by, but are apparently dictated by, the style and his meditations on it.

Conclusion

So there is Adam Usk's secret: a trick of style by which he could make his chronicle act like an unwilling informant, imperfectly concealing knowledge too dangerous to declare. He had discovered the resources for it in the rhetorical discipline of his professional community, a discipline that enforced a habit of predictable decorum, performing conclusion at moments of conclusion and signaling authorial control thereby. By disrupting those concluding gestures, Usk found, he could perform surprise and failure instead; he could create the illusion that authorial control has been ambushed by panic, that his choices are really accidents, and the ostensible reasons for them really suppressed or repressed causes. Doing so was his deliberate accomplishment, as the traces of design show. It achieved several things for him. It let him make his narration seem to emerge from thoughts incompletely reported, hinting that an unconscious not reliably accessible even to himself was leaking through in symptoms. It let him portray himself as a mechanism of precipitant impulse, flattering himself that he thinks his thoughts when in reality they think him. It let him portray other selves as such mechanisms also. It let him mobilize these mechanized selves into a preassembled repertory of dramatic ironies, deflating failures, and purposes which no precaution could shield from self-subversion. It presented to him, as an idea already formed, the sense that precautions against disaster are especially prone to disaster: they succeed only in cheating the mind with the hope that disaster is avoidable, and leave the very attempt to shed naivety naive. And it gave him a lexicon of complacent violence and suggested the gory uses to which he might put it.

He did not plant this secret for any actual audience to find; nothing suggests that he even conceived the possibility that any might. But he also did not plant pointers that would point even a notional, ideal audience—perhaps the only one he ever conceived—toward it. It is therefore not a banal joke on credulous readers ("the secret is that there is no secret");[1] it is simply the operation that makes readers want to look. It is an empty secret: a device and a MacGuffin. What look like symptoms bestrewing his discourse are not in fact symptoms, but effects made to look like them.

Nothing further is needed to explain the secret. Our investigation is therefore concluded with this answer.

~

That is my claim, anyhow, but it sounds fishy. It suggests suspicious haste (move on folks, this question's done, no more to see here) and a vain or defensive desire for the last word—that at best, and probably something worse. It runs afoul of critical good manners and of the conventional assumptions that have underwritten them: assumptions about the multivalence of all utterances; their mutual dependence in a chain of linguistic difference that never stops; the correspondingly disseminal character of all linguistic performance and the centrifugal proliferation of possible interpretative acts; the framing of all percepts and concepts by social interests and perspectives, and the irreducible multiplicity of those interests and perspectives; the resulting impossibility of honestly resolving any of them into a single focus; the democratic equality of all lines of inquiry. All these, some plainly true and all widely treated as axiomatic, have informed the mood in which interpretation seems in principle unbounded and so does the mastery it promises: it can move freely among artifacts and systems alike, now reading poems, now posters, now culture itself: tug anywhere, keep pulling, you might unravel anything. The literary text can be read as a microscopic abridgment of its world, the world as a macroscopic text; whatever; it all hangs together.[2] Thus the injunction against injunctions, the determination to disallow determinations: you just cannot insist that reading *stop*. You will never find an end of connection, resonance, homology; you can therefore give no reason for making it stop; and if you are trying to, what are you afraid of? The very attempt to do it sounds like anxiety or bad faith.

But this store of practical assumptions has always stood on shaky legs; indeed, its most potent postulate causes the problems. As Sartre cleverly remarked, reading a work as literature ("as a text" is our phrase) *stipulates* its boundlessly coherent interpretability: no matter how recondite, involved, and apparently fantastical the designs the reader imagines he has found, "he has a guarantee, namely, that they have been expressly willed."[3] A memorable anecdote by Stanley Fish would later make this point.[4] Reading something as "literature" metabolizes what would seem even its baldest failures and mistakes as studied effects: "The most beautiful disorders are effects of art, that is, again order."[5] Call this "Sartre's law." He was talking about a stance of reading, a contractual willingness in the literary reader. Interpretative literary criticism, making a discipline of itself in the anglophone academy even as Sartre wrote, had already incorporated that stance as its habitual posture: claiming that any element of any work was *not* meaningful came to be recognized quickly as by nature a losing move. Every interpretative conclusion could be unfolded into further interpretation: you could always say more about the book in front of you. Attentive undergraduates of the later twentieth century found that you could always win a seminar debate by explaining apparent fault as cunning effect. ("It's boring." "That's the *point*.") They did not need Sartre to discover Sartre's law; it yielded itself to all comers. Nothing of substance changed in the years when the category of "literature" was shunned and denied; the law's logic did not lean on anything so flimsy as as a *name*. It was quite able to look after itself; the field had no other tools to work with, because they constitute the field. Nothing of substance changed when New Criticism bracketed intention, when psychoanalysis and Marxism fragmented it, when historicism made culture itself a text.[6] Indeed, these developments seemed to find in this stance a source of endlessly renewable energy: it could apply the same tools of interpretation to works and world, to texts and their surround, and therefore could pass at will from one to the other and back again. It looked easy.

It looked easy because the same methods of reading can work on discourse and on cultures once each has been stipulated as literature ("as text"). But that is the tricky part. The homology between work and culture we embraced as a heuristic: not a claim about the ontology of the things we interpreted, but a procedure pointedly agnostic about ontologies and justified by the rich crop of insight it bore. But ontology, driven out at the door, flew in by the window. To make the homology between text and world habitual and defining as we did—conventionally available, without the need to demonstrate their connection in each particular case—you need to assume that discourse and culture are, not similar objects, but the same object: that the work ("the text") *just is*, in miniature or metonymy, the cultural system that produced it. That is, our heuristic, whenever it spoke, found itself saying that the objects themselves (literature/text, culture/society) had natures, were adjacent units of the same category, shared a continuous border wholly porous or a structure comparable at every point. Only on that assumption could the passage between them carry such frequent and casual traffic as we have sent over it. Criticism quietly, unwittingly, and despite everyone's best intentions, drew ontological conclusions from procedural premises.

Better than this ontological faith would be logical investigation, and the moment it begins it finds problems The problem illustrated by the case of Usk's secret is that what makes it so easy to generate readings of either a text or a culture is precisely what makes it hard reasonably to adduce a reading of one as evidence for reading the other: the sheer endless unfoldability of interpretation, its incapacity to show that it is done. You start by "reading" a literary work; at a certain point you wish to use some result of your reading as a datum for drawing a historical conclusion applicable outside the bounds of that work. Whether you want to find in it an interpretable homology ("new historicism"), a diagnosable symptom ("symptomatic reading"), or a countable token ("just reading") does not much matter. You must in any of these cases decide that some aspect of some discursive detail was an inadvertent byproduct of composition: unexplainable by reference to the work's internal logic and therefore knowable as the trace of something alien and unmetabolized, a detail that brings the easy routine of interpretation up short. (The old "new historicism" disassociated itself from ideological analysis and surface reading in this respect, and claimed to respect the integral structures of artifacts, inferring from them the larger structures of cultural possibility on which they depend. I will address this claim shortly.) That is, you need to decide that interpretation has reached an impasse. But interpretation, if given voice for a moment, could retort "What impasse?" It could object that it was working just fine, because it always works just fine. It could absorb the incongruous detail you want to use as a symptom or instance, because it can absorb all details without missing a beat. So it could ask on what grounds you suddenly declare that it has met its match and has thereby registered an unprocessed trace of unthinkable conflict or unthought obviousness. To identify such an impasse, to locate a symptom rationally and defensibly, interpretation must discover that it is no longer able to continue on its own terms, must encounter some misfire—some gap or incoherence or mistake—that the design it was tracing cannot metabolize. But in the "normal science" of our business, continuing on its own terms is what interpretation is best at.

It is easy to crack jokes about literary interpretation's compulsiveness, its inability to conclude, but the comedy does not make it ridiculous. It would become ridiculous only if we thought that, on its own, it should be able to conclude. Why should it? Literary interpretation is a disciplinary tool, useful, resilient, and incomplete. It is not reason itself. The criticism of the last two generations has largely been, as I said a moment ago, an unavowed tribute to the enduring utility of the tools it inherited from the New Criticism, however its tone of voice, axioms, and announced ends have differed as it used them. This little book was written partly to offer that tribute avowedly and consistently and with full recognition of its powers, acknowledging that such "New Critical" procedures of reading are the usual means of getting from one idea to the next in criticism present and past. Its tools remain durable not because they are conventional; they remain conventional because they have proved durable, because they demonstrate in their use a flexible, responsive repertory of analytic moves that are well adapted, when presented with a designed and interpretable artifact, to interpret it and explain its design. But it does have the habit of treating whatever it set before it as an interpretable artifact, and this book was also written to show how constrained and narrow criticism must be if it has no tools but these. If we try to derive from criticism's "normal-science" logic a path that will take us from literature to history and back again, all paths we find take us deeper into literature.

Now one could object that, like it or not, getting from literature to history and back *is* our normal science these days: we do it all the time. But to unfold the logic of literary interpretation on a work until it you find yourself pleased to interrupt that logic, and then to declare your own interruption as evidence of a misfire evidencing some disruption, is not the normal science of literary study, but its normal superstition. Misfires must be demonstrated, not decreed. This is not to say that they do not happen, or even that they are hard to detect when they do. It only is to say that the disciplinary practices of literary and cultural interpretation are not the instruments for their detection, that these are quite blind to the *differentiae* that distinguish the sudden from the involuntary, the impish from the inconsequential, the audacious from the pathological, the unmarked from the obvious.

A stronger objection is that taking this seriously makes the author a kind of apotropaic charm against historical inference; dictating constant recourse to the question, "But what if that is just what he *wants* me to think?" sounds like a smug catch-22 designed to stop inquiry in its tracks. But that question is already implied, as a categorical though usually tacit decision, not merely in every symptomatic reading but in every historical inference, because that is just what historical inference in this sense is. To conclude that Hoccleve's poetry illustrates the impossible conditions of court authorship under Henry IV is to imply that Hoccleve has not set out to portray that condition—if he has, then what we see may be only the fanciful or bathetic invention of one who does not find it impossible at all—but that he has, either without grasping it or without wishing to reveal it, betrayed the condition; it is not a conclusion about Hoccleve's *opinion*. Usually, in fact, the question "But does he just want me to think that?" can be answered as routinely as it is put. This point is too obvious to insist on. A related one is a little less obvious: there is a difference between investigating an author's intentional choices and obeying his directions. The argument of this book illustrates what I mean. Yes, my discussion claims to piece together the structure of Usk's intentional acts in designing and deploying his secret. But doing so means pursuing an inquiry Usk does not authorize, and this for the simple reason that it is one he cannot conceive: the possibility of posing the questions that have borne these answers comes from an intellectual and disciplinary practice that Usk could not anticipate, that of literary history and interpretation as now practiced. When you seek the intentional properties of intentional artifacts, you do not hand the reins of inquiry to authors, who have no power in this matter to endorse or prescribe: their job is done when they have written. An intention is not an empire: it is inquiry's object, not its law. (This is one reason I have preferred phrases like "intentional act" to the plain noun "intention." The latter so long tempted criticism to empty arguments about whether intention should regulate interpretation that it became a red herring.)

But a pragmatic objection to what I have been urging cuts deepest: as things stand presently, the bar to showing that something has misfired seems unscalably high. Because before you have grounds for claiming that something has misfired, you have to know what it would look like if it fired: offering to explain *why* something went wrong, you must show *that* it went wrong, which means knowing what it would be if it went right. So using misfires to find the unmeant traces of history in an intentional performance, to diagnose or to count them, requires you to produce a standard of rationality, or of goodness or beauty or appropriateness, against which a performance must be measured, and to know which standard is pertinent to the case. If you want to take the expression of an extravagant sentiment as an indication that Adam Usk has lost control of a moment in his chronicle, such that we can see in it the duress of history, you will need to establish what other sentiment, or what degree of the same sentiment, would be appropriate. This may seem an impractical expectation in a discipline reluctant to acknowledge norms of reasonability, appropriateness, and substantive coherence, much less norms of goodness and beauty. In this book, I have embraced that reluctance, have tried at all points to understand what Usk wrote from within the conventions of literary criticism; I have abstained as far as possible from holding Usk to criteria of rationality, affective appropriateness, moral clarity, or aesthetic goodness and therefore from asking whether he could possibly have meant to effect what he effected. As it happens, I conclude that he did mean it; and while I do think (as I said a moment ago) that how I got there shows what a rich array of resources criticism has for answering its own questions, you could reasonably ask whether, given that abstention, I could have concluded anything else. I could have; but only by invoking the criteria I foreswore. (You could also ask whether the thing was worth the doing. We will notice that question shortly.)

Of course, even if I am right that the apparent symptoms in Usk's chronicle are not actually symptoms and therefore cannot disclose repressed matter to diagnosis, that need not forestall, and could even supply material to, a different symptomatic reading. You might wonder where this strange idea of faking symptoms for a nonexistent audience came from; you might consider the possibility that it is so strange as to be *itself* a tell-tale disturbance registering the presence of something unrecognized or undisclosed. But this maneuver merely relocates, it does not escape, the need to give reasons for a diagnosis. For then you would still need to show that something has gone wrong or something needed has not been done. There is no escaping the need to justify diagnostic discussions by demonstrating that there is something inappropriate about the choice, and therefore the related and steeper requirement to specify what would be appropriate. If you want to diagnose Usk's choice to lay interpretative traps that never spring, you need to suggest what he should have done instead.

Even a reader otherwise sympathetic might object at this point against treating the diagnosis of unrecognized or unacknowledged motives as representative cases of historical inference. After all, part of the originating mission of the "new historicism" was a protest as much against the diagnostic reduction of literary works as against their aesthetic trivialization. "The new historicist project . . . is concerned with finding the creative power that shapes literary works *outside* the narrow boundaries in which it had hitherto been located, as well as *within* those boundaries" is the description of two of its best practitioners:[7] it meant to allow art its freedom while still exploring the determinations within which that freedom is exercised. The best new historicist work lives up fully and honorably to both parts of the ambition they describe. But is the creative power "*within*" different from the creative power "*outside*" or the same? If it is the same, then there is no creative power "*within*"; invoking it is an empty piety and works are tokens or symptoms after all. If it is different, then the sophistication and generosity with which it is elucidated do not change the logical requirement that challenges those who want to pass from it to that creative power "*outside*": in trying to find in an artifact where the creative power "*outside*" has shaped it, you must have a reason to find that somewhere the creative power "*within*" has reached the limit of its capacities. And to have that, you must have a norm that will underwrite such reasons. Until you do, Sartre's law bars the way.

~

Disciplines like literary criticism are structures of conventional procedures and conventional stipulations—*conventional* in the richest and least reductive sense of the adjective: procedures and stipulations that convene discussion. They have been assembled empirically: they have been found to work; the odds are with them. But while they can show the odds, they cannot do more. If you obey rigorously your discipline's procedures, you must be dogged by the knowledge that those odds are all you've got going for you; and sometimes the unlikely proves right. But then if you decide to spurn those procedures, you must be dogged by the knowledge that the odds are now against you. (Textual criticism gives neat instances. You say, "*Difficilior lectio potior.* So *solider Aristotle* and not *soldier Aristotle*, *receiving naughts* and not *receiving naught*."[8] But you know that the principle of *difficilior lectio* is no more than a rule of thumb. So then you say, "Still, *receiving naughts* is stupid" and emend it to "*receiving naught*." Now you know that you haven't got even the rule of thumb any more.) Always playing the odds will win more bets, but it is guaranteed to lose bets too. Since a "bet" in this metaphor is a scholarly conclusion that rests upon the possibility of mistake; and since the point of a scholarly conclusion is to build other inquiries and other conclusions upon it, and a bad bet early on will weaken the whole structure, prospects for collapse under the weight are always high. Disciplinary stipulations are those that have found to work; but also, disciplines come tacitly to prescribe them because, without them, systematic evaluation, the life of disciplinary discourse, becomes impossible. And without that, there is no way for later inquiries even to try to building upon earlier ones. Conclusions based on these are bets empirically grounded and necessary for intellectual and professional reasons alike, but still face the severe logic of combined probability.

Over the space of a few pages I have said both that staying within formal disciplinary conventions is the only way to stay coherent without appealing to extrinsic ideas of the reasonable and the good, and that staying within formal disciplinary conventions is bound eventually to lead you wrong. These are not contradictory points, but the same point put in different ways. Both are worth stressing. Abandon the logic of those procedures and you get a game without rules and therefore no game at all, only the bright ideas of perpetual amateurs; but hew to it absolutely and you confuse the game's rules with reason itself. Ignore the conventions at will and you risk being capricious; observe them without exception and you risk being *small*—you risk producing books as constrained and unambitious as *Adam Usk's Secret*. Without normative judgments and rational ways of forming them, we have no way to halt the stubborn logic of method; no way, for that matter, of knowing what the knowledge that method secures is good for. About either its limits or its use, literary criticism on its own has not got a right to an opinion. Of course no other discipline does, either; just thinking enjoys that right

Abbreviations

Boas	*Disticha catonis*. Ed. Marcus Boas and Henrik Jan Botschuyver. Amsterdam: North Holland, 1952.
BRUO	A. B. Emden. *A Biographical Register of the University of Oxford to A.D. 1500*. 3 vols. Oxford: Clarendon Press, 1957.
CCR	*Calendar of Close Rolls*
CCCM	*Corpus christianorum continuatio medievalis*
CCSL	*Corpus christianorum series latina*
CPR	*Calendar of Patent Rolls*
Fasti	John Le Neve, *Fasti ecclesiae anglicanae 1300-1541*. London: Athlone, 1962-67.
G-W	*The Chronicle of Adam Usk*. Ed. Chris Given-Wilson. Oxford: Clarendon, 1997.
PL	*Patrologia, cursus completus, series latina*
PROME	*The Parliament Rolls of Medieval England*. Ed. Chris Given-Wilson et al. Internet version, at http://www.sd-editions.com/PROME.
RS	Rolls Series
Thompson	*Chronicon Adae de Usk*. Ed. Edward Maunde Thompson. London: Henry Frowde, 1904.

Notes

INTRODUCTION

1. Sharon Marcus, *Between Women: Friendship, Desire, and Marriage in Victorian England* (Princeton, N.J.: Princeton University Press, 2007), 75–76.

2. Paul de Man, *The Resistance to Theory* (Minneapolis: University of Minnesota Press, 1986), 24. See also Derek Attridge, *J. M. Coetzee and the Ethics of Reading: Literature in the Event* (Chicago: University of Chicago Press, 2004), 32–64.

3. Paul Freedman and Gabrielle M. Spiegel, "Medievalisms Old and New: The Rediscovery of Alterity in North American Medieval Studies," *American Historical Review* 103 (1998): 700.

4. See the special issue, "The Way We Read Now," ed. Stephen Best and Sharon Marcus, *Representations* 108 (2009); also Heather Love, "Close But Not Deep: Literary Ethics and the Descriptive Turn," *New Literary History* 41 (2010): 371–91.

5. A familiar account is Marjorie Levinson, "What Is New Formalism?," *PMLA* 122 (2007): 558–69; an intelligent one is Susan J. Wolfson, "Introduction," in *Reading for Form*, ed. Susan J. Wolfson and Marshall Brown (Seattle: University of Washington Press, 2006), 3–24.

6. What follows is summarized from Steven Justice, "Literary History," in *Chaucer: Contemporary Approaches*, ed. David Raybin and Susanna Fein (University Park: Pennsylvania State University Press, 2009), 195–210.

7. The phrase seems to have emerged into general use from Louis Althusser and Étienne Balibar, *Reading "Capital"*, trans. Ben Brewster (London: New Left Books, 1970).

8. "Regem de cetero michi prius in ipsius potencia ignotum et eius leges timui ipsum, per maxillis meis frenum imponendo"; G-W 16. All quotations are taken from Given-Wilson's edition; for reasons explained later in this introduction, I supply my own translations.

9. The image is from Ezechiel: "ponam frenum in maxillis tuis" (29:4, 38:4). Jerome, commenting, notices both the silence and the pain it suggests: "Ponit autem Dominus in maxillis draconis istius frenum et perforat labia ejus atque constringit armillae circulo, quando per ecclesiasticos viros, qui scripturis sanctis eruditi sunt, imponit ei silentium, et universa perversitatis dogmata dissolvuntur "; Jerome, *Commentariorum in Hiezechielem libri xiv*, CCSL 75 (Turnhout: Brepols, 1964), 404, 406–7; Jerome's comment is picked up in Raban Maur's commentary, *Commentariorum in Ezechielem libri viginti*; *PL* 110:796, 798.

10. The passage is further discussed, and its grammatical difficulty explained, below, ch. 8, n. 28.

11. G-W 68; "Et sic—ut quid mora?—licet seipsum deposuerat ex habundanti, ipsius deposicionis sentencia, in scriptis redacta, consensu et auctoritate totius parliementi per magistrum Iohannem Treuar de Powysia, Assauen' episcopum, palam, publice et solempniter lecta fuit ibidem."

12. G-W lxxix–lxxxiv.

13. G-W 52, 56.

14. G-W 62; Michael Bennett, *Richard II and the Revolution of 1399* (Stroud: Sutton, 1999), 6. This is perhaps the most important single testimony Usk gives for the political history of England; it has therefore been very widely discussed. See ch. 5, n. 17 and the discussion there.

15. G-W 102–14.

16. G-W 250; see ch. 7, n. 2 and the discussion there.

17. G-W 218; "uenit unus globus igneus, maior magno dolio, quasi illuminans mundum; in cuius aduentu omnes attoniti timebant perimi uillam, sed directe transit contra campanile sancte Marie, et ex ictu diuisus in duas partes, ipsas ante hostia dictorum comitis et domini eas dimittit, ad maximum ipsorum, ut apparuit postea, ruine presagium."

18. G-W 48; "iusto Dei iudicio, misit Deus magnum scismatis chaos, iuxta illud prophecie unde uersus, 'Iudice celorum, rumpetur turba malorum"; see also the citations at G-W 16 and the prophecies of the Eagle, G-W 50–52. On the Bridlington hoax see Rupert Taylor, *The Political Prophecy in England* (New York: Columbia University Press, 1911), 51–52 and Michael J. Curley, "The Cloak of Anonymity and the *Prophecy of John of Bridlington*," *Modern Philology* 77 (1980): 361–69; on its satirical energies, A. G. Rigg, "John of Bridlington's Prophecy: A New Look," *Speculum* 63 (1988): 596–613.

19. For the bizarre notes that use the "prophecies of Merlin," see ch. 4, nn. 5ff.

20. G-W 226; "Item inueni ibi in cronica Martini . . ."

21. G-W 126; "Finitur istud parliamentum decimo die mensis Marcii, quo tamen die, modicum ante presens, audiui plurima aspera contra Wallen' ordinanda agitari,

scilicet de non contrahendo matrimonium cum Anglicis, nec de adquirendo aut inhabitando in Anglia, et alia plura grauia. Et, sicut nouit me Deus, nocte preuia me excitauit a sompno uox ita auribus meis insonans, 'Supra dorsum meum fabri[cauerunt],' etc., 'Dominus iustus,' etc., ut in psalmo, 'Sepe expugnauerunt.' Vnde expergefactus timens michi eo die aliquid infortunii contingere, me Spiritus Sancti gubernacioni specialiter timidus commisi." On the events this passage touches on and for a discussion, see below, ch. 6, n. 43 and the discussion there.

22. G-W 194; "Prope iam palacium sancti Petri hospitatus, luporum et canum, de nocte sepius ad hoc surgens, condiciones inspexi. Nam canibus pro domorum tutamine in dominorum suorum hostiis latrantibus, lupi in medio maiorum minores canes secum in predam abstulerunt, et, licet sic ablati, per maiores defendi sperantes, forcius inde murmurarent, de locis suis tamen, alcius ob hoc licet latrantes, nullatenus se mouebant. Et sic cogitaui quod consimilis liga inter fortes patrie et exules silue in partibus dinoscitur esse."

23. G-W 54–6; "Demum per Solopiam transiens, ibi per duos dies mansit, ubi fecit proclamari quod exercitus suus se ad Cestriam dirigeret, tamen populo et patrie parceret eo quod per internuncios se sibi submiserant. . . . Set modicum patrie ualuit proclamacio, ut infra apparebit. . . . pratisque et segetibus non parcendo, patriamque undique depredando . . . pernoctauit."

24. See ch. 3, n. 13.

25. Ch. 2 treats this story at length; for its text, see n. 5 there.

26. "hermeneutic terms . . . structure the enigma according to the expectation and desire for its solution. . . . Between question and answer there is a whole dilatory area whose emblem might be named 'reticence.' . . ."; Roland Barthes, *S/Z*, trans. Richard Howard (New York: Hill and Wang, 1974), 75. See also Barbara Herrnstein Smith, *Poetic Closure: A Study of How Poems End* (Chicago: University of Chicago Press, 1968); Frank Kermode, *The Genesis of Secrecy: On the Interpretation of Narrative* (Cambridge, Mass.: Harvard University Press, 1979), Peter Brooks, *Reading for the Plot: Design and Intention in Narrative* (New York: Knopf, 1984).

27. See ch. 1, n. 1.

CHAPTER 1. THE FIRST SECRET

1. Andrew Galloway, "Private Selves and the Intellectual Marketplace in Late Fourteenth-Century England: The Case of the Two Usks," *New Literary History* 28 (1997): 308.

2. G-W xxx–xxxiii, and Galloway, "Private Selves," 312–13. This fact, detailed and discussed below, can hardly be said to have been hidden away—since it appears in the

register of Robert Hallum—but it seems to have lain entirely unnoticed until these two studies.

3. At the top of the second leaf, narrating the early growth of Lollardy in the 1370s, he glances forward to "tempore secundi parlementi Henrici regis quarti, infrascripti"; at this time the Lollards planned a massive uprising, he says, but Archbishop Arundel, forewarned, prepared a suitable remedy, "ut inferius liquebit" (G-W 8). The parliament referred to in this passage (which is written in the main scribe's hand in the body of the text) opened 26 January 1401. That would then be the earliest point at which this sentence, which appears at the beginning of the manuscript copy, might have been composed.

4. On his home parish, see G-W 118, and his will, G-W 272. For the name "Adam Porter," see *CPR 1381–85*, 115, 307, noticed by James Tait, review of *Calendar of the Patent Rolls (1377–1385), English Historical Review* 13 (1898): 355.

5. G-W 158 reports the capture of that Edmund (Mortimer) "who put me to school." Alastair Dunn, *The Politics of Magnate Power in England and Wales, 1389–1413* (Oxford: Clarendon, 2003), 26 takes this as an exemplary instance of the opportunities opened by aristocratic networks of influence.

6. He relinquished the church of Trou, in Mortimer's gift, to Hugh Wacham in September 1385; *CPR 1381–85*, 22.

7. G-W 6–8.

8. G-W 12; he was also present there for the riots of 1388 and 1389 (G-W 14–16; see ch. 8, n. 27).

9. See ch. 7, n. 9.

10. *CPR 1396–1399*, 23.

11. The deaths of these two men, and only these two, are reported in his chronicle as having occurred "longe ante michi optatum"; G-W 46 (Mortimer) and 246–48 (Arundel). For the latter, see ch. 6, n. 49 and ch. 7, n. 1 and the discussions there.

12. *CPR 1391–1396*, 695; *CPR 1396–1399*, 23; *CPR 1399–1401*, 231.

13. E.g., G-W 96, where he represents Thomas, Lord Morley.

14. See above, Introduction n. 15.

15. What a civilian might do there is summarized in Simon Walker, "Between Church and Crown: Master Richard Andrew, King's Clerk," *Speculum* 74 (1999): 961.

16. See ch. 2, n. 2 and the discussion there.

17. "Item, lego Edwardo ap Adam, consanguineo meo, unum librum uocatum 'Policronica'"; G-W 272. For the date of probate, see Edward Owen, "The Will of Adam of Usk," *English Historical Review* 18 (1903): 316.

18. V. H. Galbraith, "An Autograph MS of Ranulph Higden's *Polychronicon*," *Huntington Library Quarterly* 23 (1959): 2.

19. C. T. Allmand, "The Civil Lawyers," in *Profession, Vocation, and Culture in Later Medieval England: Essays Dedicated to the Memory of A. R. Myers*, ed. Cecil H. Clough (Liverpool: Liverpool University Press, 1982), 167.

20. John Taylor, *The Universal Chronicle of Ranulf Higden* (Oxford: Clarendon, 1966).

21. This remaining gathering is housed at Belvoir castle; G-W xxxviii–xxxix.

22. See ch. 4, nn. 5ff. and the discussion there.

23. G. H. Martin, "Narrative Sources for the Reign of Richard II," in *The Age of Richard II*, ed. James L. Gillespie (Stroud: Sutton, 1997), 61.

24. Some aspects of orthography are consistently eccentric through the chronicle, remaining constant through changes of scribes; as Given-Wilson notes, this clearly indicates that they were copying a written draft; G-W xci.

25. Two minor qualifications to this and what follows do not bring the point into question. (1) It is possible that he employed the same scribe on two successive stints, and that a marked change in color of ink, especially when it coincides with a narrative episode, might mark a break between two campaigns of copying by the same scribe, and therefore possibly between two campaigns of composition by Usk. (2) Usk could have allowed more than one stint of composition to elapse before giving the material to a scribe for copying; this would be undetectable. These two considerations apply chiefly to the two longest sections of composition.

26. ". . . usque ad magnum eiusdem regni confucionem, ipsiusque Ricardi regis sibique nimis uoluptuose adherencium finalem destruccionem," G-W 6. On the date of Richard's death, see Nigel Saul, *Richard II* (New Haven, Conn.: Yale University Press, 1997), 425–26.

27. Usk himself dates the death of Warwick to Good Friday, 1 April, and refers back to a jailbreak in Usk on Passion Sunday, 20 March. He dates the betrayal of the rebels William and Rhys ap Tudor, who had been holding Castle Conway, to 28 May, and mentions the pardon that their betrayers received in response; G-W 126–28. Given-Wilson observes that the pardon, reproduced in Rymer's *Foedera*, is dated 8 July (G-W 128 n. 3).

28. G-W 152; "Iam, Deus, qui me studium Oxon' et ipsius doctoratus regimen trienale, ac demum in curia Cant' septenale aduocacionis officium, tam honorem quam utilitatem, ex tue infinitate gracie concessisti perficere, ac in aliis meis agendis quibuscumque a iuuentute mea adiuuisti usque ad senectam et senium . . . ; meumque iam . . . directum Romam aggressum, cum ibidem progressu necnon ad partes uotiuas regressu, siue aduocatorum siue auditorum numero aggregandum, ad tui nominis honorem et laudem, et mei utriusque hominis sospitatem, . . . da misericorditer consolari." The lovely phrase "land of my desire" as a translation for *partes uotiuas* is Given-Wilson's.

29. G-W 152; "Quid mora? Vndecimo kalendas Marcii anno Domini millesimo quadringentensimo primo, presencium compilator, ut, Deo disponente, proposuit, London' apud Byllyngsgate nauem ingressus, prospero flante uento et mari sulcato . . . suos gressus uersus Romam dirigendo, infra diem naturalem terre applicuit."

30. He could not have begun writing it much before 1410, for at the top of the next leaf after narrating his 1402 departure for Rome, Usk speaks of "dominum Balthasarum, tituli sancti Eustacii diaconum cardinalem, postea papam Ioannem uicensimum tercium"; G-W 154. The Council of Basel advanced Usk's "Lord Balthasar"—Baldassare Cossa, cardinal-deacon of St. Eustace—as a papal candidate (he took the name John XXIII) in 1410, which is therefore the earliest date at which Usk might have resumed his chronicle. The five words on his papacy are inserted interlinearly. But conclusively, this section reports that the body of Roger Acton, executed after Oldcastle's rebellion in January 1414, still hangs on the gallows (G-W 246); it mentions Arundel's death in February 1414, but not the death in May of John Burghill, bishop of Lichfield, about whom these leaves relate a piquant story; G-W 246–50. The next scribe's stint begins with a report of Chichele's translation to Canterbury in April 1414; G-W 250. At any rate, the scribe copying the first of these passages worked at least through February 1414, and maybe through May.

31. G-W 154; "infra quindenam in pape capellanum, palaciique apostolici auditorem, . . . exstitit sublimatus. Cui et papa infra octo dies extunc triginta magnas causas commisit ad sui audienciam delatas, ipsius industria terminandas."

32. John Taylor, *English Historical Literature in the Fourteenth Century* (Oxford: Clarendon, 1987), 11.

33. See ch. 4, n. 8 and the discussion there. Roy Martin Haines, *The Church and Politics in Fourteenth-Century England: The Career of Adam Orleton, c. 1275–1345* (Cambridge: Cambridge University Press, 1978), 7, 15–19.

34. See R. G. Davies, "Richard II and the Church in the Years of 'Tyranny,'" *Journal of Medieval History* 1 (1975), 354.

35. James Hamilton Wylie, *History of England Under Henry the Fourth* (London: Longmans, 1884), 2.200–203, and Peter McNiven, "Scrope, Richard (c.1350–1405)," *Oxford Dictionary of National Biography*, http://www.oxforddnb.com/view/article/24964 (accessed May 16, 2009).

36. See, generally, Margaret Harvey, *The English in Rome, 1362–1420: Portrait of an Expatriate Community* (Cambridge: Cambridge University Press, 1999), chs. 7–8; and see also William Swan's letter, quoted by her, 181.

37. Harvey, *English in Rome*, 138, 143–44; *Fasti*, vol. 11 (Welsh Dioceses); *Fasti*, vol. 8 (Bath and Wells), 2; Gwilym Dodd, "Henry IV's Council, 1399–1405," in *Henry IV: The Establishment of the Regime, 1399–1406*, ed. Gwilym Dodd and Douglas Biggs (York: York Medieval Press, 2003), 102.

38. Lancelot C. Sheppard, *Lacordaire: A Biographical Essay* (New York: Macmillan, 1964), 21.

39. Dorothy M. Owen, *The Medieval Canon Law: Teaching, Literature and Transmission* (Cambridge: Cambridge University Press, 1990), 11. For a lucid description of the larger structure of the curia at a slightly later point in the fifteenth century, see John F. D'Amico, *Renaissance Humanism in Papal Rome: Humanists and Churchmen on the Eve of the Reformation* (Baltimore: Johns Hopkins University Press, 1983), 19–28. The time of Usk's tenure there in the early fifteenth century falls between periods in which it is more fully documented.

40. G-W 188–90.

41. Brigide Schwarz, "*Statuta sacri causarum apostolici palacii auditorum et notariorum*: Eine neue Quelle zur Geschichte der Rota romana im späten Mittelalter," in *Studien zum 15. Jahrhundert: Festschrift für Erich Meuthen*, ed. Johannes Helmrath, Heribert Müller, and Helmut Wolff (Munich: R. Oldenbourg, 1994), 845–67; Dietrich of Niem, *Der Liber cancellariae apostolicae vom jahre 1380 und der Stilus palatii abbreviatus*, ed. Georg Erler (Leipzig: Carl Winter, 1888), 9.

42. Harvey, *English in Rome*, 169.

43. Johann Burchard, *Diarium sive rerum urbanarum commentarii (1483–1506)*, ed. Louis Thuasne (Paris: Ernest Leroux, 1883), 1.102.

44. G-W 196 "Papa in festo Purificacionis candelas benedicit, et . . . omnibus mundi principibus et principissis catholicis easdem distribuit. . . . Et ita eciam in festo cinerum, in propria persona, omnibus presentibus cineres distribuit; me teste, quia dictas candelas pro rege et regina Angl' recepi, et cinerum bassinam sibi tenui"; 202; "agnos de alba cera benedictos . . . distribuit; bassinam sepius euacuatam et tenui, et remanentes in fine pro me habui."

45. G-W 204 "michi burdando dicere solebat."

46. G-W 204 "ad pape mandatum a quodam iudeo, eius medico, Helia nomine, in grossia eius urina intoxicacione experta . . . sanitas recuperatur."

47. At least it would appear that the two different popes are involved; see n. 49 below.

48. G-W 174–76 "Anglicorum sibi resistencium inuidia suisque literis una cum intoxicacione ipsum regi, unde eciam magnis infortuniis quatuor annis in terra et in mari uelut exul cruciatus exstitit, deprauancium, non promocionem sed depressionem ac ultimatam paupertatem omnibus beneficiis et bonis, inter extraneos cum Ioseph linguam quam non nouerat audiendo, licet pro consilio auro remuneratus, reportauit priuatus."

49. G-W 188 "Vacante ecclesia London', collegium auditorum unanimiter ad papam ascendit, rogando quatinus dominum Guidonem Mone, episcopum Meneuen', ad ipsam transferret et de Meneuen' ecclesia istorum compilatori prouideret." The

proposal involved translating Moon to London, just vacated by Robert Braybrook's death. Usk does not say that it was Innocent who proposed to provide him to St. David's, and it could have been otherwise; Trefnant of Hereford died on 29 March 1404 (*Fasti*, vol. 2 [Hereford] 2) and Braybrook of London on 28 August of the same year (*Fasti*, vol. 5 [St. Paul's, London], 3), while Boniface IX did not die until 1 October, and Innocent VII, elected 17 October, was crowned 11 November. So it is possible that Rome had learned of Braybrook's death in time to be considered by Boniface. Both popes by this point knew him well: Cosimo dei Migliorati, who became Innocent VII, had examined Usk in his knowledge of law preparatory to his being engaged as an auditor; G-W 154. Usk narrates Boniface's death between mentions of the two attempts at provision. It does not affect the story.

50. G-W 188–90 "Sed, deuulgato negocio, cum clamore ualido et ore obtestantes regi ac cardinalibus in Angl' beneficiatis minando quod, si hoc permitterent, indignante rege, beneficia sua perderent; iurarunt eciam quod rex eundem compilatorem ad carceres et furcas mitteret; insuper mercatoribus, ne sibi de pecuniis prouiderent, et sub pena expellendi socios ab Anglia prohibuerunt. Et certe hic fuit summum negocii impedimentum, et ita frustratum."

51. For the relevant passages, see below, n. 76.

52. G-W 176 "In Anglia interim parliamenta celebrantur multa, in quibus . . . contra prouisiones apostolicas strictiora sunt statuta." It is not clear what counts as "meanwhile," nor therefore exactly what statutes he refers to, but on parliament's increasing severity toward provisions in these years, see William E. Lunt, *Financial Relations of the Papacy with England 1327–1534*, vol. 2, Studies in Anglo-Papal Relations During the Middle Ages (Cambridge, Mass.: Medieval Academy of America, 1962), 401–4.

53. On the background, and the contest of king and pope as episcopal patrons in just these years, see G. L. Harriss, *Cardinal Beaufort: A Study of Lancastrian Ascendancy and Decline* (Oxford: Clarendon, 1988), 41–42; for a very illuminating study of the complexity of royal-papal relations in the very best circumstances—in the years immediately after Henry V's death, when Usk's own generation of bishops was dying—see Richard G. Davies, "Martin V and the English Episcopate, with Particular Reference to his Campaign for the Appeal of the Statute of Provisors," *English Historical Review* 92 (1977): 309–44.

54. G-W 176 "propter emulorum suorum detractiones."

55. *CCR 1399–1402*, 509. G-W, xxiii, notes that this is a clear indication that his trip to Rome was in search of advancement; it is also the case that the "permission" of which Usk speaks is implied in the pledge.

56. When it was offered, "Ego uero in eo confisus, qui aspera in plana conuertere . . . potest irrigare"—more pious expressions follow—"sperans, huiusmodi

gratuitum munus, ad laudem Dei, et ut culmini regio suisque deuotis per hoc utilius obsequi possem, acceptando, illud exerceo" (G-W 176–78). Given-Wilson recognized the force of *gratuitum*: not "unearned" but "unremunerated."

57. G-W 204 "quia eciam mercator cum meis pecuniis in rumore effugerat."

58. G-W 210 "In festo sancti Barnabe, expensarum penuria, quia spoliatus ut supra, et propter amicorum ingratitudines, ut infra, a curia versus partes recedens . . ."

59. G-W 212 "Ricardus, Lancastell rex armorum, consuluit michi quod propter regem mortem michi minantem, citra eius graciam adeptam, et quam michi promisit, et pro qua ipsum expectaui in illis partibus per biennium, licet frustra, quod non intrarem Angliam consuluit omnino."

60. G-W 214 "Per dictum biennium, per Flandriam, Franciam, Normanniam et Britaniam, multorum episcoporum, abbatum et procerum consiliis satis inde lucrando, perlustraui patrias. Et bis interim, per Wallicos in quibus fiduciam habui, totaliter, saltem altera uice, dormiens usque ad braccas inclusiue, spoliatus fui. Et certe ex procerum predictorum largitate eodem die postea centum uiginti coronas habui."

61. Monastery library, G-W 218–26; companions, see below, n. 76.

62. G-W 238 "Vnde coram eodem armorum rege protestatus fuit idem compilator quod fingeret se hominem fore Oweni, ac cum gente sua ad Walliam ad ipsum transiret, et inde, captata oportunitate, ab eo ad dominum suum Powys, sub ipso graciam regis expectaturus, latenter recederet. Et factum est ita; et hec protestacio sibi saluauit uitam."

63. G-W 238 "multis ac magnis mortis et captiuitatis falsorumque fratrum famisque et sitis, noctesque nonnullas hostium inuadencium metu insompnes ducendo, periculis satis cruciatus." This catalogue is derived from 2 Cor. 11:25–28.

64. G-W 238–40 "ad eum et castrum suum de Pola noctanter et clanculum me transtuli, ubi et in eius ecclesia parochiali, extra teritorium exire non ausus, tamquam pauper capellanus, solum pro missa alimenta recipiens, ab ingratis cognatis et olim amicis nullatenus uisitatus, talem et in corde Deus nouit qualem languidam satis duxi uitam."

65. Recorded in *CPR 1408–1413*, 283: a pardon "for all treasons, adherences to the king's enemies, felonies and trespasses" committed by Usk, "who was against his will in the company of Owin de Glendorduy and the Welsh rebels and has come away from them as quickly as he could."

66. G-W 240 "tamquam denuo natus, statum ante exilium aliqualiter refigurare incepi."

67. G-W 240 "seruientes, libros, pannos et lares ut alter Iob accumulaui, quare benedicatur Deus in eternum et ultra."

68. Guillaume Mollat, "Contribution à l'histoire du sacré collège de Clément V à Eugène IV," *Revue d'Histoire Ecclésiastique* 46 (1951): 49.

69. *CPR 1408–13*, 149, for 24 January 1410, which notes the church of Castlecombe (Wilts), "forfeited to the king because Adam Uske, parson of the church, was an adherent of the king's enemies and rebels of France and Wales." It might be urged that his return to Wales and the service, pretended or otherwise, of Glendower, would itself precipitate the accusation of treason; indeed, the pardon issued in 1411 (see n. 65 above) pardons him all "treasons [and] adherences to the king's enemies." But this cuts both ways. For if, as Usk narrates, his service in Glendower's camp was undertaken with an eye to pardon, this is precisely what we would expect.

70. G-W 116 "*Duo papae per .xxii. annos.* Vnum est quod hiis diebus dolenter refero, quod duo pape, quasi monstrum in natura, iam per uiginti et duo annos tunicam Christi inconsutelem, contra id Sapiencie, 'Vna est columba mea,' neffandissime diuidendo, mundum animarum erratis, corporum diuersis cruciatorum terroribus, nimium perturbarunt. Et heu, si uerum est quod memorie reduco, scilicet illud euangelii, 'Vos estis sal terre, sed quid si sal euanuerit? Ad nichil ualet ultra, nisi ut eiciatur foras et conculcetur ab hominibus.'"

71. GW 116–18 "*Venalitas in sacerdotio.* Vnde quia sacerdocio modo quasi uenali, etc., nonne Christus ementes et uendentes in templo, facto funiculo, eiecit foras? Et unde timeo ne cum magna flagellacione et conculcacione a gloria sacerdocii eiciamur, attendens quod in ueteri testamento, postquam uenalitas sacerdocium uiolarat, funus impressibilis, ignis inextiguibilis, fetor innocissibilis, cessarunt in templo. Vt quid mora, an mater uirgo, iuxta id Apoca', a facie bestie in trono sedentis in desertum fugit cum filio. Hic me iubet quiescere Plato, cum nil sit cercius morte, nil incercius hora mortis."

72. G-W 118 "*Ornamenta ecclesie de Vsk.* Ideo benedicatur Deus, in mei originis, scilicet de Vsk, ecclesia, iam mori adiscens, memoriale meum in competentibus missali, gradali, tropario, sequencia, antiphonario, nouiter et cum nouis addicionibus et notis compositis, ac plena uestimentorum secta cum tribus capis ornanter compositorum, meis signis, scilicet nudi fodentis in campo nigro, oracionum suffragiis ibidem me comendando, relinquo; ulterius, si Deus dederit, ecclesiam eandem reparacione honestiori ad beate Virginis gloriam, in cuius natiuitatis honore est dedicata, perornare proponens; hoc ad mei laudem non reputando, quia presentis fatuitatis mee scripturam in uita mea uideri detestor."

73. Galloway, "Private Selves," 310–11.

74. Thompson; A. B. Emden, *A Biographical Register of the University of Oxford to A.D. 1500*, 3 vols. (Oxford: Clarendon, 1957), 3.1938; R. R. Davies, *The Revolt of Owain Glyn Dwr* (Oxford: Oxford University Press, 1995), 163–64.

75. Glanmor Williams, *The Welsh Church from Conquest to Reformation* (Cardiff: University of Wales Press, 1976), 226; *Fasti*, vol. 11 (Welsh Dioceses), 22 n. 2.

76. G-W 214 "Demum comes iterato ad Scociam et inde in Angliam, sub fabrica-

tis doli sigillis regnum pro se habiturus promittentibus, proditorie est seductus; ut transirem secum, magnas promociones michi promisit." Discussion below, ch. 7.

77. G-W xxxi.

78. G-W 240 "Ad instanciam . . . dicti domini et Dauid Holbech, magnifici uiri, regis graciam per suas literas . . . obtinui."

79. G-W xxv–xxvi; translated from a quotation in Harvey, *English in Rome*, 141.

80. See chs. 5, 7 below.

81. Apparently Davies, at least, would go this far; see n. 65.

82. So also Given-Wilson: "this deserves to be taken at face value. There is nothing to suggest that Usk attempted to circulate or in any sense 'publish' his chronicle"; lxxxiv–lxxxv.

83. Andrew Galloway, "Writing History in England," in *The Cambirdge History of Medieval English Literature*, ed. David Wallace (Cambridge: Cambridge University Press, 1997), 274.

84. And a little exaggerated. Arnulf of Milan expresses his determination to restrict the circulation of the *Liber gestorum recentium*: "Cuius privatum ac singulare volumen sue limina civitatis rogo nullatenus excedat"; Arnulf of Milan, *Liber gestorum recentium*, ed. Claudia Zey, MGH Scriptores 67 (Hanover: Hahnsche Buchhandlung, 1994), 118.

85. Guigo I, *Les méditations (Recueil de pensées)*, ed. un chartreux, Sources Chrétiennes 308 (Paris: Éditions du Cerf, 1983), 16–17.

86. Augustine Baker, OSB, *The Confessions of Venerable Father Augustine Baker, O.S.B., Extracted from a Manuscript Treatise preserved in the Library of Ampleforth Abbey*, ed. Justin McCann, OSB (London: Burns, Oates and Washburn, 1922), 56.

87. "Tuque, ideo, libelle, conventus hominum fugiens, mecum mansisse contentus eris, nominis proprii non immemor. *Secretum* enim *meum* es et diceris; mihique in altioribus occupato, ut unumquodque in abdito dicatum meministi, in abdito memorabis"; Francesco Petrarca, *Secretum*, ed. Ugo Dotti (Rome: Guido Izzi, 1993), 6.

88. Hans Baron, *Petrarch's Secretum: Its Making and Its Meaning*, Medieval Academy Books 94 (Cambridge: Medieval Academy of America, 1985), 185–96.

89. Edward Wilson, "An Unrecorded Middle English Version of Petrarch's 'Secretum': A Preliminary Report," *Italia medioevale e umanistica* 25 (1983); Edward Wilson and Iain Fenlon, eds. *The Winchester Anthology: A Facsimile of British Library Additional Manuscript 60577* (Woodbridge: Brewer, 1981). The copy of the translation here recorded was made perhaps fifty years after Usk wrote.

90. ". . . nil morte certius, nil hora mortis incertius"; Petrarca, *Secretum*, 36. The popularity of the phrase and the forms it took are described in Harry Vredeveld, "Notes on Erasmus's *De conscribendis epistolis*," *Journal of Neo-Latin Studies* 49 (2000): 129–30.

91. Ch. 7 below.

92. G-W 204 "amicisque propter bonorum recessum et recedentibus, aliqualiter sustentacione exstitit desolatus."

CHAPTER 2. THE STORY OF WILLIAM CLERK

1. J. M. Coetzee, *Giving Offense: Essays on Censorship* (Chicago: University of Chicago Press, 1996), 36–37.

2. G-W 122–24 "Solempnes nuncii ex parte ducis Bauerie, in imperatorem ut premittitur nouiter electi, pro regis nata sibi copulanda in Angl' aduenerunt. Quibus ad partem dixi, 'Numquid rex Boemie electus est in possessione imperii? Vnde ista noua eleccio, prima non cassata?' Vnus magnus clericus ex eis michi respondit, 'Quia inutilis fuit, et quia per papam nondum coronatus, electores in ea parte hoc fecerunt.' Tunc dixi, 'Per capitulum *Venerabilem*, extractum *De lectionibus*, ad solum papam hoc pertinere dinoscitur, quia ipse imperium a Grecis transtulit in Germanos.' Tunc episcopus Herffor' michi silencium indixit."

3. Antonia Gransden, *Historical Writing in England*, vol. 2, *C. 1307 to the Early Sixteenth Century* (London: Routledge & Kegan Paul, 1982), 176; Harvey, *English in Rome*, 142. The latter takes this to have occurred during the formal negotiations, but the words *ad partem dixi* clearly indicate informal exchange, as both editors have noticed: "aside," Thompson 223; "in conversation," G-W 123.

4. G-W 124 "A quo clerico contra symoniam, de quibus gaudeo, hos habui uersus."

5. G-W 122 "in festo carnipriuii, quidam Wyllylmus Clerk, scriptor Cant', et oriundus in comitatu Censtrie, militaris curie iudicio dampnatus, primo lingua quia in regem, hec aliis imponendo, protulerat, secundo dextra manu qua illa scripserat, priuatus, tercio pena talionis, quia false proposita non probauit, aput Turrim decapitatur."

6. G-W 86 "Hiis diebus, Vsce nascebatur uitulus habens duas caudas, duo capita, quattuor oculos et quattuor aures."

7. Paul Strohm, *England's Empty Throne: Usurpation and the Language of Legitimation, 1399–1422* (New Haven, Conn.: Yale University Press, 1998), 25–26, 55. This latter passage says that Usk's story of William Sawtry's execution, which was exactly contemporary with that of William Clerk (Sawtry is discussed below, ch. 5, n. 41), was "possibly that of an eyewitness, but recollected from later years." It has been usual to think that Usk composed all of his chronicle late in life; see, for example, Margaret Aston, "Lollardy and Sedition," *Past and Present* 17 (1960): 6. By contrast, Frank Grady, "The Lancastrian Gower and the Limits of Exemplarity," *Speculum* 70 (1995), 573; Simon Walker, "Rumour, Sedition and Popular Protest in the Reign of Henry IV,"

Past and Present 166 (2000): 60; and Lee Patterson, "'What Is Me?': Self and Society in the Poetry of Thomas Hoccleve," *Studies in the Age of Chaucer* 23 (2001): 453 without comment treat the story as historical.

8. G. D. Squibb, *The High Court of Chivalry: A Study of the Civil Law in England* (Oxford: Clarendon, 1959); Richard Firth Green, "Palamon's Appeal of Treason in the *Knight's Tale*," in *The Letter of the Law: Legal Practice and Literary Production in Medieval England*, ed. Emily Steiner and Candace Barrington (Ithaca, N.Y.: Cornell University Press, 2002), 105–14.

9. Strohm, *Empty Throne*, 25–26.

10. Ibid., 26, 2–3.

11. The account is written in the main body of the chronicle; it is not a marginal addition or on a singleton leaf, and so could not have been a later addition to the section of which it is part, and thus it was certainly written by February 1402. The pattern of copying plausibly places it closer still. The story of William Clerk is written in what Given-Wilson calls "Hand Two," whose work concludes on the next leaf with the dissolution of parliament on 10 March. The section of the narrative copied by "Hand Three" begins with the death of Warwick on 1 April, and the section copied by "Hand Four" begins with the return of Isabella, on 28 July. Since it is reasonably clear that after completion of the section copied by "Hand One" Usk composed brief sections contemporaneously and had them copied contemporaneously (see ch. 1, n. 27 and the discussion there), it is likely that the section copied by "Hand Two"—the one with which we are here concerned—was composed at the latest before the last event narrated in the section copied by "Hand Three," and more likely that it was composed before the first event in that section. On the other hand, the chronicle speaks on the same manuscript page, just prior to this report, of an inquisition that Usk and Arundel conducted in Warwickshire, which refers to a woman, still pregnant at the time of the inquisition, who gave birth "on the feast of St. Petronilla most recently past" (G-W 120; see discussion of this episode, below, ch. 3, n. 25).

12. See, for example, *CPR 1396–1399*, 28 (for "Adam Hush" read "Adam Usk," per James Tait, review of *CPR* 1386–1399, *English Historical Review* 25 (1910), 770; *BRUO*, 1937; Galloway, "Private Selves"; on Oxford and the teaching of the learned laws, see also J. L. Barton, "The Legal Faculties of Late Medieval Oxford," in *Late Medieval Oxford*, ed. Jeremy I. Catto and Ralph Evans, History of the University of Oxford (Oxford: Clarendon, 1992), 281–313.

13. G-W 120–22, 132–24; at the same time he also appeared in Chivalry on behalf of Sir John Colville del Dale in a suit with Sir Walter Bytterley.

14. In addition to the details that follow, there is also the case of the coordination between London and Cheshire rebels a year later; Peter McNiven, "The Men of

Cheshire and the Rebellion of 1403," *Transactions of the Historical Society of Lancashire and Cheshire* 129 (1979): 1–29.

15. *CPR 1399–1401*, 458.

16. "les officers des courtz de chivalrie, hostielle et de ameralle, de jour en autre par suggestions arrestent plusours des lieges nostre dit seignur le roy, al foithe les emprisonant, al foithe les mettant a respondre en les courtz suisditz"; Chris Given-Wilson, "Henry IV, Parliament of 1401: Text and Translation," Item 99, PROME.

17. Whether it can be said that Archbishop Scrope truly rebelled against Henry is unclear. Peter McNiven, "The Betrayal of Archbishop Scrope," *Bulletin of the John Rylands Library* 54 (1971): 173–213 argues that the Archbishop was very much in rebellion, but as Northumberland's stooge; Simon Walker, "The Yorkshire Risings of 1405: Texts and Contexts," in *Henry IV: The Establishment of the Regime, 1399–1406*, ed. Gwilym Dodd and Douglas Biggs (York: York Medieval Press, 2003), 161–84, seems to regard him as an agitator pincered by circumstances in his attempt to reform the king's government and broker peace between the northern earls. The point is that Henry still could portray him as a rebel leader.

18. John G. Bellamy, *The Law of Treason in England in the Later Middle Ages* (Cambridge: Cambridge University Press, 1970), 165.

19. Thomas Gascoigne, *Loci e libro veritatum: Passages selected from Gascoigne's Theological Dictionary illustrating the Condition of Church and State 1403–1458* (Oxford: Clarendon, 1881), 225–26. This story of William Gascoigne's refusal is accepted in the *Oxford DNB* entry on Scrope—McNiven, "Scrope, Richard (c.1350–1405)"—and entertained by that on Gascoigne—Edward Powell, "Gascoigne, Sir William (c.1350–1419)," *Oxford Dictionary of National Biography*, http://www.oxforddnb.com/view/article/10427, accessed April 2, 2008. But the observation of Keen (who accepts the account) that William Fulthorpe, who obeyed the king's instruction to pass judgment, was the constable's lieutenant, makes a plausible scenario; Maurice H. Keen, "Treason Trials Under the Law of Arms," *Transactions of the Royal Historical Society* 5th ser. 12 (1962), 87n.

20. The execution of Scrope cost Henry even more than that of Clerk; Michael Bennett, "Henry IV, the Royal Succession and the Crisis of 1406," in *The Reign of Henry IV: Rebellion and Survival, 1406–1413*, ed. Gwilym Dodd and Douglas Biggs (York: York Medieval Press, 2008), 15–16.

21. Statute of 25 Edward III, in *Statutes of the Realm* (London: HMSO, 1810), 2.319–20; Bellamy, *Law of Treason*, 116–22.

22. Given-Wilson, "Henry IV: Parliament of 1399: Text and Translation," Item 70, PROME; Bellamy, *Law of Treason*, 116. The scope of treason remained a live issue in the struggle of Richard and the appellants, see Michael Bennett, *Richard II and the Revolution of 1399* (Stroud: Sutton, 1999), 28–29.

23. This seems to be the unspoken association leading Usk to juxtapose the story of Clerk's execution with the story of William Sawtry's, which immediately precedes it. Sawtry, whose death is much better documented (a fact that will concern us below), was burnt for heresy in anticipation of the statute *Against the Lollards*; lacking the statute's authority, the execution took place as the result of royal command.

24. The history of *talio* is complex, and, despite expert help from Richard Perruso, I cannot feel confident that I have mastered it. But it is clear that Usk would have known talion, by this name, as a specifically Roman procedure meant to discourage fraudulent accusation by imposing on an accuser the punishment sought against the accused. The *lex talionis* is described as such as early as the Twelve Tables, and can be found in fundamental texts of the civil law, whence it found its way also into canon law; *Decretum*: Emil Friedberg, *Corpus iuris canonici* (Leipzig: Bernhard Tauchnitz, 1879), 2.14.1.2 and 2.23.5.1. The latter shows that it is the Roman concept in question: "nolumus passiones servorum Dei, quasi vice talionis, paribus suppliciis vindicari." Theological sources often associate it with the more general principle of precise and limited retribution enforced by Exodus 21:24 ("oculum pro oculo, dentem pro dente"); see uses in Augustine, *De civitate Dei*, ed. B. Dombart and A. Kalb, CCSL 47–48, 1955), 777 ("talio . . . agit, ut hoc patiatur quisque quod fecit"), and Peter Damian, *Die Briefe des Petrus Damiani*, ed. Kurt Reindel, Die Briefe der deutschen Kaiserzeit 4 (Munich: 1983), 51 (letter 96).

25. Derek W. Whitfield, "Conflicts of Personality and Principle: The Political and Religious Crisis in the English Franciscan Province, 1400–1409," *Franciscan Studies* 17 (1957): 321–62, which relates the case of R. Frisby that follows. Both Richard and Roger Frisby were Franciscans and both were involved in the conspiracy; Whitfield notes that it is unclear which one's confession is reported in the *Eulogium*, on which see Frank Scott Haydon, ed., *Eulogium historiarum sive temporis*, RS 9 (London: Longman, Green, Longman, Roberts, and Green, 1863), 3.328 n. 21.

26. "Electio nulla est, vivente possessore legitimo. Et si mortuus est, per vos mortuus est. Et si per vos mortuus est perdidistis titulum, et omne jus quod habere potestis ad regnum"; Haydon, *Eulogium historiarum*, 3.392.

27. "Per caput istud, tu perdes caput tuum"; Haydon, *Eulogium historiarum*, 3.392.

28. Archbishop Scrope's manifesto similarly describes Henry as excommunicate for the perjury, treason, and murder against his lord; James Raine, *The Historians of the Church of York and Its Archbishops*, RS 71 (London: Longman, 1879), 2.297–98.

29. G-W lxxxv.

30. The case of Thomas Usk, whom Northampton's faction employed to "write their bills" because he was of their faction, suggests the common-sense likelihood that a scribe might come to work for, and be trusted by, such an enterprise because already sympathetic with it and already implicated in its activities; R. W. Chambers

and Marjorie Daunt, eds., *A Book of London English* (Oxford: Oxford University Press, 1931), 23.

31. Annabel Patterson, *Censorship and Interpretation: The Conditions of Writing and Reading in Early Modern England* (Madison: University of Wisconsin Press, 1984), 18; used, e.g., in Kathryn Kerby-Fulton, *Books Under Suspicion: Censorship and Tolerance of Revelatory Writing in Late Medieval England* (Notre Dame, Ind.: University of Notre Dame Press, 2006), 19–20.

32. E.g., Sheila Delany, "Politics and the Paralysis of Imagination in *The Physician's Tale*," *Studies in the Age of Chaucer* 3 (1981): 47–60; S. Sanderlin, "Chaucer and Ricardian Politics," *Chaucer Review* 22 (1988): 171–84; Mel Storm, "Speech, Circumspection, and Orthodontics in the *Manciple's Prologue* and *Tale* and the Wife of Bath's Portrait," *Studies in Philology* 96 (1999): 109–25, and next n.

33. See, for example, Walker, "Rumour, Sedition and Popular Protest in the Reign of Henry IV," 52, saying that prophecies offered a useful vehicle for the expression of dissent because "they placed a vital distance between their seditious message and the messenger who bore them: they were neutral texts, apt for idiosyncratic elaboration, that furnished a supernatural authority for action while allowing individual exegetes to disclaim direct responsibility for their interpretations." The notion is endorsed also by Chris Given-Wilson, *Chronicles: The Writing of History in Medieval England* (Hambledon: Hambledon Press, 2004), 45; John Barnie, *War in Medieval English Society: Social Values in the Hundred Years War, 1337–1399* (Ithaca, N.Y.: Cornell University Press, 1974), 142–45; Antonia Gransden, "Silent Meanings in Ranulf Higden's *Polychronicon* and in Thomas Elmham's *Liber Metricus de Henrico Quinto*," *Medium Ævum* 46 (1977): 231–40; James Simpson, "The Constraints of Satire in 'Piers Plowman' and 'Mum and the Sothsegger'," in *Langland, the Mystics and the Medieval English Religious Tradition: Essays in Honour of S. S. Hussey*, ed. Helen Phillips (Cambridge: Brewer, 1990), 11–30, but also his reconsideration: *Oxford English Literary History*, vol. 2, *Reform and Cultural Revolution, 1350–1547* (Oxford: Oxford University Press, 2002), 342.

34. Quotations are from the F-prologue; this and all Chaucer quotations taken from Larry D. Benson, ed. *The Riverside Chaucer* (Boston: Houghton Mifflin, 1987). I have repunctuated these lines better to accord with what I take to be the real syntax of the sentence of which they are part. Part of the joke of this passage, not strictly to my purpose here, is that Alceste and the god of love argue over Chaucer's poems without having read them: she urges him to hear the accused, since "This man to yow may falsly ben accused" (350), which in the context could only mean, "This man may not even have said in those works what he is said to have said," which in turn could only mean that Alceste does not know, and knows that the god of love does not know, precisely what is in those works.

35. Paul Strohm, *Hochon's Arrow: The Social Imagination of Fourteenth-Century Texts* (Princeton, N.J.: Princeton University Press, 1992), 111–18.

36. "Nec Londonienses nec illi de Holbourn voluerunt testes esse. Et ideo fecerunt venire duodenam de Hysildon' et Heygate, qui dixerunt fratres reos esse"; Haydon, *Eulogium historiarum*, 3.393.

37. William Lyndwood, *Provinciale, seu constitutiones Angliae* (Oxford: H. Hall, 1679), 64–68.

38. On what is clearly the same principle, a Scottish king of arms (Usk later relates) was sentenced by Chivalry later in the year (30 June 1401) to be paraded through London and to have his tongue cut out "propter obloquia sua de rege Henrico in regno Francie habita" (132). But his nationality and his status as a herald place him indisputably under the jurisdiction of the *curia militaris*. This prompts the further observation that, since Usk thinks the episode worth the narration, even a punishment indisputably legal and at at least formally less than capital (though trauma, blood loss, and infection must have made this mutilation in effect an execution) of a foreigner under military law is extraordinary enough, even early in Henry IV's reign, to make the story worth the telling. In this case, he goes on to say, the herald was pardoned the offense and returned *graciose* to his king, "cum literis ex causa ipsius herawd ignominiosa missiuis."

39. "Hoc exemplo terribili alii complices sui haereses suas in Cruce Sancti Pauli personaliter revocabant"; Haydon, *Eulogium historiarum*, 3.387–88.

40. Strohm, *Empty Throne*, 25–26. Peter McNiven, *Heresy and Politics in the Reign of Henry IV: The Burning of John Badby* (Woodbridge: Boydell, 1987), 88–92 also assumes Sawtry was meant to die in the public eye and with a deterrent effect.

41. David Wilkins, ed., *Concilia Magnae Brittanie et Hibernie* (London: 1737), 3.258–60; Given-Wilson, "Parliament of 1401," Item 29; Thomas Walsingham, *Historia anglicana*, RS 28:2 (London: Longman, Green, Longman, Roberts, and Green, 1864), 247.

CHAPTER 3. FEAR

1. E.g., Strohm, *Empty Throne*, 196–97; John M. Bowers, "Thomas Hoccleve and the Politics of Tradition," *Chaucer Review* 36 (2002): 363.

2. "In art and poetry these particulars always appear as incommensurates: details, persons, events which the work's own (reflected) conceptual formulas and ideologies must admit, but which they cannot wholly account for"; Jerome J. McGann, "Introduction," in *Historical Studies and Literary Criticism* (Madison: University of Wiscon-

sin Press, 1985), 15. Hoccleve "tries to respond to the very issues he raises," Strohm, *Empty Throne*, 146.

3. G-W 70 "Veniente coronacionis die, omnes heroes regni, in rubio, scarleto et herminio ornanter induti, ad coronacionem huiusmodi magno gaudio uenerunt."

4. G-W 72 "Regem ante recepcionem corone domino Cant' iurare audiui quod populum suum in misericordia et ueritate omnino regere curaret."

5. Hope Traver, *The Four Daughters of God: A Study of the Versions of this Allegory with Especial Reference to those in Latin, French, and English* (Philadelphia: John C. Winston, 1907); Samuel C. Chew, *The Virtues Reconciled: An Iconographic Study* (Toronto: University of Toronto Press, 1947).

6. G-W 78 "Iohannes Halle, familiaris ducis Northefolchie, quia ducis Glocestr' morti consenciendo interfuit, per parliementum dampnatus trahitur, suspenditur ac, eius uisceribus extractis et coram eo crematis adhuc uiuus, decapitatur et quatripercitur; cuius quarta pars dextram manum continens ultra pontem London' in palo ponitur." In this passage I have rendered the historical present, ordinarily natural in Latin, as an English present tense; following on a passage given consistently in the preterite, Usk's present here is striking. As we will see, it is not the only place that Usk experiments with verb tenses for such a purpose.

7. "le dit Johan Halle soit treinez del Tourhill' jesqes a les Fourkes de Tybourne, et la bowelez, et ses bowels arcz devaunt luy, et puis soit penduz, decollez, et quarterez; et soun teste envoie a Caleys ou le mourdre fuist fait, et les quartres envoiez as autres lieux, ou le roy plerra"; Given-Wilson, "Parliament of 1399," Item 16.

8. "lì vid' io / de le mie vene farsi in terra laco"; *Purgatorio* 5.83–84; ed. Petrocchi, as printed in Dante Alighieri, *The Divine Comedy*, ed. C. S. Singleton (Princeton, N.J.: Princeton University Press, 1970).

9. Valentin Groebner, *Defaced: The Visual Culture of Violence in the Late Middle Ages*, trans. Pamela Selvyn (New York: Zone, 2004), 151.

10. G-W 78 "duo regis ualetti, London' cenantes, in quinque ouis quibus eis seruiebatur appertissimas hominum facies in omnibus similitudinem continentes inuenerunt, que loco crinium habuerunt albedinem a faciebus separatam ultra uerticem coagulatam et ad mentum per fauces descendentem; quorum unum uidi." I use Given-Wilson's translation here, both because it clearly and elegantly renders this sentence and because his cleverness in working out its precise sense deserves recognition.

11. G-W 78 "circa medie noctis obscurissime silencium per Thames' euectus, ululando et cum clamore se natum fuisse doluit. Cui unus miles ibi excistens dixit, 'Cogites quod eodem modo comitem Arundell' per omnia malignissime tractasti.'"

12. Reuben Brower describes Latin's special aptness for "strong vocal effect," as "perhaps inevitable, certainly much more natural, in a language rich in words like

plangoribus, ululant, clamor"; Reuben A. Brower, *Hero and Saint: Shakespeare and the Graeco-Roman Heroic Tradition* (Oxford: Clarendon, 1971), 92.

13. G-W 88 "ubi, in crastino epiphanie, plebeiorum pagensium tumultu decapitati fuerunt; et plures cum eis inuenti, Oxon' ducti, ibi suspensi et decapitati extiterunt, quorum cadauera, partita ad modum ferinarum carnium uenacione occupatarum, partim in sacculis, partim inter duos super humeros in baculis, London' deferri, et postea sale condiri, uidi."

14. G-W 88 "De quibus rex domino meo Cant' scripsit, unde ipse, sub isto themate, 'Nuncio uobis magnum gaudium,' per modum sermonis hoc clero et populo London' puplicauit, et cantato ymno, 'Te Deum laudamus,' Deo regraciando per ciuitatem cum solempni transiuit processione."

15. For accounts of Sawtry's execution and the politics behind it, see K. B. McFarlane, *John Wycliffe and the Beginnings of English Nonconformity* (London: English Universities Press, 1952); McNiven, *Heresy and Politics*, 79–92. But for suggestions of another element contributing to his choice, see Strohm, *Empty Throne*, 58–59.

16. See ch. 6, n. 41.

17. Inevitably my description depends on Elaine Scarry, *The Body in Pain: The Making and Unmaking of the World* (New York: Oxford University Press, 1985). I drop to the notes to anticipate an obvious objection, that the emotional effect I ascribe to these passages is impressionistic and anachronistic, and that these passages *revel* in the payback that tears at the bodies of heretics and traitors, while revulsion at torture, dismemberment, and violent death bespeaks a modern queasiness at pain and degradation. The example of the *Inferno* and the justice of its *contrapasso* could be easily cited. And yet Dante's most audacious gambit there is forcing readers to confront its punishments as just and therefore as beautiful; that gambit would be pointless and vulgar if he expected readers to find them entertaining rather than aversive. As Robert Mills argues, *Suspended Animation: Pain, Pleasure and Punishment in Medieval Culture* (London: Reaktion Books, 2005), e.g., 28–31, 61, medieval artistic representations of torture depend on making the reader or viewer anticipate, and thereby imaginatively "feel," the pain represented, a technique that would be pointless if it was anticipated with delight. If I read it rightly, a similar effect is described in David Lawton, "Titus Goes Hunting and Hawking: The Poetics of Recreation and Revenge in *The Siege of Jerusalem*," in *Individuality and Achievement in Middle English Poetry*, ed. O. S. Pickering (Cambridge: Brewer, 1997), 105–6.

18. See n. 13 above. There is no real reason to doubt Usk's eyewitness claim, but, literally taken, it is a little strange. He says that he saw them *both* being carried to London *and* being pickled, the two passive infinitives forming parallel constructions both governed by *uidi*. This produces the admittedly improbable picture of Usk join-

ing the procession of the bodies and remaining with it until it reached its London destination and began the preservation.

19. A. D. Nuttall, *Why Does Tragedy Give Pleasure?* (Oxford: Clarendon, 1996), 77.

20. See Introduction, n. 21.

21. G-W 126 "Ordinatum fuit in isto parliament quod homines marchie contra Wallen' sibi indebitatos uel eos ledentes . . . represaliis possent usitare."

22. Psalm 128:3–4, with the Douay-Reims translation of v. 4 rendered with a little more of the Vulgate's luridness.

23. The confession, made in convocation, is printed in Wilkins, *Concilia*, 3.262.

24. G-W 120 "super diuersis criminibus, heresibus et erroribus ibidem per eum, ut diffamabatur, tanquam a colubro sub sanctitatis simulate specie, nequiter perpetratis."

25. G-W 120 "Vbi et quando inuenimus unam monialem, ipsius Roberti extraordinaria libidine, more sodomico, per seminis lapsum et non per instrumenti ingressum, tam per confessionem eiusdem monialis quam literas dicti Roberti, quam eciam inspexione corporis impregnate ante partum per matronas fact, fuisse impregnatam."

26. Though a reader attending to the rubrics would be alerted to it: "Per sodomiticum seminis lapsum fit impregnacio."

27. G-W lxxxiii.

28. "ab initio macrocosmi usque ad nostram aetatem non solum juxta temporum seriem, verum etiam juxta singulorum annorum supputationem congruentem aliqua compilarem"; Ranulph Higden, *Polychronicon*, ed. Churchill Babington and Joseph Rawson Lumby, RS 41 (London: Longman, 1865), 1.8.

29. Ibid., 2.436.

30. In the *Didascalicon*, Hugh of St.-Victor describes a property of biblical narrative he fears will confound students: it "keeps neither to a natural nor to a continuous order of speech . . . because it often connects even things which are separated from each other by an interval of time, as if one followed right on the heels of the other, so that it seems as if no lapse of time stood between those events which are set apart by no pause in the discourse" (VII.vii).

31. G-W 246 "Iste miles . . . , calcaribus aureis adornari obtinuit. Post tamen in ipsos tamquam ingratus recalcitrari non eribuit." Alertly noticed by Robert Epstein, "Literal Opposition: Deconstruction, History, and Lancaster," *Texas Studies in Literature and Language* 44 (2002): 27.

32. G-W 246 "dominus Rogerus Acton, miles de Salopia, adhuc et per mensem in patibulo stat suspensus."

33. See ch. 6, n. 41.

34. "In every thing sudden, we are apt to start; that is, we have a perception of danger, and our nature rouses us to guard against it"; Edmund Burke, *A Philosophical*

Enquiry into the Origin of our Ideas of the Sublime and Beautiful (New York: Columbia University Press, 1958), 83.

35. See ch. 1, n. 72.

36. Erich Auerbach, *Mimesis: The Representation of Reality in Western Literature*, trans. Willard R. Trask (Princeton, N.J.: Princeton University Press, 1953), 498–99.

CHAPTER 4. PROPHECY

1. See ch. 3, n. 10.

2. "Tincture" is Christopher Ricks's term for a tonal association accomplished by proximity rather than logic; Christopher B. Ricks, *Milton's Grand Style* (Oxford: Clarendon, 1963).

3. Gransden, *Historical Writing*, 130–31, 221; Grady, "Lancastrian Gower"; Strohm, *Empty Throne*, 11–14; Helen Barr, *Socioliterary Practice in Late Medieval England* (Oxford: Oxford University Press, 2001); Stephen Yandell, "Prophetic Authority in Adam of Usk's *Chronicle*," in *Prophet Margins: The Medieval Vatic Impulse and Social Stability*, ed. E. L. Risden, Karen Moranski, and Stephen Yandell (New York: Peter Lang, 2004), 79–100; David R. Carlson, "English Poetry, 1399 July–October, and Lancastrian Crime," *Studies in the Age of Chaucer* 29 (2007): 375–418.

4. "Adam Usk took himself seriously as a historian, and understood that history was a discipline which made diagnostic demands upon the writer," who necessarily, and particularly in the early fifteenth century, was "preoccupied with the interpretation of 'signs.'" Usk seems (to quote the same scholar) to cultivate portentousness with especial intensity, since his work "includes more than thirty 'abnormal' events (portents, miracles, dreams, prophecies), a significantly higher proportion than most English chronicles of the later middle ages," Given-Wilson, *Chronicles*, 22, 29, 46. For the assumption that medieval chroniclers were preoccupied with discerning providence, see William J. Brandt, *The Shape of Medieval History: Studies in Modes of Perception* (New Haven, Conn.: Yale University Press, 1966); Janet Coleman, *Ancient and Medieval Memories: Studies in the Reconstruction of the Past* (Cambridge: Cambridge University Press, 1992), 278; David Wallace, *Chaucerian Polity: Absolutist Lineages and Associational Forms in England and Italy* (Stanford, Calif.: Stanford University Press, 1997), 239.

5. G-W xli n. 117 "Ecce, omnis miserie reiciendo uangam, quam gloriosus uirtutibus efficitur Adam! Vsk: de isto cognomine canit uates Merlinus, 'Fluuius Vsk per septem menses feruebit, cuius calore pisses morientur et serpentes grauabunt'—serpentes in bona parte sumendo, ut intelligo, iuxta illud euangelii, 'Estote prudentes sicut serpentes.' Sed de quo ista canit Merlinus? Credo quod <de> domine Marchie."

6. See ch. 1, n. 71, and the discussion later in this chapter.

7. G-W xli, n. 113.

8. "Ade felicibus translacionis assencibus a Herefordiensi ad Wygorniensem, et a Wygorniensi ad Wyntoniensem, canit quidam emulus: 'Trigamus est Adam talem suspendere vadam. / Thomam neglexit, Wolstanum non bene rexit, / Swythinum maluit. Cur? Quia plus valuit'"; Thompson, viii.

9. G-W xl, n. 111, "Ade quamuis, propter sui uirtutes omni carentis miseria, finaliter principiis obstet inuidia, tamen praecipua in eo reperitur gracia, ut patet Genesi .i.; qui, expulsus paradiso per inuidiam diaboli, fuit restitutus celo per sanguinem Dei filii. Et quamuis per inuidiam cuiusdam militis fuit priuatus beneficio, ecce quam solempnis fuit eius restitucio, exacta de testimonio ex parte Ade. Et, quamuis uenatorum inuidia eorum ducis concilio expellebatur et consorcio, ecce quam gloriosa eciam eius reparacio, exacta de iurribus: ueniens Adam iuxta naturam Aprilis, in quo fuit creatus, primo uarias et asperas aurarum et turbinum subeuntis procellas, tamen finaliter Maii ac tocius estatis flores causantis et dilicias"

10. See ch. 6, n. 40.

11. Given-Wilson refers to Minnis's discussion of *compilatio* as one of the available conceptualizations of authorial responsibility, referring to Alastair J. Minnis, *Medieval Theory of Authorship* (Philadelphia: University of Pennsylvania Press, 1988), 94ff, noting however that Usk's practice seems "more exalted" than what Bonaventure describes.

12. G-W 90 "In coronacione istius domini, tria regalitatis insignia tria sibi infortunia portentebant: primo, in processione unum de coronacionis sotularibus perdidit, unde et primo plebei, contra ipsum insurgentes, ipsum post per totam uitam suam detestabantur; secundo, unum de calcaribus aureis ab eo cecidit, unde et militares secundo sibi rebellando aduersabantur; tercio, in prandio subitus uenti impetus coronam a capite deposuit, unde tercio et finaliter a regno depositus et per regem Henricum supplantatus fuit." The story of the lost slipper appears elsewhere also, and was acknowledged by Richard; in 1390, he offered a pair in replacement; L. C. Hector and Barbara Harvey, eds. *The Westminster Chronicle, 1381–1394* (Oxford: Clarendon, 1966), 414–16; V. H. Galbraith, ed. *The Anonimalle Chronicle, 1333–1381* (Manchester: Manchester University Press, 1927), 111.

13. He quotes them on the evils of Edward III's taxation (G-W 16) and on the conflict between Richard and the appellants (G-W 48).

14. G-W 116 "*Fit imperator dux Bauarie.* Dux Bauarie, frater regine Francie, Boemie rege, a diu imperium occupante, quia inutili et nondum per papam coronato contempto, Francorum auxilio in imperatorem erectus, cum pluribus Francis campestri bello per dictum regum deuincitur."

15. G-W 116 "*Campane per se pulsant.* Quatuor campanelle ad quatuor angulos

tumbe sancti Edwardi aput Westm' affixe propriis motibus, et multo plus quam uiribus humanis pulsate, ad magna conuentus terrores et prodigia, quater in uno die mirabiliter sonuerunt."

16. G-W 116 "*Fons manat sanguine.* Fons in quo caput Llewelini ap Gr' Wallen' principis ultimi, in pago de Buellt situato, post eius amputacionem lotum extitit, per diem naturalem integrum merissimo sanguine manauit."

17. See ch. 1, n. 70.

18. See ch. 1, n. 71.

19. See the discussions at ch. 1, n. 70, ch. 7, n. 13.

20. Both well attested; on the former, see Dillian Gordon, *Making and Meaning: The Wilton Diptych* (London: National Gallery, 1993), 54; on the latter, Davies, *Revolt of Owain Glyn Dwr*, 160–61.

21. The deposition appears on f. 163r, p. 68 in G-W; Richard's death on f. 165v, p. 90.

22. The delay and surprise result from deliberate delay, not from a mere habit of delaying the verb. Usk elwhere delays monstrous or significant details that are revealed by other elements of the sentence, as in the prepositional phrase that concludes the story of the boy born at Llanbadoc (86): "Nascitur eciam in parochia de Lanpadock unus puer masculus" (so far merely the birth) "cum uno oculo tantum" (at this point what is recorded could be merely the misfortune of a missing eye) "in fronte situato" (here sentence and episode end: this is not just an eye lacking, but one prodigiously and horribly located mid-forehead).

23. Compare the three instances of the adverb "thrice" (*ter*) at *Aeneid* 8:230–32; noted by John V. Fleming, *Classical Imitation and Interpretation in Chaucer's Troilus* (Lincoln: University of Nebraska Press, 1990), 102.

24. G-W 158 "O Deus, quam dolenter iam ecclesia duobus, et imperium tribus, presidentibus mutuis se infestant et deuastant cladibus."

25. The image was used famously in Boniface VIII's bull *Unam sanctam*: "Ecclesiae unius et unicae unum corpus, unum caput, non duo capita quasi monstrum," Heinrich Denzinger and Peter Hünermann, eds. *Enchiridion symbolorum definitionum et declarationum de rebus fidei et morum* (Freiburg: Herder, 1991), 872.

26. G-W 80 "Et sic Thomas et Rogerus, si fas est dicere, duo archiepiscopi in una ecclesia, quasi duo capita in uno corpore."

27. Hélène Millet, "Le grand schisme d'occident selon Eustache Deschamps: un monstre prodigieux," in *Miracles, prodiges et merveilles au moyen âge: XXVe Congrès de la S.H.M.E.S (Orléans, juin 1994)* (Paris: Publications de la Sorbonne, 1995), 215–26. A similar conception, derived from this, is implied in portrayals of disorder as peoples "without a head"; see, e.g., Robert E. Lerner, *The Powers of Prophecy: The Cedar of Lebanon Vision from the Mongol Onslaught to the Dawn of the Enlightenment* (Berkeley: University of California Press, 1983), 109–10.

28. He refers to John XXIII as pope, "aliis duobus, scilicet Gregorio et Benedicto, secum, licet monstruose, concurrentibus," G-W 254, and to the schism as "Christianitatis orbem aliquando quatuor, aliquando tribus, aliquando duobus monstruose et dolenter presedentibus disturbans."

29. Dietrich of Niem, *Dialog über Union und Reform der Kirche 1410 (De modis uniendi et reformandi ecclesiam in concilio universali)*, ed. Hermann Heimpel (Leipzig: Teubner, 1933), 4. How commonplace it was and remained is illustrated by Joinville's use of it in the iconography of Pentecost (Lionel J. Friedman, *Text and Iconography for Joinville's Credo* (Cambridge, Mass.: Medieval Academy of America, 1958), 23 and plate XX) and by the Roman Catechism's use of it as the single biblical authority for the unity and uniqueness of the Church; *Catechismus ad parochos ex decreto Concilii Tridentini editus* (London: Nathanael Thompson, 1687), 81.

30. The rubric makes the same point: "Duo pape per .xxii. annos," G-W 116.

31. Usk uses the formula *campestri bello* also at G-W 210, where it also engages a tacit rhyme: *capellano, campestri bello.*

32. G-W 2 "Isti Ricardi regni sui tempore plura uotiue inclita ferebantur." See ch. 7, n. 21 and the discussion there.

33. See Introduction, n. 17.

CHAPTER 5. UTILITY

1. "Multum in melius exemplum format alius / Et iuvat alterius vita probata prius," Kuratorium Singer, ed. *Thesaurus proverbiorum medii aevi [Lexikon der Sprichwörter des romanisch-germanischen Mittelalters]* (Berlin: W. de Gruyter, 1995), 1.177.

2. Boas 3.13; "vita est nobis aliena magistra." All quotations from Cato's *Distichs* here and elswhere are taken from this edition and given by book and number.

3. Anne Middleton, "Langland's Lives: Reflections on Late-Medieval Religious and Literary Vocabulary," in *The Idea of Medieval Literature: New Essays on Chaucer and Medieval Culture in Honor of Donald R. Howard*, ed. James M. Dean and Christian K. Zacher (Newark: University of Delaware Press, 1992), 227–42.

4. Higden, *Polychronicon* 1:2,6.

5. Augustine says that history "narrates deeds accurately and usefully," "facta narrat fideliter atque utiliter," Augustine, *De doctrina christiana*, ed. Joseph Martin, CCSL 32 (Turnhout: Brepols, 1962), 63, and Hobbes that its "principal and proper work" is "to instruct and enable men, by the knowledge of actions past, to bear themselves prudently in the present and providently towards the future," Hobbes's forward to Thucydides, *The Peloponnesian War: The Complete Hobbes Translation*, (Chicago:

University of Chicago Press, 1989), xxi. See Coleman, *Ancient and Medieval Memories*, 301–3; Given-Wilson, *Chronicles*, 2.

6. See ch. 3, n. 11 and ch. 6, n. 47.

7. Strictly, there are a few exceptions to this in the account of the 1397 parliament, most memorably the single word with which he silences Arundel before he can speak in his own defense: "Cras" (G-W 22). But this long section is shared almost verbatim with the Monk of Evesham, and is certainly not Usk's composition; C. Given-Wilson, "Adam Usk, the Monk of Evesham and the Parliament of 1397–1398," *Historical Research* 66, 161 (1993): 329–35. In the Monk of Evesham's version, Richard says "Cras respondere debes"; George B. Stow, Jr., ed., *Historia vitae et regni Ricardi secundi* (Philadelphia: University of Pennsylvania Press, 1977), 139; if their shared original read thus, Usk has revised even it to make Richard as tight-lipped as possible.

8. G-W 64 "Vbi et quando idem rex in cena dolenter retulit confabulando sic dicens, 'O deus, hec est mirabilis terra et inconstans, quia tot reges, tot presules, totque magnates exulauit, interfecit, destrucit et depredauit, semper discencionibus et discordiis mutuisque inuidiis continue infecta et laborans.' Et recitauit historias et nomina uexatorum a primeua regni inhabitacione." On the episode, see Gransden, *Historical Writing*, 186; and esp. Given-Wilson, "Adam Usk," 369, which observes that, by showing that Richard knew in September what would happen to him, Usk confirms the counter-Lancastrian account in "The Manner of King Richard's Renunciation" that describes Richard coerced into his resignation. That Usk does report this confirms the point, which should have been clear enough, that he does not write as a Lancastrian ideologue.

9. G-W 6 "Cuius magistri Iohannis, ut Machomdus, discipuli . . . , multas clades, insidias, rixas et contenciones et sediciones adhuc durantes et, ut timeo, usque ad regni confusionem duraturas, nefandissime seminarunt."

10. G-W 6 "et timeo ita finaliter contingere, ut sic prius contingebat quod plures London' fideles contra dictum ducem Lancastrie . . . insurrexerant." My translation assumes that *London'* records a genitive or dative rather than a locative, and that *fideles* appears not in an absolute sense ("the faithful," i.e., Christians) but in relation to a particular object of fidelity ("those faithful to London"). But it does not matter. Given-Wilson skillfully leaves the reading open: "various of the London faithful," 7.

11. G-W 90 "timeo quod gladii posessionem, eis iam tolleratam contra ordinis rationem, in dominos magis in futurum uibrare causabuntur."

12. G-W 160 "Quare, sicut ueteris testimenti . . . tria cessarunt miracula . . . , timeo quod in nouo testamento et ita continget."

13. In the articles of complaint against Richard II in 1399, and in the articles of resignation to which Richard was forced to agree, one way that Bolingbroke's men portrayed Richard's tyranny was by avowing the terror he is supposed to have in-

spired: he ruled "per minas et terrores" so that his lieges were led into action by fear ("metu ductos"); Given-Wilson, "Parliament of 1399," Item 39. The charges against Exeter at that time also mentioned that "pur poure et doute de sa morte," he did not dare resist the king's command; Given-Wilson, "Parliament of 1401," Placita, Item 5. Not only here, however, where the greatest men in the kingdom found it convenient to discover that they had been afraid of Richard, but in the most ordinary of petitionary language, the place of fear is the place of claims.

14. G-W 270 "Vtinam non sit dominus meus suppremus gladii furoris Domini, cum Iulio, cum Assuro, cum Alexandro, cum Ectore, cum Siro, cum Dario, cum Machabeo, finaliter particeps."

15. G-W 62 "Item, per sertos doctores, episcopos et alios, quorum presencium notator unus extiterat, deponendi regem Ricardum et Henricum Lancastrie ducem subrogandi in regem materia, et qualiter et ex quibus causis iuridice, committebatur disputanda."

16. G-W 62 "per capitulum *Ad apostolice*, extractus de *Re iudicata* in *Sexto*, cum ibi notatis."

17. Gerard E. Caspary, "The Deposition of Richard II and the Canon Law," in *Proceedings of the Second International Congress of Medieval Canon Law: Boston College, 12–16 August 1963*, ed. Stephan Kuttner and J. Joseph Ryan (Vatican City: Sacra Congregatio de Seminariis et Studiorum Universitatibus, 1963), 201.

18. Edward Peters, *The Shadow King:* Rex inutilis *in Medieval Law and Literature, 751–1327* (New Haven, Conn.: Yale University Press, 1970).

19. G-W 62 "periuria, sacrilegia, sodomidica, subditorum exinnanitio, populi in seruitutem redactio, uecordia, et ad regendum inutilitas, quibus rex Ricardus notorie fuit infectus."

20. Given-Wilson, "Parliament of 1399," Item 13.

21. For Usk's explanation that Wenzel was deposed "quia inutili et nondum per papam coronato," see ch. 4, n. 14; for the passage from the pope's decree of deposition declaring Wenzel "inutilem," see below, n. 25.

22. Peters suggests that it contributed to developing an idea of princely power as such, as distinct from its institutional embodiments; Peters, *Shadow King*, 20 and ch. 6.

23. St. Dominic apparently reported himself worthy of deposition: "Ego sum dignus depositione, quia ego sum inutilis et remissus"; *Relatio juridica, in qua novem testes . . . ex OP narrant pia gesta et miracula S. Dominici, Acta sanctorum* (August 1), 640.

24. Siegfried Wenzel, *The Sin of Sloth: Acedia in Medieval Thought and Literature* (Chapel Hill: University of North Carolina Press, 1967), 88–96.

25. G-W 166 "Tandem electores ipsi, uidentes moram ipsius infinita dispendia causare, et exortaciones predictas frustra fore et inanes, ad hanc rem tam sanctam et

Christianitati necessariam penitus obduratas, ipsumque W ad regimen dicti imperii esse omnino inutilem, et ne bona imperii ipsius desidia tenderent irreparabiliter in collapsum, nobis per eorum nuncium significari curarunt quod, prefati W segnicia diligenter inspecta, ex qua mundo pullularunt discrimina, ipso amoto, ad alterius eleccionem qui eis potenter occurreret procedere disposuerunt."

26. It is also a failure to measure up to the pattern of a just prince, as suggested in Hildebrand's utterances, which lie at the bottom of much "useless king" theory; see Walter Ullmann, *The Growth of Papal Government in the Middle Ages: A Study in the Ideological Relation of Clerical to Lay Power* (London: Methuen, 1965), 287–89. Still the declarations seem much more concerned with the adequacy to meet present needs in a world that requires action than with the relatively attenuated and abstract ideas of spiritual appropriateness, or of the *cohaerentia* implied in the idea of an organic utility in the image of the "social body"; Ullmann, 425–26.

27. Given-Wilson, "Parliament of 1399," Items 54–55. 1 Sam 9:17, "cumque aspexisset Samuhel Saulem Dominus ait ei ecce vir quem dixeram tibi iste dominabitur populo meo." See also n. 37 below.

28. G-W 14 ". . . rixae, contenciones, et hominum sepe interfecciones extiterunt."; "quam expulsionem presencium compilatori multum imposuerunt"; G-W 16 (see ch. 8, n. 27).

29. See n. 28 above; ch. 2, n. 2.

30. G-W 62 "Sic per omnia de isto Ricardo contigebat; cuius produccioni natalium, quasi non ex patre regalis prosapie set ex matre lubrice uite dedita, multum sinistri predicabatur in uulgo, ut de multis auditis, taciam." Credit for the inspired translation "given to slippery ways of life" goes to Thompson, 181.

31. Ch. 1, n. 71 and G-W 184 "Christus fuit humilis et eius uicarius piscator quam mitis. Sed hic me Plato quiescere iubet, etc."

32. See ch. 8, n. 27 and the discussion there.

33. G-W 62 "in dicta turri ubi rex Ricardus in custodia fuerat, ipsius cene, presencium notator interfuit, ipsius modum et gesturam explorando, per dominum Wyllelmum Beauchamp ad hoc specialiter inductus."

34. G-W 64 "Videns animi sui turbacionem, et qualiter nullum sibi specialem aut famulari solitum, set alios extranios sibi totaliter insidiantes, ipsius obsequio deputatos, de antiqua et solita eius gloria et de mundi fallaci fortuna intra me cogitando, multum animo meo recessi turbatus."

35. Bennett, *Revolution of 1399*, 177.

36. See ch. 1, n. 24.

37. G-W 10 "Alias in coronacione tua, fili, gaudebam me tanti nati in regem coronati matrem promeruisse fieri. Set iam doleo quia tui ruinam uideo imminere per maledictos adulatores tuos tibi causatam."

38. Gordon, *Wilton Diptych*, 22–24. Eccl 10:16, "Woe to thee, O land, when thy king is a child, and when the princes eat in the morning." Walsingham, *Historia anglicana*, 2.97; *Piers Plowman* B.Prol.196, ed. Kane and Donaldson (London: Athlone, 1975) and C.Prol.209, ed. Russell and Kane (London: Athlone, 1997); and some have found the sentiment echoed in the confrontation of the young Arthur of *Sir Gawain and the Green Knight*; see John M. Bowers, *The Politics of Pearl: Court Poetry in the Age of Richard II* (Woodbridge: Brewer, 2001), 17 and n. 40 below.

39. See n. 27 above. On the device, see recently Jenni Nuttall, *The Creation of Lancastrian Kingship: Literature, Language and Politics in Late Medieval England* (Cambridge: Cambridge University Press, 2007), 13–14; and, more ambitiously, Christopher Fletcher, *Richard II: Manhood, Youth, and Politics 1377–99* (Oxford: Oxford University Press, 2008).

40. Christine Chism, *Alliterative Revivals* (Philadelphia: University of Pennsylvania Press, 2002), 69.

41. Sylvia Wright, "The Author Portraits in the Bedford Psalter-Hours: Gower, Chaucer, and Hoccleve," *British Library Journal* 18 (1992): 195–96.

42. "legere et non intellegere parum prodest. Unde scire verba non est scire leges, sed scire vim et potestatem ipsarum"; Richard M. Hazelton, "Two Texts of the *Disticha Catonis* and its Commentary, with Special Reference to Chaucer, Langland, and Gower" (Ph.D. dissertation, Rutgers University, 1956), 103.

43. On the importance of Cato in literary composition, see nn. 44, 45. On the use of glosses in elementary education, see Suzanne Reynolds, *Medieval Reading: Grammar, Rhetoric and the Classical Text* (Cambridge: Cambridge University Press, 1996), 7–16.

44. Richard Hazelton, "The Christianization of 'Cato': The *Disticha Catonis* in the Light of Late Medieval Commentaries," *Mediaeval Studies* 19 (1957): 157–73; Hazelton, "Chaucer and Cato," *Speculum* 35 (1960): 357–80.

45. We are told, correctly, that Cato's works were usually encountered in no pure state in the Middle Ages; they traveled in the company of other didactic works and a tradition of commentary, both written and encountered in the practices of the schoolroom; see especially Aage Brusendorff, "'He Knew Nat Catoun for his Wit Was Rude,'" in *Studies in English Philology: A Miscellany in Honor of Frederick Klaeber*, ed. Kemp Malone and Martin B. Ruud (Minneapolis: University of Minnesota Press, 1929), 320–39, Marjorie Curry Woods and Rita Copeland, "Classroom and Confession," in *The Cambridge History of Medieval English Literature*, ed. David Wallace (Cambridge: Cambridge University Press, 1999), 380–81; Jill Mann, "'He knew nat Catoun': Medieval School-Texts and Middle English Literature," in *The Text in the Community: Essays on Medieval Works, Manuscripts, Authors, and Readers*, ed. Jill Mann and Maura Nolan (Notre Dame, Ind.: University of Notre Dame Press, 2006),

41–74. But the clarity of his *stylistic* identity is witnessed in every aspect of his influence.

46. "Nunc te, fili carissime, docebo, quo pacto morem animi tui componas"; Boas, 4. Indeed, rubrics often describe the work as a paternal address to a son whose character remains to be made: "Incipiunt dicta Marci Catonis ad filium suum."

47. 1.3; "Virtutem primam esse puta compescere linguam; / proximus ille deo est, qui scit ratione tacere." See Chaucer, *Troilus* 2.294, "thise wise clerkes that ben dede / Han evere yet proverbed to us yonge, / That 'firste vertu is to kepe tonge.'"

48. 1.14b, "Dissimula laesus . . . / qui celare potest odium, post laedere quem vult."

49. 1.12, "Rumores fuge, ne incipias novus auctor haberi,/ Nam nulli tacuisse nocet, nocet esse locutum."

50. 1.13, "Spem tibi promissi certam promittere noli; / Rara fides ideo est, quia multi multa loquuntur."

51. 2.7, "Quod pudeat, socios prudens celare memento"; 2.21a, "quod tacitum esse vis dicere noli"; 4.20, "Perspicito cuncta tacitus, quid quisque loquatur; / sermo hominum mores et celat et indicat idem."

52. 2.18, "Insipiens esto, cum tempus postulat ipsum; / stultitiam simulare loco, prudentia summa est."

53. 4.31, "Demissos animo et tacitos vitare memento: / quod flumen placidum est, forsan latet altius unda."

54. "Multiloquium est stultiloquium"; Hazelton, "Two Texts of the *Disticha Catonis*," 22.

55. Hazelton, "Christianization of 'Cato.'"

56. In general the commentaries perform on the *Distichs* the technique of "reverent exposition" described in M.-D. Chenu, *La théologie au douzième siècle* (Paris: Vrin, 1957), 364–65—making the text mean what it must mean, despite its attempt to mean something else; this of course entails the recognition that such reverent exposition is required. But sometimes they find the moral advice beyond recuperation, and deploy something analogous to the modern concept of culture to explain the differences. In response to the most notorious of the counsels, quoted above—"thus fraud is confounded by fraud," *sic ars deluditur arte*—they hurry to qualify this advice: "Haec scientia est secularis," this is the wisdom of the world, says one commentary, while another almost equivalently: "Secularium est sententia ista, et non perfectorum"; Hazelton, "Two Texts of the *Disticha Catonis*," 48. A similar example of the recognition of Cato's own limitations is the confrontation between his advice on almsgiving and that of Pope St. Gregory in *Piers Plowman* B.7; on which, see the comment of David Aers, *Community, Gender, and Individual Identity: English Writing 1360–1430* (London: Routledge, 1988), 50.

57. 1.31, "stultum petere est quod possit jure negari"; 2.3, "nam stultum est, tempore in omni, / dum mortem metuas, amittere gaudia vitae." See also: 2.16, "Nec te conlaudes nec te culpaveris ipse: / hoc faciunt stulti, quos gloria vexat inanis"; 4.14, "stultitia est morte alterius sperare salutem."

58. 3.4, "Sermones blandos blaesosque cavere memento: / simplicitas veri fama est, fraus ficta loquendi"; 3.17, "Quod merito pateris, patienter ferre memento"; 1.14, "Cum te aliquis laudat, judex tuus esse memento; / plus aliis de te, quam tu tibi, credere noli." Compare also: 1.15, "Officium alterius multis narrare memento, / at quaecumque aliis benefeceris ipse, sileto"; 1.20, "Exiguum munus cum dat tibi pauper amicus, / accipito placide, plene laudare memento"; 1.21, "Infantem nudum cum te natura crearit, / paupertatis onus patienter ferre memento"; 2.1, "Si potes, ignotis etiam prodesse memento"; 2.6, "Quod nimium est fugito, parvo gaudere memento: / tuta mage puppis est, modico quae flumine fertur"; 2.7 (for which see n. 51); 2.13, "Invidiam nimio cultu vitare memento"; 2.19 (for which see n. 59); 3.23, "Uxoris linguam, si frugi est, ferre memento: / namque malum est, non velle pati nec posse tacere"; 4.5, "Cum fueris locuples, corpus curare memento"; 4.7, "Res age quae prosunt, rursus vitare memento, / in quibus error inest, nec spes est çerta laboris"; 4.26, "Tranquillis rebus semper adversa timeto: / rursus in adversis melius sperare memento"; 4.31, "Demissos animo et tacitos vitare memento: / quod flumen placidum est, forsan latet altius unda"; 4.44, "Cum servos fueris proprios mercatus in usus / et famulos dicas, homines tamen esse memento."

59. 2.19, "Luxuriam fugito, simul et vitare memento / crimen avaritiae; nam sunt contraria famae."

60. 4.30, "Cum Venere et Baccho vis est et juncta voluptas; / quod lautum est animo complectere, sed fuge lites." Thus Boas, but the commentaries regularly report the variant that reads *lis* ("contention") for *vis* ("power").They then understand the "contention" as the effects of alcohol on sexual performance. Though both commentaries edited by Hazelton offer a more moralizing interpretation—"lis procedit de Venere, ut pote inter duos amantes; . . . de Baco, id est de vino, ut pote inter duos ebrios," Hazelton, "Two Texts of the *Disticha Catonis*," 124–25; but a few lines later the same commentary quotes quite unambiguous lines from the *Cato novus*: "Baco frigescit, Baco Venus ipsa calescit"—it provokes the desire and takes away the performance. The commentator understands the literal reference of Cato's words, which he interprets acceptably. Cato's advice, then, is to measure the indulgence in both so that neither pleasure interferes with the other; .

61. 1.19; "Cum dubia et fragilis sit nobis vita tributa, / in mortem alterius spem tu tibi ponere noli."

62. 2.3, "stultum est tempore in omni / dum mortem metuas, amittere gaudia vitae."

63. 3.22, "Fac tibi proponas mortem non esse timendam, / quae bona si non est, finis tamen illa malorum est."

64. "Ridebam et dicebam in corde meo: 'Sic ars deluditur arte,'" Jocelin of Brakelond, *Chronica*, ed. H. E. Butler (New York: Oxford University Press, 1949), 72.

65. 3.23, "Uxoris linguam, si frugi est, ferre memento" = "Suffre thy wives tonge, as Caton bit" (Chaucer, Merchant's Tale 1377).

66. See above, n. 58.

67. See above, n. 49.

68. "Natura bestiarum et serpentum ac volucrum et ceterorum domatur et a natura humana domita sunt, linguam autem suam nemo domare potest"; Albertano of Brescia, *Liber de doctrina dicendi et tacendi: La parola del cittadino nell'Italia del Duecento*, ed. Paola Navone, (Florence: SISMEL Edizioni del Galluzzo, 1998), 2, citing James 3:7–8.

69. Paola Navone, "La 'Doctrina loquendi et tacendi' di Albertano da Brescia. Censimento dei manoscritti," *Studi Medievali* 35 (1994): 895–930 lists 238 manuscripts of this work.

70. "Tu igitur, fili carissime, cum loqui desideras, a temetipso incipere debes, ad exemplum galli, qui antequam cantet, ter se cum alis percutit in principio"; Albertano, 2.

71. "Nam sicut super abecedario scripturae omnes volvuntur, ita super hoc dicto versiculo quicquid dici vel taceri debet, fere posset inflecti"; Albertano, 42.

72. "Requiras quid dicere vis, utrum sit efficax an inane"; Albertano, 12 compare also: "Pro omnibus vero prædictis libentius verba fundas utilia, videlicet pro Dei servitio et humano commodo et amici utilitate," 32.

73. "Cato instruit ergo filium suum, et quemlibet sub persona filii sui"; Hazelton, "Two Texts of the *Disticha Catonis*," 4; thus also the *Accessus ad auctores*: "..cum videret juvenes et puellas in magno errore versari, scripsit hunc libellum ad filium suum, insinuans ei rationem bene vivendi et per eum docens cunctos homines ut juste et caste vivant"; R. B. C. Huygens, ed., *Accessus ad auctores; Bernard d'Utrecht; Conrad d'Hirsau, Dialogus super auctores* (Leiden: Brill, 1970), 21.

74. William Caxton, *Here begynneth the prologue or prohemye of the book callid Caton*, STC 4853 (Westminster: William Caxton, 1484), iir.

75. Manciple's Tale, 359–60.

76. The phrase appears ten times in the last fifty lines of the tale: 318, 319, 321, 322, 325, 329, 335, 346, 351, 359.

77. 317–19, "thus taughte me my dame: / My sone, thenk on the crowe, a goodes name! / My sone, keep wel thy tonge, and keep thy freend." On the learned character of "proverbial" lore, see Mann, "'He knew nat Catoun.'"

78. G-W 20 "Set quare illam nondum septennem, licet cum maximis expensis et

seculi pompis Caliciis sibi nuptam, preelegit? Dicitur quia regis Francie auxilio et fauore latens suum uenenum effundere affectando sibi exosos destruere proposuit." On the events, and Usk's relatively good information about them, see J. J. N. Palmer, "The Background to Richard II's Marriage to Isabel of France," *Bulletin of the Institute for Historical Research* 44 (1971): 13–14.

79. It is unclear whether Henry's challenge to the throne after Richard's deposition actually relied on his claim to hereditary right; see the account given by "The Manner of King Richard's Renunciation," edited in G. O. Sayles, "The Deposition of Richard II: Three Lancastrian Narratives," *Bulletin of the Institute of Historical Research* 54 (1981): 257–70. What cannot be argued, and what would have been obvious to any observer, is that even a minor direct male heir of Richard's would have constituted some difficulty for his challenge; to this Usk, who seems to have maintained some allegiance to the Mortimer interest, would have been alert.

80. "Quis, quaeso, unquam audivit factum tale? aut quis vidit huic simile? Tu, qui Anglicus es et audis, obstupesce," James Raine, *The Historians of the Church of York and Its Archbishops*, RS 71 (London: Longman, 1879), 2.298.

CHAPTER 6.GRIEF

1. "Tanque le mond soit le mielx estable," Mary Dominica Legge, ed. *Anglo-Norman Letters and Petitions from All Souls MS. 182*, Anglo-Norman Text Society 3 (Oxford: Blackwell, 1941), 113; Chaucer, "Lak of Stedfastnesse," 1, 5, Benson, *Riverside Chaucer*, 654.

2. G-W 10 (see ch. 5, n. 37 above); 36 "tamen ad modum statui Nabocodonosor in maxima eius uanagloria ruit parliementum cum eius fautoribus" (not the idolatrous statue Nebuchadnezzar erects in Daniel 3, but the "statua" he sees in a dream in Daniel 2:31, which is crushed by a great stone); G-W 48 "Rex continue usque ad eius ruinam . . . , habuit secum in familia sua quadringentos excessiuos uiros de comitatu Cestr'. . . . quos rex in tantum fouebat ita ut nullum contra eos querelantem audire dignaretur, ymmo illum tamquam exosum pocius dedignaretur, quod fuit causa ipsius ruina maxima"; G-W 60–62 "de . . . infimis in magnates, et de ydeotis in pontifices quampluribus per eum exaltatis, postea ruina propter eorum inordinatum saltum depressis"; G-W 172 "eciam ecclesiis non parcendo, unde et ad ruinam finaliter deuenit."

3. See n. 49 below.

4. G-W 16 "ille nobilis miles dominus Iohannes Arundele, uersus partes Francie debellandas cum florida iuuentute patrie directus, quassata classe in uigilia sancti Nicholai—pro dolor—miserabili maris intemperie peremptus extitit."

5. G-W 16 "Idem de rege Edwardo condigit, qui collectatus clero et populo cum magno excersitu Franciam inuadere affectans, aduersante uento, licet iuxta maritima eius prosperitatem per sex menses expectans, inutiliter rediit cum excersitu."

6. For the plans and the size of the becalmed army, see J. W. Sherborne, "Indentured Retinues and English Expeditions to France, 1369–1380," *English Historical Review* 79 (1964): 725.

7. See the official accusations in Chris Given-Wilson, "Richard II: Parliament of October 1383: Text and Translation," Item 13, PROME, and the account in G. H. Martin, ed., *Knighton's Chronicle 1337–1396* (Oxford: Clarendon, 1995), 324–28; Margaret Aston, "The Impeachment of Bishop Despenser," *Bulletin of the Institute of Historical Research* 38 (1965): 127–48.

8. G-W 14 "episcopus Norwyc' cum cruciata in Flandream transiit, et ibidem Flandrenses circa nouem mille, quia Gallicis scismaticis adherentes, bellicoso peremit insultu; tamen partes deserere et ad propriam remeare regis Francie et eius exercitus potencia, pluribus Anglicis ad tunc uentris fluxu morientibus."

9. "Ce q'est einsi avenuz ne doit mye par reson estre surmys en son defaute, meement come ce est avenuz pluis par l'aventure de Dieux qe en autre manere"; Given-Wilson, "Parliament of October 1383," Item 19, PROME.

10. G-W 8 "sed—pro dolor—ad infrascripta tedia, prefecti extiterunt. . . . Ex quo—pro dolor—quanti dolores et tedia fuerunt insecuta, et presertim de morte illorum nobilium ducis Glowcestrie et comitis Arundelie, plenius infra liquebit"; G-W 16 (see n. 4 above); G-W 18 "Et sic—pro dolor—labi dinoscitur"; G-W 46 "Demum . . . pro dolor, casu quodam quo omnia tendunt in occasum, longe ante michi optatum terminum, tanta sui nobilitate mundum reliquit orbatum"; G-W 248 (see n. 49 below).

11. "Heu, prodolor" are the two equivalents the *Catholicon anglicum* gives for "Alas"; Sidney J. H. Herrtage, ed. *Catholicon anglicum: An English Latin Wordbook Dated 1483*, Camden Society n.s. 30 (Westminster: Camden Society, 1882), s.v. The one book we know Usk owned, the *Rationale* of William Durand of Mende, begins with it: "Sed, pro dolor, ipsi hodie, ut plurimum de his que usu cotidiano in ecclesiasticis contractant rebus, et proferunt officiis, quid significent, et quare instituta sint, modicum apprehendunt aut nihil," William Durandus, *Rationale divinorum officiorum*, ed. A. Davril, O.S.B. and T. M. Thibodeau, CCCM 140 (Turnhout: Brepols, 1995). Matthew Paris can scarcely let a year go by without using it: see, for instance, *Chronica majora*, ed. Henry Richards Luard, RS 57 (London: Longman, 1880), 5.38 (for 1248), 67 (for 1249), 163 and 173 (for 1250).

12. On this visit, see Donald M. Nichol, "A Byzantine Emperor in England: Manuel II's Visit to London in 1400–1401," *University of Birmingham Historical Journal* 12 (1970): 204–25.

13. G-W 120 "O Deus, quid tu facis, Romana olim gloria? Tui imperii magnalia notorie sunt hodie scissa, unde tibi poterit id Ieremie merito dici, 'Princeps prouinciarum facta est sub tributo.' Quis umquam crederet quod ad tantam deuenires miseriam, que in solio maiestatis residere solens toti mundo principabas, iam Christiane fidei nequaquam succursum prestare ualendo?" A useful list of the English reports appears in David R. Carlson, "Greeks in England, 1400," in *Interstices: Studies in Middle English and Anglo-Latin Texts in Honour of A. G. Rigg*, ed. Richard Firth Green and Linne R. Mooney (Toronto: University of Toronto Press, 2004), 88–93.

14. See ch. 4, n. 24; G-W 182 "O Deus, Cesaris et Augusti, Salamonis et Alexandri, Assueri, Darii et Constantini magni, quo pertransiuit gloria?"

15. G-W 4 "O quantus regni desolati tunc uibrabatur luctus"; G-W 6 "uelud Iudei ad Montem Oreb propter uitulum conflatilem . . . mutuo in se reuertentes, uiginti tres milium de suis miserabilem pacientes casum merito doluerunt, Anglici inter se de fide antiqua et noua altercantes omni die sunt in pincto quasi mutuo ruinam et sedicionem inferendi"; G-W 60 "dictus Vnfredus . . . , ad magnum regni luctum, sic ueniendo moriebatur"; G-W 156 "Dux iste . . . subita peste ad magnum peregrinorum dolorem succubuit, quia in uirga ferrea terras suas regendo, tutum uiantibus prestabat transitum per easdem."

16. G-W 158 (see ch. 4, n. 24 above); G-W 170 "dictus dominus Henricus, milicie Christiane flos et gloria, cum dicto patruo suo dolenter occubuit"; G-W 242 "Henricus quartus, . . . dolenter intoxicatus, . . . diem suum clausit extremum"; G-W 266 "sisma Christianitatis orbem aliquando quatuor, aliquando tribus, aliquando duobus monstruose et dolenter presedentibus disturbans."

17. G-W 38 "Et rex fecit eum per ducem Lanc' proditorem adiudicari, sed uitam concessit ei perpetuo lugendam carceribus" (this instance, however, Usk apparently draws from his source; see Stow, *Historia vitae et regni*, 145); G-W 188 "O Deus, in quantum Roma est dolenda"; in this case, the adverb is introduced by the gerundive form discussed in the next paragraph almost immediately: "quam dolenter noscitur desolata."

18. Chris Given-Wilson, "Richard II, Parliament of 1391: Text and Translation," Item 24, PROME: "Item, suppliont voz poveres liges les possessours des niefs parmy le roialme: qe come sibien en vostre temps come es temps des voz nobles progenitours, grantz prosperite, honours et profitz ont eschuez al roialme d'Engleterre par la navye du dit roialme; quelle navie, si remede ne soit hastivement ordeine, est a poi destruit, et les possessours d'icelle navye anientiz a toutz jours, dont dolour est et grant pite."

19. Chris Given-Wilson, "Richard II, Parliament of January 1397: Text and Translation," Item 16, PROME, "Et illoeqes ovek tout humilite et obeissance q'ils purroient,

faisant grant :dolour, [come aparust par] lour chier, de ce qe le roy avoit pris tiel conceit envers eux."

20. Given-Wilson, "Parliament of 1399," Item 66, "En quel parlement, et auxint par l'auctorite suisdite, diverses estatutz, juggementz, ordinances, et establissementz furent faitz, ordeignez, et renduz erronousement et tresdolorousement, en grant disheritesoun, et final destruccioun et anientisement des plusours honurables seignours, et autres lieges du roialme, et de leur heirs as toutz jours."

21. Given-Wilson, "Parliament of 1401," Item 44, "a tresgrand dolour et desolacioun de seinte esglise."

22. E.g., "Dum contemplationis dulcedinem alte describitis, ruinae meae mihi gemitum renovastis, quia audivi quid intus perdidi, dum foris ad culmen regiminis immeritus ascendi. Tanto autem me percussum moerore agnoscite, ut vix loqui sufficiam, oculos enim mentis meae doloris tenebrae obsident," Letter 6, *PL* 77: 450–51.

23. E.g., Matthew Paris, *Chronica majora*, 4.38 (1248), 4.67 (1249), 4.163 (1250), 4.184 (1250, this in a section he heads "Querula exclamatio), and so on; Walsingham, *Historia anglicana*, 1.326, 328 (1377), 2.104 (1383), 2.183 (1383), 2.212 (1392).

24. 1.14a, "Perde semel socium, quem ingratum noveris esse; / saepe dato bonis, scieris bene ponere quod des."

25. 1.26 (restoring the familiar reading), "sic ars deluditur arte."

26. 1.19, "dubia et fragilis nobis sit vita"; cf. 1.33, "dubia incertis versetur vita periclis."

27. 1.40, "Dapsilis interdum notis et carus amicis, / dum fueris dando, semper tibi proximus esto."

28. See Introduction, n. 22.

29. See ch. 1, n. 64.

30. G-W 240 "illud uulgare quod 'non propter me sed propter mea alii dilexerunt,' unde infortunia labente me neclexerunt."

31. Cicero's injunctions against the appearance of premeditation—"suspicio quaedam apparitionis atque artificiosae diligentiae . . . , quae maxime orationi fidem, oratori adimit auctoritatem," Marcus Tullius Cicero, *Rhetorici libri duo de inventione*, ed. E. Stroebel (Stuttgart: Teubner, 1977), 23—became a standard of medieval rhetoric. On medieval familiarity with *De inventione*, see James J. Murphy, *Rhetoric in the Middle Ages: A History of Rhetorical Theory from St. Augustine to the Renaissance* (Berkeley: University of California Press, 1974), 106–23. The Ciceronian advice appears in, e.g., Brunetto Latini: "Il y doit avoir un petit de doreure de jeu et de consonances, porce que de ces choses naist sovent une sospecon comme de chose pensée par grant maistrie, en tel maniere que li oierres se doute de toi, et ne croit pas à tes paroles"; Brunetto Latini, *Li livres dou tresor*, ed. P. Chabaille (Paris: Imprimerie Impériale, 1863), 503. The prejudice against the premeditated is not unrelated to the

"antitheatrical prejudice"; Jonas A. Barish, *The Antitheatrical Prejudice* (Berkeley: University of California Press, 1981); a startling (though now familiar) contemporary statement is Roland Barthes, *Camera Lucida: Reflections on Photography* (New York: Hill and Wang, 1981), on which see Michael Fried, "Barthes's *Punctum*," *Critical Inquiry* 31 (2005): 539–75.

32. See ch. 5, n. 34.

33. "Antequam spiritus ad os tuum verba producat, te ipsum et omnia verba in hoc versiculo posita requiras"; Albertano, *De doctrina dicendi*, 2.

34. "Verbum ad cor pertinet; vox ad aurem"; "Sancti Augustini sermones post Maurinos reperti," in *Miscellanea agostiniana; testi e studi, pubblicati a cura dell'Ordine cremitano di s. Agostino nel XV centenario dalla morte del santo dottore*, ed. Germain Morin (Rome: Tipgrafia poliglotta vaticana, 1930), 227.

35. "ut autem perferatur ad tuum cor, quod in meo corde jam natum est, ministerium vocis adsumit"; "Sermones post Maurinos reperti," 227; "necessaria est vox quasi quoddam vehiculum verbi," Sermo 196, *PL* 39:2112.

36. "Nihil itaque agimus per membra corporis in factis dictisque nostris quibus vel approbantur vel improbantur mores hominum quod non verbo apud nos intus edito praevenimus. Nemo enim aliquid volens facit quod non in corde suo prius dixerit"; Augustine, *De trinitate libri xv*, CCSL 50 (Turnhout: Brepols, 1968), 304.

37. See, e.g., Guigo I: "Non norunt invicem motus suos animae, nisi per signa corporea"; Guigo I, *Méditations*, 204.

38. "Ecce, ex corde tuo credis cordi non tuo, et quo nec carnis nec mentis dirigis aciem, accommodas fidem"; Augustine, *Liber de fide rerum invisibilium*, ed. M. P. J. van den Hout, CCSL 46 (Turnhout: Brepols, 1969), 3.

39. G-W 216 "ipsos in campo contriuit decapitauitque, ac eorum capita ultra London', pontem inde posita, ad regem Henricum transmisit. Quo audito, presencium compilator de sua a retro remanencia futurorum regraciabatur scrutatori."

40. G-W 214 "ut transirem secum, magnas promociones michi promisit. Visitauit Deus cor meum, et cogitaui, 'Tu, Adam, positus in labrintho, disponas te cum Deo.' Malignum misit Deus spiritum, et merito, inter regem et istum comitem, ad modum Abymalech, ut legitur in libro Iudicum. Et sic, uerti mantellum, ac ad dominum meum de Poisia, regis et regni graciam expectaturus, si Deus daret, gressus meos dirigere disposui; et factum est ita." Given-Wilson's decision about the bounds of the quotation in which Usk addresses himself, as it appears in this note, follows Thompson's. As my translation shows, I disagree. There is no diegetic signal that the quotation ends until the "Et sic" of the following sentence, and Usk elsewhere quotes himself citing texts in the manner that Judges is here mentioned.

41. G-W 122 "*Heredicus crematur.* In couocacione quidam dominus Wyllylmus Sawtri, capellanus, de heresi conuictus et condempnatus, domino meo Cant' statim

lata contra ipsum huiusmodi sentencia, magno impetu dixit ista uerba, 'Ego, missus a Deo, dico tibi, quod tu et totus clerus tuus, et eciam rex, estis in breui mala morti morituri, et extranea nacionis lingua in regno superauerit regnatura, et hoc est in hostio proxime expectans.' Qui quidem, sic dampnatus, primo solempniter degradatus, postea in Smythfeld London' posti derecte stando catenatus ac dolio, ignitis focalibus circumdatis, in cineres redactus existit."

42. The record of Sawtry's interrogation does give testimony to deliberately riddling and mocking speech; Wilkins, *Concilia*, 3.255–57.

43. G-W 146: "Decretum destruccionis lingue Wallice"; see also G-W 126, which twice mentions the parliamentary initiatives against the Welsh living in England. For these proposals, see Given-Wilson, "Parliament of 1401," Items 102–7; for discussions of this and other early fifteenth-century anti-Welsh legislation, see Davies, *Revolt of Owain Glyn Dwr*, 283–92; Philip Morgan, "Cheshire and Wales," in *Power and Identity in the Middle Ages: Essays in Memory of Rees Davies*, ed. Huw Pryce and John Watts (Oxford: Oxford University Press, 2007), 208–10.

44. Aquinas remarks in passing, as something obvious, the equivocation implied in the idea of *impetus* as he explains contradictory lections in the text of the *Metaphysics*: "Illud ergo dicitur esse violentum, quod est *praeter* impetum, id est praeter inclinationem rei naturalis. . . . Alia littera habet et hoc est . . . *secundum* impetum. Violentia enim est cum aliquid agit secundum impetum exterioris agentis, contra voluntatem vim passi"; Thomas Aquinas, *In duodecim libros metaphysicorum Aristotelis expositio* (Turin: Marietti, 1950), book 5, lect. 6, n. 3.

45. G-W 132 (and for the last sixteen words of the translation, I have used Given-Wilson's version, which could not be bettered) "a Londoniis uersus patrem, pluribus tractatibus intermediis ad hoc habitis, recessit, nigris induta, regi Henrico multum depressum et maleuolum in recessu, uix os apperiens, exhibendo uultum."

46. I have explored this mechanism, at much greater length and in a writer much greater than Usk, in "Chaucer's History-Effect," in *Answerable Style: The Idea of the Literary in Medieval England*, ed. Frank Grady and Andrew Galloway (Columbus: Ohio State University Press, 2013), 169–94.

47. See ch. 3, n. 11; G-W 86 "et post depossicionem regis Ricardi, ad ipsum idem leoprarius ductus, eum alio modo quam unum priuatum sibi incognitum respicere non curauit, quod idem tunc depositus dolenter ferebat"; G-W 90 "usque ad sui mortem lugendo condoluit."

48. "Si etenim perspicaciter consideramus quid cum loquimur intendamus, patet quod nihil aliud quam nostrae mentis enucleare aliis conceptum"; Dante Alighieri, *De vulgari eloquentia*, ed. Steven Botterill (Cambridge: Cambridge University Press, 1996), 4.

49. G-W 246–48 "*Mors archiepiscopi Cant'*. Mensis Februarii undeuicesimo die,

anno Domini millesimo quadringentesimo terciodecimo, dominus meus illustrissimus, domini nostri regis et fratrum suorum, necnon Marchie, Arundellie et Notynghamie ac Stafford' comitum, necnon de Bergaueny et Spenser, patruus, comitis Arundellie defuncti filius, dominus Thomas de Arundell', Cant' archiepiscopus, totius Angl' primas et apostolice sedis legatus, uirtus, lampas et sophia populi, lucerna ac delicie cleri ecclesieque, fidei Christiane columpna inpressibilis, qui michi de Kemsynge in Cancia et de Merstham in Suthreya, cum prebenda de Landogy in Wallia, bonas ecclesias contulit, et per quem me ad maiora, prout ita promiserat, promoueri sperabam, casu quodam quo omnia tendunt in occasum subita mutacione preventus, dies suos longe ante optatum michi terminum—pro dolor—Cantuar' terminauit, regis celestis illam dulcedinis uocem, 'Serue bone et fidelis, intra in gaudium domini tui,' cum eternitatis gaudio recepturus."

CHAPTER 7. THEORY OF HISTORY

1. G-W 248 "Quam terminacionem eadem nocte London' in uisione habui, scilicet quod ipse, relicta tota familia, et in curtis uestibus quasi remote transiturus, uelocissime currebat solus; et cum ego omni nisu ipsum insequi laborarem, tradidit michi unam ceream candelam dicens, 'Scindas istam in medio inter nos duos,' et sic a uisu meo disparuit; et sic euigilans intellexi quod diuisi eramus de cetero, et pro anima sua quam dolenter missam celebraui; et postea de morte sua certioratus fui."

2. G-W 248–50 "Frater Iohannes Burghhull, uir auarissimus de ordine predicatorum, episcopus Lychfelden', ad scandalosam eius per totum regnum famam, magnam summam auri in quodam camere sue foramine abscondit. Et quia in alia parte foramen erat apertum, due monedule, merito a moneta dicte, uolentes in eo nidificare, aurum per arbores et gardinum dispergentes, et foramen eo ad multorum comodum euacuauerunt."

3. G-W 80 "idem dominus Thomas iterato propria textorum artis subtilitate arma et insignia restituit; dictique Rogeri, ut premittitur, sublata tunc uidi sub scannis in derisum habita iacere, et per famulos extra fenestras proici pariter et iactari." By the same token, the vice of Roger Walden that is punished in the contemptuous treatment narrated here is not luxury (a few lines later, Usk calls him "modestus, pius, et affabilis"), but usurpation.

4. He reports John Trevor, bishop of St. Asaph, condemning the economies parliament would force on the king as tending to "tenacitatem, quod omni regalitati contrarium existit," G-W 82. Cicero's *De inventione*, a source frequently cited for the cardinal virtues (Rosamond Tuve, "Notes on the Virtues and Vices," *Journal of the*

Warburg and Courtauld Institutes 26 [1963]: 268), listed magnificence as "rerum magnarum et excelsarum cum animi ampla quadam et splendida propositione cogitatio atque administratio," Cicero, *De inventione*,149, 2.163, but the content of those lofty things brilliantly imagined tended to follow the Aristotelian definition requiring "great expenses": "magnos sumptus," Thomas Aquinas, *Summa theologiae* IIa IIae, q. 134 a. 3 co.; "grans despens," Brunetto Latini, *Tresor*, 285.

5. "magna solacia"; see n. 8 below.

6. "des coureurs qui tombent et des naïfs qu'on mystifie, coureurs d'idéal qui trébuchent sur les réalités, rêveurs candides que guette malicieusement la vie"; Henri Bergson, *Le rire: essai sur la signification du comique* (Paris: Presses Universitaires de France, 1981), 10–11.

7. Stanley Cavell, *Must We Mean What We Say?* (Cambridge: Cambridge University Press, 1976), 278. "In this sense," because there is another: Steven Justice, "'Shameless': Augustine, After Augustine, and Way After Augustine," *Journal of Medieval and Early Modern Studies* 44 (2014): 17–43.

8. G-W 250 "una die in mensa dicti domini mei, ad magna solacia per nonnullos conuiuas regni magnates, fabulatum audiui."

9. G-W 250 "Ad sedem transfertur Cant' magister Henricus Chychley, legum doctor, Meneuen' tunc episcopus, cui et subrogatur in Meneuen' magister Iohannes Kedryk; dicto, iam Cant', in recessu meo ab Oxon' cathedram meam ciuilem dimisi. Demum, et infra medietatem anni extunc, predicto fratri Iohanni Burchhill ab hac uita subtracto, et sibi N. de Patryngton', ordinis Carmelitarum, subrogatur in sedibus." Catterick was provided to St. David's 27 April 1414 (*Fasti*, vol. 11 [Welsh Diocese], 54), and translated to Coventry and Lichfield, 1 February 1415 (*Fasti*, vol. 10 [Coventry and Lichfield], 2); in 1419 he would be translated to Exeter; *Fasti*, vol. 9 (Exeter), 2.

10. See ch. 1, n. 49.

11. See ch. 6, n. 49.

12. See ch. 6, n. 10.

13. See ch. 1, nn. 71–72.

14. Leicester explains it most clearly in "Newer Currents in Psychoanalytic Criticism, and the Difference 'It' Makes: Gender and Desire in the Miller's Tale," *ELH* 61, 3 (1994): 473–99.

15. See ch. 1, n. 26.

16. G-W 2 "Predicto gracioso Edwardo in uigilia natalis sancti Iohannis baptiste anno regni sui quinquagesimo secundo ab hac uita subtracto, ipsius nepos Ricardus, Edwardi principis Wallie dicti regis primogeniti filius, undecim annorum pupilus, inter omnes mortales ac si secundus Apsalon pulcherimus, ei successit aput Westm' in festo sancti Kenelmi coronatus. Isti Ricardi regni suit tempore plura uotiue inclita

ferebantur. Et quia tenere etatis existebat, alii ipsius et regni curam habentes lasciuias, extorciones et alias intolorabiles iniurias regno irrogare non desistebant."

17. See ch. 4, n. 12 and the discussion there.

18. See ch. 6, n. 47.

19. See ch. 4, n. 12.

20. G-W 90 "Nunc, Ricarde, uale, ymmo rex, si fas est dicere, ualentissime, cum post mortem laudare licitum sit cuique, si cum Deo et populi tui releuamine acta tua disposuisses, merito laudande. Sed, quamuis cum Salamone dapsilis, cum Absalone pulcher, cum Assuero gloriosus, cum Belino magno precellens edificator existens, ad modum Cosdre regis Persarum in manus Eraclii, sic in medio glorie tue, rota labente fortune, in manus ducis Henrici miserrime, cum interna populi tui maledictione, cecidisti."

21. Nuttall, *Creation of Lancastrian Kingship*, 28–33.

22. *Vale*, "farewell," formally is the imperative mood (second singular) of *valere*, "to prosper, to fare well"; Usk plays with the fact that *valens*—"powerful, effective"—is the same verb's present participle, and emerges with the conceit that *valentissimus* is therefore the superlative form of "farewell." The "excuse" he offers for his kind words here, that one may legitimately praise the dead, then provides the next vocative, as he imagines in a counterfactual the conditions that would have allowed him to be praiseworthy (*merito laudande*, rightly to be praised).

CHAPTER 8. ADAM USK'S SECRET

1. "Si latet, ars prodest: adfert deprensa pudorem, / Atque adimit merito tempus in omne fidem"; *Ars amatoria*, in Ovid, *Amores [etc.]*, ed. Rudolf Ehwald, Bibliotheca scriptorum Graecorum et Romanorum Teubneriana (Lipsiae: Teubner, 1887), 2.313–14. See Paolo D'Angelo, "'Celare l'arte': per una storia del precetto 'Ars est celare artem,'" *Intersezioni* 6 (1986): 323–30 on the relevant classical sources.

2. There is an enormous scholarly literature on the dictamen. Good places to start are Ronald G. Witt, "The Arts of Letter-Writing," in *The Cambridge History of Literary Criticism*, vol. 2, *The Middle Ages*, ed. Alastair J. Minnis (Cambridge: Cambridge University Press, 2005), 68–83, and Martin Camargo, *Ars dictaminis, ars dictandi*, Typologie des Sources du Moyen Âge Occidental 60 (Turnhout: Brepols, 1991); Martin Camargo, "The Waning of Medieval Ars Dictaminis," *Rhetorica* 19 (2001): 135–40. Witt's work has helpfully refuted a traditional assertion—associated especially with Kristeller and Quentin Skinner—that the dictamen gave rise to humanist rhetorical and literary concerns—see esp. Ronald G. Witt, *"In the Footsteps of the Ancients": The Origins of Humanism from Lovato to Bruni* (Leiden: Brill,

2000)—but it has also shown the importance of the dictamen in other aspects of medieval culture.

3. Augusto Gaudenzi, "Sulla cronologia dei dettatori Bolognesi," *Bolletino dell' Istituto Storico Italiano* 14 (1895): 118ff.; Helene Wieruszowski, "*Ars dictaminis* in the Time of Dante," *Medievalia et Humanistica* 1 (1943): 97; G. P. Cuttino, *English Diplomatic Administration, 1259–1339* (Oxford: 1971), 116–17; Nigel Ramsay, "Scriveners and Notaries as Legal Intermediaries in Later Medieval England," in *Enterprise and Individuals in Fifteenth-Century England*, ed. Jennifer Kermode (Stroud: Sutton, 1991), 124; Martin Camargo, *Medieval Rhetorics of Prose Composition: Five English Artes Dictandi and Their Tradition* (Binghamton, N.Y.: Medieval and Renaissance Texts and Studies, 1995), 18; Witt, "Arts of Letter-Writing."

4. "Romane curie vestigiis inherentes eius stili non indigne magisterium imitamur," Thomas of Capua, *Die Ars dictandi des Thomas von Capua*, ed. Emmy Heller (Heidelberg: C. Winter, 1929), 11; "qui gratiam apostolicae sedis venantur," *De dictamine et dictatorio syllogismorum* in John of Limoges, *Opera omnia*, ed. Constantin Horváth, OCSO (Veszprém: Egyházmegyei Könyvnyomda, 1932), 3.

5. H. M. Schaller, "Studien zur Briefsammlung des Kardinals Thomas von Capua," *Deutsches Archiv für Erforschung des Mittelalters* (1965): 390. Schaller mentions the telling detail that the best evidence for the business of the papal chancery is the collection of model letters assembled for instruction in the art, 380.

6. Guido Faba, *Summa dictaminis*, ed. Augusto Gaudenzi, *Il propugnatore* 2.3 (1890), 293.

7. H. G. Richardson, "Business Training in Medieval Oxford," *American Historical Review* 46 (1941): 259–80; H. G. Richardson, "Letters of the Oxford *Dictatores*," in *Formularies Which Bear on the History of Oxford c. 1204–1420*, ed. H. E. Salter, W. A. Pantin and H. G. Richardson, Oxford Historical Society (Oxford: Clarendon, 1942), 331–450.

8. The formulary in Oxford, All Souls College MS 182, for example, was associated with Henry Chichele, Usk's successor in the chair of civil law at Oxford, and Guy Mone; E. F. Jacob, "Verborum florida venustas," *Bulletin of the John Rylands Library* 17 (1933): 282–84.

9. Augustine refers to them in passing as *numerosae clausulae*, and regrets that they are not to be found much in Christian authors: "hunc elocutionis ornatum, qui numerosis fit clausulis, deesse fatendum est auctoribus nostris"; Augustine, *De doctrina christiana*, 148.

10. The cursus has been massively discussed, and much of the important bibliography appears in the footnotes to follow. An especially efficient and flexible description of the most common prescribed cadences is in Camargo, *Ars dictaminis*, 25–26. What makes these cadences so successful poses a challenge to analyzing them, bril-

liantly summarized in Tore Janson, *Prose Rhythm in Medieval Latin from the 9th to the 13th Century*, vol. 20 (Stockholm: Almqvist & Wiksell International, 1975), 10–13: because they are so neatly tailored to the natural rhythms of Latin, it is hard to know whether an author has deliberately chosen, or merely lucked into, any particular instance. Janson devises a statistical approach that I do not use here because the dramatic moments of choice will, I think, make the larger-scale analysis unnecessary and (anyhow) call its application to this work into question.

11. Léonce Couture, "Le 'cursus' ou rhythme prosaïque dans la liturgie et la littérature," *Revue des Questions Historiques* 51 (1892): 253–61 gives one important reason why.

12. "Contiones saepe exclamare vidi, cum apte verba cecidissent"; Marcus Cicero, *Orator*, ed. P. Reis (Leipzig: Teubner, 1932), 64.

13. Credit for discovering the cursus as a regular practice of papal writing offices belongs to the doctoral thesis of Noël Valois, *De arte scribendi epistolas apud gallicos medii ævi scriptores rhetoresve* (Paris: Picard, 1880), 70–80; and focused and expanded the next year in Noël Valois, "Étude sur la rhythme des bulles pontificales," *Bibliothèque de l'École des Chartes* (1881): 164–272.

14. See Richardson, "Letters," 333.

15. Ian Cornelius, "The Rhetoric of Advancement: *Ars dictaminis*, *Cursus*, and Clerical Careerism in Late Medieval England," *New Medieval Literatures* 12 (2010): 289–330.

16. "Est ergo dictamen digna verborum et artificiosa congeries, cum pondere sententiarum et ordine dictionum, nihil intra se sustinens diminutum, nihil concipiens otiosum . . .. 'Ordo dictionum' ideo inseritur, quia ordinandae sunt in dictamine dictiones, sicut notabiliter inferius exprimetur"; Thomas of Capua, *Die Ars dictandi des Thomas von Capua*, 12–13.

17. Samuel Holt Monk, "'A Grace Beyond the Reach of Art,'" *Journal of the History of Ideas* 5 (1944).

18. In a typically obscure and penetrating remark, Blackmur said that "the characteristic intellectual monument of the Roman Empire was law. The *Institutes* of Justinian took up the slack in those of Quintilian"; R. P. Blackmur, "The Lion and the Honeycomb," *Hudson Review* 3 (1951): 488.

19. G-W 19.

20. N. Denholm-Young, "The *Cursus* in England," in *Oxford Essays in History Presented to H. E. Salter* (Oxford: Clarendon, 1934), 47.

21. The following catalogue includes full stops (which the editor has or could have marked with a period) in the first pages, omitting only those in which an abbreviation of a place-name (in this case "London'") leaves uncertain whether an inflectional ending is meant and which one, and therefore what the rhythm is. I am using a mod-

erately conservative standard for judging what counts as a proper rhythm: I include as rhythmical the so-called *cursus trispondaicus* (/ x || x x / x), but I exclude those that observe the rhythmical pattern but not the word-limits. The results show, of forty-seven periods, forty-one that are rhythmical using these criteria:

"Kenélmi coronátus" (trispondaicus); "irrogáre non desistébant" (velox); "prímo venérunt" (planus); "perpétuum duratúre" (velox); "décapitáti" (planus); "fúgam arrípuit" (tardus); "fécit proclamári" (trispondaicus); "deturpáre iactábant" (planus); "dicióreṁ spoliábat" (trispondaicus); "ad própria remeárunt" (velox); "ad mília trucidárunt" (velox); "sine próle defúnctam" (planus); "per pápam radificáre" (**irregular**); "transmíttitur coronánda" (velox); "finálem destrucciónem" (**irregular**); "extitérunt corrúpte" (planus); "nefandíssime seminárunt" (velox); "sediciónem inferéndi" (trispondaicus); "uíuus evásit" (planus); "uenírent reponsúri" (trispondaicus); "irrúere properántes" (velox); "pénitus destruxísse" (velox); "inférius liquébit" (**irregular**); "preféċti extitérunt" (trispondaicus, though with hiatus); "infestáre non cessáuit" (trispondaicus); "ínfra liquébit" (planus); "proposuérunt" (planus); "accédo dispósuit" (**irregular**); "habére procurárunt" (trispondaicus); "íter arrípuit" (tardus); "síbi indúxit" (planus, though with hiatus); "gubernári consílium" (tardus); "tíbi causátam" (planus); "reconciliáuit" (trispondaicus); "sécum addúxit" (planus); "intériit propulérunt" (velox); "exílio periérunt" (velox); "cómites tenébant" (**irregular**); "cláues transmísit" (planus); "dediciónem obsidérunt" (trispondaicus); "custódiis tradidérunt" (velox); "Hybérniam deportárunt" (velox); "decapitárunt" (planus); "compellebátur" (planus); "mórbo amísit" (planus); "pacificátus" (planus); "éxtitit subórta" (**irregular**).

22. G-W 74. Thompson translates, "This rough translation out of French into Latin does not pretend to be exact; and so, reader, be lenient"; Thompson 189. Given-Wilson comes closer: "This translation from French into Latin does no justice to the style of the original, therefore be tolerant, reader," G-W 75.

23. G-W 18 "Ordini annorum hucusque in gestis parcat lector, quia solum que uidi et audiui, forcius ex ueritate facti quam ex temporis ordine, memorie comendaui."

24. "narratio dicitur vitiosa si sit confusa; quod accidit cum ordo rei gestae omittitur"; "Lucida est, cum usitatis significationibus, rerum ordine servato, et non longo circuito res monstrantur"; Guido Faba, *Summa dictaminis*, 293, 332.

25. "Aperta autem narratio poterit esse, si, ut quidque primum gestum erit, ita primum exponetur, et rerum ac temporum ordo servabitur"; Cicero, *De inventione*, 26, I.28.

26. "Prosa est producta oratio et a lege metri soluta. Prosum enim antiqui 'productum' dicebant, et 'rectum' . . . quae non est perflexa numero, sed recta, prosa oratio dicitur, in rectum producendo"; Isidore of Seville, *Isidori Hispalensis Episcopi Etymologiarvm sive originvm libri XX* (Oxford: Clarendon, 1911), 1.88 (n.p.).

27. G-W 16 "Vt quid mora? Pacificari non potuimus quousque nostrum quamplures de insurrexione proditoria indictati fuimus, inter quos presencium compulator tanquam principalis Wallencium dux et fautor, et forte non immerito, indictatus fuerat; sicque indictati, uix per duodenam nos obtinuimus coram regis iusticiario liberari. Regem de cetero michi prius in ipsius potencia ignotum et eius leges timui ipsum, per maxillis meis frenum imponendo."

28. Probably for this reason, Thompson silently omitted the preposition, as he also omitted the interlined *ipsum*, rendering the clause "et eius leges timui, maxillis meis frenum imponendo," Thompson 8.

29. "de insurrexione," "proditoria indictati," "non immerito indictatus," "sicque indictati," "potencia ignotum," "timui ipsum."

30. A classic example is "Rector Xerxes, rex Xerxes bonus"; Guido Faba, *Summa dictaminis*, 291.

31. Defending the child who produces the construction "Irai-je-t-y?": "Remarquez de plus avec quelle adresse il évitait l'hiatus de *irai-je-y* ou *y irai-je*?" Jean-Jacques Rousseau, *Émile, ou de l'éducation*, ed. T. L'Aminot (Paris: Garnier, 1999), 54. Medieval warnings against hiatus include Vincenzo Licitra, "La 'Summa de arte dictandi' di Maestro Goffredo," *Studi medievali* 3 ser. 7 (1966), 910; John of Limoges, *De dictamine*, 18.

32. G-W 82 "Ista peticio inciuílis est et iniústa [velox], quia concludit ad régis tenacitátem [planus], quod omni regalitati contrárium exístit [**irregular**]. Cui potius largitatis affluencia conueníre denóscitur [tardus]. Concludit eciam quod subditi suum regem a sui innata bonitáte restríngerent [tardus], que michi non uidéntur honésta [planus]. Ideo non ipse, sed iniuste et indigne petens, ueniat pótius puniéndus [velox]."

33. G-W 94 "Subditus meus es. In uetito stas examine coram non tuo iudice. Veni mecum."

34. Benedetto Croce, *Storia della età barocca in Italia: pensiero, poesia e letteratura, vita morale*, 2nd ed. (Bari: Laterza, 1946), 24.

35. This difference is most marked in longer and especially in narrative compositions. In poetic meters defined by patterns of multiple lines—like the elegaic couplet—major syntactic units tend to measure themselves to the length of couplet or stanza. That is just why these work less well for extended poetic discourse and especially narrative discourse than (say) the hexameter. Even so, the phenomenology of stanzaic verse is different from that of the prose cursus: following the unrolling of thought through sapphics (for instance), and watching the utterance reveal its sense and shape, the stanza cultivates a suspense about just how the sense will complete itself within the patterns of a matrix already recognized as fixed.

36. Guido Faba, *Summa dictaminis*, 292; see also Alberic, *Flores rhetorici*, 47;

Alberic of Monte Cassino, *Flores rhetorici*, ed. Mauro Inguanez and H. M. Willard, Miscellanea Cassinese 14 (Rome: Arti Grafiche e Fotomeccaniche Sansaini, 1938), 47.

37. Guido Faba, *Summa dictaminis*, 292.

38. "viciosum facit prolatorem viciosa prolatio, quando puncta non fiant ubi fieri deberent, quia nihil adeo bene dictatum quin male narrando possit depravari"; Licitra, "La 'Summa de arte dictandi' di Maestro Goffredo," 911. Licitra allows that the attribution to Geoffrey is uncertain; 873–74, 877–78. But see Martin Camargo, "Toward a Comprehensive Art of Written Discourse: Geoffrey of Vinsauf and the *Ars dictaminis*," *Rhetorica* 6 (1988): 174.

39. "Cautus itaque dictator provideat ut per singulas constructiones suae cursum prolationis castiget, et distinctiones pertinentes ad eundem ordinem construendi proferat et quibusdam morulis nunc longis, nunc brevibus, nunc elevata voce, nunc mediocriter quiescenti, nunc sono depressiori globos constructionum discriminet vel disjungat"; Licitra, "La 'Summa de arte dictandi' di Maestro Goffredo," 911.

40. See ch. 3, n. 6.

41. G-W 56 "Tercio die aduentus sui ibidem, magni malefactoris reputati Perkyn de Lye caput amputari, et in palo ultra portam orientalem affigi, fecit." Indeed, through the whole of the episode telling of Perkyn's malefactions, only a single period slides into the cursus, the one assuring the reader that his death was universally unmourned ("scio quod de eius morte neminem ad tunc dolére perpéndi" [*planus*]).

42. See ch. 3, n. 13.

43. G-W 90; G-W 94.

44. G-W 98.

45. "nec est pulchrum . . . aliquid ab impetu incipere vel cum impetu terminare"; Licitra, "La 'Summa de arte dictandi' di Maestro Goffredo," 912.

46. See ch. 6, n. 41.

47. See ch. 4, n. 16.

48. G-W 154–56; having said that he saw a portentous comet in the sky at this time, he adds that the duke's "arma terribilia, quia serpentem blauium hominem rubium et nudum in campo albo deuorantem, eciam in aere sepius fuerant tunc uisa."

49. See ch. 3, n. 25.

50. It is interesting that Alberic of Monte Cassino joins the faults of stylistic suddenness with the vileness of matter, using the example of "strange copulation"; Alberic, *Flores rhetorici*, 36.

51. See Introduction, n. 21.

52. See ch. 3, n. 10.

53. G-W 180.

54. See ch. 7, n. 1.

55. G-W 194 "Prope iam palacium sancti Pétri hospitátus [trispondaicus], lupo-

rum et canum, de nocte sépius ad hoc súrgens [velox], condiciónes inspéxi [planus]. Nam canibus pro domorum tutamine in dominorum suorum hóstiis latrántibus [**irregular**], lupi in medio maiorum minores canes secum in prédam abstulérunt [trispondaicus], et, licet sic ablati, per maiores deféndi sperántes [planus], forcius índe murmurárent [trispondaicus], de locis suis tamen, alcius ob hoc lícet latrántes [planus], nullaténus se mouébant [trispondaicus]."

56. See n. 27 above.

57. Alberic, *Flores rhetorici*, 43; "Quare diligentius hunc modum inspicias, inspectum exerceas, exercitum freno moderationis regas."

58. See n. 27 above.

59. Bonifatius Fischer and Robert Weber, eds. *Biblia sacra iuxta Vulgatam versionem* (Stuttgart: Württembergische Bibelanstalt, 1975), 1096.

60. "Prosa est producta oratio, et a lege metri soluta"; *Etymologies* 1.38.

61. See quotations or close paraphrases in Eberhard of Béthune, *Graecismus*, ed. Johannes Wrobel (Bratislava: Wilhelm Koebner, 1887), 11.40, p. 92 and Hugh of St.-Victor, *Opera propaedeutica*, ed. Roger Baron (Notre Dame, Ind.: University of Notre Dame Press, 1966), 139.

62. Carl Sutter, *Aus Leben und Schriften des Magisters Boncompagno: ein Beitrag zur italienischen Kulturgeschichte im dreizehnten Jahrhundert* (Freiburg: Akademische Verlagsbuchhandlung von J. C. B. Mohr, 1894), 63. See Ronald G. Witt, *Boncompagno and the Defense of Rhetoric* (Durham, N.C.: Duke University Press, 1986), 14–15.

63. "Dictamen est orationum series perfectarum intervallis intercisa distantibus, nullis metrorum legibus obligata"; Licitra, "La 'Summa de arte dictandi' di Maestro Goffredo," 885.

64. Janson, *Prose Rhythm*, 37.

65. "assuetudine, quae altera natura est"; John of Limoges, *De dictamine*, 4.

CONCLUSION

1. I mean the kind of secret that "is always the same because it is the fact of fiction itself, its way of construction a secret, that is the last word. These fictions are demonstrations of the power of fiction"; Jacques Rancière, *Mute Speech: Literature, Critical Theory, and Politics*, trans. James Swenson (New York: Columbia University Press, 2011), 116.

2. David Simpson, *The Academic Postmodern and the Rule of Literature: A Report on Half-Knowledge* (Chicago: University of Chicago Press, 1995).

3. Jean-Paul Sartre, *"What Is Literature?"and Other Essays* (Cambridge, Mass.: Harvard University Press, 1988), 60.

4. Stanley Fish, *Is There a Text in This Class? The Authority of Interpretive Communities* (Cambridge: Harvard University Press, 1980), 322–36.

5. Sartre, *What Is Literature?* 60.

6. It is also the case that culture came unwittingly, by that same logic, to be treated as having an immanent logic tacitly indistinguishable from intention. The first volume of Foucault's *History of Sexuality, An Introduction*, trans. Robert Hurley (New York: Pantheon, 1978), made this crisply clear. The modification of this position in later volumes does not modify his theoretical justification, but abandons theoretical justification. But this is an argument for another time.

7. Catherine Gallagher and Stephen Greenblatt, *Practicing New Historicism* (Chicago: University of Chicago Press, 2000), 12.

8. Two familiar textual cruces that feature a more difficult and a less difficult reading: Yeats's "Among School Children" and Shakespeare's sonnet 44.

Bibliography

PRIMARY

Alberic of Monte Cassino. *Flores rhetorici*. Ed. Mauro Inguanez and H. M. Willard. Miscellanea Cassinese 14. Rome: Arti Grafiche e Fotomeccaniche Sansaini, 1938.

Albertano of Brescia. *Liber de doctrina dicendi et tacendi: La parola del cittadino nell'Italia del Duecento*. Ed. Paola Navone. Florence: SISMEL Edizioni del Galluzzo, 1998.

Arnulf of Milan. *Liber gestorum recentium*. Ed. Claudia Zey. MGH Scriptores 67. Hanover: Hahnsche Buchhandlung, 1994.

Augustine. *De civitate Dei*. Ed. B. Dombart and A. Kalb. CCSL 47–48. Turnhout: Brepols, 1955.

—. *De doctrina christiana*. Ed. Joseph Martin. CCSL 32. Turnhout: Brepols, 1962.

—. *De trinitate libri xv*. Ed. W. J. Mountain and François Glorie. CCSL 50. Turnhout: Brepols, 1968.

—. *Liber de fide rerum invisibilium*. Ed. M. P. J. van den Hout. CCSL 46. Turnhout: Brepols, 1969.

—. "Sancti Augustini sermones post Maurinos reperti." In *Miscellanea agostiniana; testi e studi, pubblicati a cura dell'Ordine cremitano di s. Agostino nel XV centenario dalla morte del santo dottore*, ed. Germain Morin. Rome: Tipografia poliglotta vaticana, 1930.

Baker, Augustine, OSB. *The Confessions of Venerable Father Augustine Baker, O.S.B., Extracted from a Manuscript Treatise preserved in the Library of Ampleforth Abbey*. Ed. Justin McCann, OSB. London: Burns, Oates and Washburn, 1922.

Benson, Larry D., ed. *The Riverside Chaucer*. Boston: Houghton Mifflin, 1987.

Brunetto Latini. *Li livres dou tresor*. Ed. P. Chabaille. Paris: Imprimerie impériale, 1863.

Burchard, Johann. *Diarium sive rerum urbanarum commentarii (1483–1506)*. Ed. Louis Thuasne. Paris: Ernest Leroux, 1883.

Catechismus ad parochos ex decreto Concilii Tridentini editus. London: Nathanael Thompson, 1687.

Caxton, William. *Here begynneth the prologue or prohemye of the book callid Caton*. STC 4853. Westminster: William Caxton, 1484.

Chambers, R. W. and Marjorie Daunt, eds. *A Book of London English*. Oxford: Oxford University Press, 1931.

Cicero, Marcus Tullius. *Orator*. Ed. P. Reis. Leipzig: Teubner, 1932.

—. *Rhetorici libri duo de inventione*. Ed. E. Stroebel (Stuttgart: Teubner, 1977)

Dante Alighieri. *The Divine Comedy*. Ed. C. S. Singleton. Princeton, N.J.: Princeton University Press, 1970.

—. *De vulgari eloquentia*. Ed. Steven Botterill. Cambridge: Cambridge University Press, 1996.

Denzinger, Heinrich and Peter Hünermann, eds. *Enchiridion symbolorum definitionum et declarationum de rebus fidei et morum*. Freiburg: Herder, 1991.

Dietrich of Niem. *Dialog über Union und Reform der Kirche 1410 (De modis uniendi et reformandi ecclesiam in concilio universali)*. Ed. Hermann Heimpel. Veröffentlichungen der Forschungsinstitute an der Universität Leipzig: Institut für Kultur- und Universalgeschichte 3. Leipzig: Teubner, 1933.

—. Dietrich of Niem. *Der Liber cancellariae apostolicae vom jahre 1380 und der Stilus palatii abbreviatus*, ed. Georg Erler. Leipzig: Carl Winter, 1888.

Eberhard of Béthune. *Graecismus*. Ed. Johannes Wrobel. Bratislava: Wilhelm Koebner, 1887.

Fischer, Bonifatius and Robert Weber, eds. *Biblia sacra iuxta Vulgatam versionem*. Stuttgart: Württembergische Bibelanstalt, 1975.

Fish, Stanley. *Is There a Text in This Class? The Authority of Interpretive Communities*. Cambridge, Mass.: Harvard University Press, 1980.

Friedberg, Emil. *Corpus iuris canonici*. Leipzig: Bernhard Tauchnitz, 1879.

Friedman, Lionel J. *Text and Iconography for Joinville's Credo*. Cambridge, Mass.: Medieval Academy of America, 1958.

Gascoigne, Thomas. *Loci e libro veritatum: Passages selected from Gascoigne's Theological Dictionary illustrating the Condition of Church and State 1403–1458*. Ed. James E. Thorold Rogers. Oxford: Clarendon, 1881.

Gregory I. *Epistolae*. *PL* 77: 431–1367.

Guido Faba. *Summa dictaminis*. Ed. Augusto Gaudenzi. Il propugnatore 2.3 1890.

Guigo I. *Les méditations (Recueil de pensées)*. Ed. un chartreux. Sources Chrétiennes 308. Paris: Éditions du Cerf, 1983.

Haydon, Frank Scott, ed. *Eulogium historiarum sive temporis*. RS. 9.3. London: Longman, Green, Longman, Roberts, and Green, 1863.

Hazelton, Richard. "Two Texts of the *Disticha Catonis* and its Commentary, with

Special Reference to Chaucer, Langland, and Gower." Ph.D. dissertation, Rutgers University, 1956.

Hector, L. C. and Barbara Harvey, eds. *The Westminster Chronicle, 1381–1394*. Oxford: Clarendon, 1966.

Herrtage, Sidney J. H., ed. *Catholicon anglicum: An English-Latin Wordbook Dated 1483*. Camden Society n.s. 30. Westminster: Camden Society, 1882.

Higden, Ranulph. *Polychronicon*. Ed. Churchill Babington and Joseph Rawson Lumby. London: Longman, 1865.

Hugh of St.-Victor. *Opera propaedeutica*. Ed. Roger Baron. Notre Dame, Ind.: University of Notre Dame Press, 1966.

Huygens, R. B. C., ed. *Accessus ad auctores; Bernard d'Utrecht; Conrad d'Hirsau, Dialogus super auctores*. Leiden: Brill, 1970.

Isidore of Seville. *Isidori Hispalensis Episcopi Etymologiarvm sive originvm libri XX*. Ed.W. M Lindsay. Oxford: Clarendon, 1911.

Jerome. *Commentariorum in Hiezechielem libri xiv*. Ed. François Glorie. CCSL75. Turnhout: Brepols, 1964.

Jocelin of Brakelond. *Chronica Jocelini de Brakelonda*. Ed. H. E. Butler. New York: Oxford University Press, 1949.

John of Limoges. *De dictamine et dictatorio syllogismorum*. In *Opera omnia*, ed. Constantin Horváth, OCSO. Veszprém: Egyházmegyei Könyvnyomda, 1932.

Kane, George and E. T. Donaldson, eds. *Piers Plowman: The B Version*. London: Athlone, 1975.

Martin, G. H., ed. *Knighton's Chronicle 1337–1396*. Oxford: Clarendon, 1995.

Kuratorium Singer, ed. *Thesaurus proverbiorum medii aevi [Lexikon der Sprichwörter des romanisch-germanischen Mittelalters]*. Berlin: W. de Gruyter, 1995.

Legge, Mary Dominica, ed. *Anglo-Norman Letters and Petitions from All Souls MS. 182*. Anglo-Norman Text Society 3. Oxford: Blackwell, 1941.

Licitra, Vincenzo. "La 'Summa de arte dictandi' di Maestro Goffredo." *Studi Medievali* 3 ser. 7 (1966): 865–913.

Lyndwood, William. *Provinciale, seu constitutiones Angliae*. Oxford: H. Hall, 1679.

Matthew Paris. *Chronica majora*. Ed. Henry Richards Luard. RS 57. London: Longman, 1880.

Ovid. *Amores [etc.]*. Ed. Rudolf Ehwald. Bibliotheca scriptorum Graecorum et Romanorum Teubneriana. Lipsiae: Teubner, 1887.

Peter Damian. *Die Briefe des Petrus Damiani*. Ed. Kurt Reindel. Die Briefe der deutschen Kaiserzeit 4. Munich: MGH, 1983.

Petrarca, Francesco. *Secretum*. Ed. Ugo Dotti. Rome: Guido Izzi, 1993.

Rabanus Maurus. *Commentariorum in Ezechielem libri xx*. *PL* 110: 493–1084.

Relatio juridica, in qua novem testes oculati et jurati ex OP narrant pia gesta et miracula S. Dominici. Acta sanctorum (August 1). 632–45.

Rousseau, Jean-Jacques. *Émile, ou de l'éducation*. Ed. T. L'Aminot. Paris: Garnier, 1999.

Russell, George and George Kane, eds. *Piers Plowman: The C Version*. London: Athlone, 1997.

Statutes of the Realm. 11 vols. London: HMSO, 1810.

Stow, George B., ed. *Historia vitae et regni Ricardi secundi*. Philadelphia: University of Pennsylvania Press, 1977.

Thomas Aquinas. *In duodecim libros metaphysicorum Aristotelis expositio*. Turin: Marietti, 1950.

—. *Secunda secundae Summae theologiae a quaestione CXXIII ad quaestionem CLXXXIX*. Ed. Dominican friars. Leonine ed. 10. Rome: Typographia Polyglotta S. C. de Propaganda Fide, 1899.

Thomas of Capua. *Die Ars dictandi des Thomas von Capua*. Ed. Emmy Heller. Heidelberg: C. Winter, 1929.

Thucydides. *The Peloponnesian War: The Complete Hobbes Translation*. Chicago: University of Chicago Press, 1989.

Walsingham, Thomas. *Historia anglicana*. RS 28:2. London: Longman, Green, Longman, Roberts, and Green, 1864.

Wilkins, David, ed. *Concilia Magnae Brittanie et Hibernie*. London: 1737.

William Durandus. *Rationale divinorum officiorum*. Ed. A. Davril, O.S.B. and T. M. Thibodeau. CCCM 140. Turnhout: Brepols, 1995.

SECONDARY

Abbate, Carolyn. "Outside Ravel's Tomb." *Journal of the American Musicological Society* 52 (1999): 465–530.

Aers, David. *Community, Gender, and Individual Identity: English Writing 1360–1430*. London: Routledge, 1988.

Allmand, C. T. "The Civil Lawyers." In *Profession, Vocation, and Culture in Later Medieval England: Essays Dedicated to the Memory of A. R. Myers*, ed. Cecil H. Clough, 155–80. Liverpool: Liverpool University Press, 1982.

Althusser, Louis and Étienne Balibar. *Reading "Capital."* Trans. Ben Brewster. London: New Left Books, 1970.

Aston, Margaret. "Lollardy and Sedition." *Past and Present* 17 (1960): 1–44.

—. "The Impeachment of Bishop Despenser." *Bulletin of the Institute of Historical Research* 38 (1965): 127–48.

Attridge, Derek. *J. M. Coetzee and the Ethics of Reading: Literature in the Event*. Chicago: University of Chicago Press, 2004.

Auerbach, Erich. *Mimesis: The Representation of Reality in Western Literature*. Trans. Willard R. Trask. Princeton, N.J.: Princeton University Press, 1953.

Barish, Jonas A. *The Antitheatrical Prejudice*. Berkeley: University of California Press, 1981.

Barnie, John. *War in Medieval English Society: Social Values in the Hundred Years War, 1337–1399*. Ithaca, N.Y.: Cornell University Press, 1974.

Baron, Hans. *Petrarch's Secretum: Its Making and Its Meaning*. Medieval Academy Book 94. Cambridge, Mass.: Medieval Academy of America, 1985.

Barr, Helen. *Socioliterary Practice in Late Medieval England*. Oxford: Oxford University Press, 2001.

Barthes, Roland. *S/Z*. Trans. Richard Howard. New York: Hill and Wang, 1974.

—. *Camera Lucida: Reflections on Photography*. New York: Hill and Wang, 1981.

Barton, J. L. "The Legal Faculties of Late Medieval Oxford." In *Late Medieval Oxford*, ed. Jeremy I. Catto and Ralph Evans, 281–313. Oxford: Clarendon, 1992.

Bellamy, John G. *The Law of Treason in England in the Later Middle Ages*. Cambridge: Cambridge University Press, 1970.

Bennett, Michael. *Richard II and the Revolution of 1399*. Stroud: Sutton, 1999.

—. "Henry IV, the Royal Succession and the Crisis of 1406." In *The Reign of Henry IV: Rebellion and Survival, 1406–1413*, ed. Gwilym Dodd and Douglas Biggs, 9–27. York: York Medieval Press, 2008.

Bergson, Henri. *Le rire: essai sur la signification du comique*. Paris: Presses Universitaires de France, 1981.

Best, Stephen and Sharon Marcus, eds. "The Way We Read Now." *Representations* 108 (2009).

Blackmur, R. P. "The Lion and the Honeycomb." *Hudson Review* 3 (1951): 487–507.

Bowers, John M. *The Politics of Pearl: Court Poetry in the Age of Richard II*. Woodbridge: Brewer, 2001.

—. "Thomas Hoccleve and the Politics of Tradition." *Chaucer Review* 36 (2002): 352–69.

Brandt, William J. *The Shape of Medieval History: Studies in Modes of Perception*. New Haven, Conn.: Yale University Press, 1966.

Brooks, Peter. *Reading for the Plot: Design and Intention in Narrative*. New York: Knopf, 1984.

Brower, Reuben A. *Hero and Saint: Shakespeare and the Graeco-Roman Heroic Tradition*. Oxford: Clarendon, 1971.

Brusendorff, Aage. "'He Knew Nat Catoun for his Wit Was Rude.'" In *Studies in English Philology: A Miscellany in Honor of Frederick Klaeber*, 320–39. Minneapolis: University of Minnesota Press, 1929.

Burke, Edmund. *A Philosophical Enquiry into the Origin of our Ideas of the*

Sublime and Beautiful. Ed. J. T. Boulton. New York: Columbia University Press, 1958.

Camargo, Martin. "Toward a Comprehensive Art of Written Discourse: Geoffrey of Vinsauf and the *Ars dictaminis*." *Rhetorica* 6 (1988): 167–94.

—. *Ars dictaminis, ars dictandi*. Trans. L. Genicot. Typologie des Sources du Moyen Âge Occidental 60. Turnhout: Brepols, 1991.

—. *Medieval Rhetorics of Prose Composition: Five English Artes Dictandi and Their Tradition*. Binghamton, N.Y.: Medieval and Renaissance Texts and Studies, 1995.

—. "The Waning of Medieval Ars Dictaminis." *Rhetorica: A Journal of the History of Rhetoric* 19, 2 (2001): 135–40.

Carlson, David R. "Greeks in England, 1400." In *Interstices: Studies in Middle English and Anglo-Latin Texts in Honour of A. G. Rigg*, ed. Richard Firth Green and Linne R. Mooney, 74–98. Toronto: University of Toronto Press, 2004.

—. "English Poetry, 1399 July–October, and Lancastrian Crime." *Studies in the Age of Chaucer* 29 (2007): 375–418.

Caspary, Gerard E. "The Deposition of Richard II and the Canon Law." In *Proceedings of the Second International Congress of Medieval Canon Law: Boston College, 12–16 August 1963*, ed. Stephan Kuttner and J. Joseph Ryan, 189–201. Vatican City: Sacra Congregatio de Seminariis et Studiorum Universitatibus, 1963.

Cavell, Stanley. *Must We Mean What We Say?* Cambridge: Cambridge University Press, 1976.

Chenu, M.-D. *La théologie au douzième siècle*. Paris: Vrin, 1957.

Chew, Samuel C. *The Virtues Reconciled: An Iconographic Study*. Toronto: University of Toronto Press, 1947.

Chism, Christine. *Alliterative Revivals*. Philadelphia: University of Pennsylvania Press, 2002.

Coetzee, J. M. *Giving Offense: Essays on Censorship*. Chicago: University of Chicago Press, 1996.

Coleman, Janet. *Ancient and Medieval Memories: Studies in the Reconstruction of the Past*. Cambridge: Cambridge University Press, 1992.

Cornelius, Ian. "The Rhetoric of Advancement: *Ars dictaminis*, *Cursus*, and Clerical Careerism in Late Medieval England." *New Medieval Literatures* 12 (2010): 289–330.

Couture, Léonce. "Le 'cursus' ou rhythme prosaïque dans la liturgie et la littérature." *Revue des Questions Historiques* 51 (1892): 253–61.

Croce, Benedetto. *Storia della età barocca in Italia: pensiero, poesia e letteratura, vita morale*. 2nd ed. Bari: Laterza, 1946.

Curley, Michael J. "The Cloak of Anonymity and the *Prophecy of John of Bridlington*." *Modern Philology* 77 (1980): 361–69.

Cuttino, G. P. *English Diplomatic Administration, 1259–1339*. Oxford: Oxford University Press, 1971.

D'Amico, John F. *Renaissance Humanism in Papal Rome: Humanists and Churchmen on the Eve of the Reformation*. Baltimore: Johns Hopkins University Press, 1983.

D'Angelo, Paolo. "'Celare l'arte': per una storia del precetto 'Ars est celare artem.'" *Intersezioni* 6 (1986): 321–41.

Davies, Richard G. "Martin V and the English Episcopate, with Particular Reference to his Campaign for the Appeal of the Statute of Provisors." *English Historical Review* 92 (1977): 309–44.

—. "Richard II and the Church in the Years of 'Tyranny.'" *Journal of Medieval History* 1 (1975): 329–62.

Davies, R. R. *The Revolt of Owain Glyn Dwr*. Oxford: Oxford University Press, 1995.

Delany, Sheila. "Politics and the Paralysis of Imagination in *The Physician's Tale*." *Studies in the Age of Chaucer* 3 (1981): 47–60.

de Man, Paul. *The Resistance to Theory*. Minneapolis: University of Minnesota Press, 1986.

Denholm-Young, N. "The *Cursus* in England." In *Oxford Essays in History Presented to H. E. Salter*, 68–103. Oxford: Clarendon, 1934.

Dodd, Gwilym. "Henry IV's Council, 1399–1405." In *Henry IV: The Establishment of the Regime, 1399–1406*, ed. Gwilym Dodd and Douglas Biggs, 95–115. York: York Medieval Press, 2003.

Dunn, Alastair. *The Politics of Magnate Power in England and Wales, 1389–1413*. Oxford: Clarendon, 2003.

Emden, A. B. *A Biographical Register of the University of Oxford to A.D. 1500*. 3 vols. Oxford: Clarendon, 1957.

Epstein, Robert. "Literal Opposition: Deconstruction, History, and Lancaster." *Texas Studies in Literature and Language* 44 (2002): 16–33.

Fleming, John V. *Classical Imitation and Interpretation in Chaucer's Troilus*. Lincoln: University of Nebraska Press, 1990.

Fletcher, Christopher. *Richard II: Manhood, Youth, and Politics 1377–99*. Oxford: Oxford University Press, 2008.

Foucault, Michel. *The History of Sexuality*. Vol. 1, *An Introduction*. Trans. Robert Hurley. New York: Pantheon, 1978.

Freedman, Paul and Spiegel, Gabrielle M. "Medievalisms Old and New: The Rediscovery of Alterity in North American Medieval Studies." *American Historical Review* 103 (1998): 677–704.

Fried, Michael. "Barthes's *Punctum*." *Critical Inquiry* 31 (2005): 539–75.

Galbraith, V. H., ed. *The Anonimalle Chronicle, 1333–1381*. Manchester: Manchester University Press, 1927.

—. "An Autograph MS of Ranulph Higden's *Polychronicon*." *Huntington Library Quarterly* 23 (1959): 1–18.

Gallagher, Catherine and Stephen Greenblatt. *Practicing New Historicism*. Chicago: University of Chicago Press, 2000.

Galloway, Andrew. "Private Selves and the Intellectual Marketplace in Late Fourteenth-Century England: The Case of the Two Usks." *New Literary History* 28 (1997): 291–318.

—. "Writing History in England." In *The Cambridge History of Medieval English Literature*, ed. David Wallace. Cambridge: Cambridge University Press, 1997, 255–83.

Gaudenzi, Augusto. "Sulla cronologia dei dettatori Bolognesi." *Bolletino dell' Istituto Storico Italiano* 14 (1895): 85–174.

Given-Wilson, Chris. "Adam Usk, the Monk of Evesham and the Parliament of 1397–1398." *Historical Research* 66 (1993): 329–35.

—. *Chronicles: The Writing of History in Medieval England*. Hambledon: Hambledon Press, 2004.

Gordon, Dillian. *Making and Meaning: The Wilton Diptych*. London: National Gallery, 1993.

Grady, Frank. "The Lancastrian Gower and the Limits of Exemplarity." *Speculum* 70 (1995): 552–75.

Gransden, Antonia. "Silent Meanings in Ranulf Higden's *Polychronicon* and in Thomas Elmham's *Liber Metricus de Henrico Quinto*." *Medium Ævum* 46 (1977): 231–40.

—. *Historical Writing in England*. Vol. 2, *C. 1307 to the Early Sixteenth Century*. London: Routledge & Kegan Paul, 1982.

Green, Richard Firth. "Palamon's Appeal of Treason in the *Knight's Tale*." In *The Letter of the Law: Legal Practice and Literary Production in Medieval England*, ed. Emily Steiner and Candace Barrington, 105–14. Ithaca, N.Y.: Cornell University Press, 2002.

Groebner, Valentin. *Defaced: The Visual Culture of Violence in the Late Middle Ages*. Trans. Pamela Selvyn. New York: Zone Books, 2004.

Haines, Roy Martin. *The Church and Politics in Fourteenth-Century England: The Career of Adam Orleton, c. 1275–1345*. Cambridge: Cambridge University Press, 1978.

Harriss, G. L. *Cardinal Beaufort: A Study of Lancastrian Ascendancy and Decline*. Oxford: Clarendon, 1988.

Harvey, Margaret. *The English in Rome, 1362–1420: Portrait of an Expatriate Community*. Cambridge: Cambridge University Press, 1999.

Hazelton, Richard. "The Christianization of 'Cato': The *Disticha Catonis* in the Light of Late Medieval Commentaries." *Mediaeval Studies* 19 (1957): 157–73.

—. "Chaucer and Cato." *Speculum* 35 (1960): 357–80.

Jacob, E. F. "Verborum florida venustas." *Bulletin of the John Rylands Library* 17, 2 (1933): 264–90.

Janson, Tore. *Prose Rhythm in Medieval Latin from the 9th to the 13th Century*. Studia Latina Stockholmiensia 20. Stockholm: Almqvist & Wiksell, 1975.

Justice, Steven. "Literary History." In *Chaucer: Contemporary Approaches*, ed. David Raybin and Susanna Fein, 195–210. University Park: Pennsylvania State University Press, 2009.

—. "Chaucer's History-Effect." In *Answerable Style: The Idea of the Literary in Medieval England*, ed. Frank Grady and Andrew Galloway, 169–94. Columbus: Ohio State University Press, 2013.

—. "'Shameless': Augustine, After Augustine, and Way After Augustine." *Journal of Medieval and Early Modern Studies* 44 (2014): 17–43.

Keen, Maurice H. "Treason Trials Under the Law of Arms." *Transactions of the Royal Historical Society* 5th ser. 12 (1962): 85–103.

Kerby-Fulton, Kathryn. *Books Under Suspicion: Censorship and Tolerance of Revelatory Writing in Late Medieval England*. Notre Dame, Ind.: University of Notre Dame Press, 2006.

Kermode, Frank. *The Genesis of Secrecy: On the Interpretation of Narrative*. Cambridge, Mass.: Harvard University Press, 1979.

Lawton, David. "Titus Goes Hunting and Hawking: The Poetics of Recreation and Revenge in *The Siege of Jerusalem*." In *Individuality and Achievement in Middle English Poetry*, ed. O. S. Pickering, 105–17. Cambridge: Brewer, 1997.

Leicester, H. Marshall. "Newer Currents in Psychoanalytic Criticism, and the Difference 'It' Makes: Gender and Desire in the Miller's Tale." *ELH* 61, 3 (1994): 473–99.

Lerner, Robert E. *The Powers of Prophecy: The Cedar of Lebanon Vision from the Mongol Onslaught to the Dawn of the Enlightenment*. Berkeley: University of California Press, 1983.

Levinson, Marjorie. "What Is New Formalism?" *PMLA* 122 (2007): 558–69.

Love, Heather. "Close But Not Deep: Literary Ethics and the Descriptive Turn." *New Literary History* 41 (2010): 371–91.

Lunt, William E. *Financial Relations of the Papacy with England 1327–1534*. Studies in Anglo-Papal Relations During the Middle Ages 2. Cambridge, Mass.: Medieval Academy of America, 1962.

Mann, Jill. "'He knew nat Catoun': Medieval School-Texts and Middle English Literature." In *The Text in the Community: Essays on Medieval Works, Manuscripts, Authors, and Readers*, ed. Jill Mann and Maura Nolan, 41–74. Notre Dame, Ind.: University of Notre Dame Press, 2006.

Marcus, Sharon. *Between Women: Friendship, Desire, and Marriage in Victorian England.* Princeton, N.J.: Princeton University Press, 2007.

Martin, G. H. "Narrative Sources for the Reign of Richard II." In *The Age of Richard II*, ed. James L. Gillespie, 51–69. Stroud: Sutton, 1997.

McFarlane, K. B. *John Wycliffe and the Beginnings of English Nonconformity.* London: English Universities Press, 1952.

McGann, Jerome J. "Introduction." In *Historical Studies and Literary Criticism*, 3–21. Madison: University of Wisconsin Press, 1985.

McNiven, Peter. "Scrope, Richard (c.1350–1405)." *Oxford Dictionary of National Biography.* http://www.oxforddnb.com.

—. "The Betrayal of Archbishop Scrope." *Bulletin of the John Rylands Library* 54 (1971): 173–213.

—. "The Men of Cheshire and the Rebellion of 1403." *Transactions of the Historical Society of Lancashire and Cheshire* 129 (1979): 1–29.

—. *Heresy and Politics in the Reign of Henry IV: The Burning of John Badby.* Woodbridge: Boydell, 1987.

Middleton, Anne. "Langland's Lives: Reflections on Late-Medieval Religious and Literary Vocabulary." In *The Idea of Medieval Literature: New Essays on Chaucer and Medieval Culture in Honor of Donald R. Howard*, ed. James M. Dean and Christian K. Zacher, 227–42. Newark: University of Delaware Press, 1992.

Millet, Hélène. "Le grand schisme d'occident selon Eustache Deschamps: un monstre prodigieux." In *Miracles, prodiges et merveilles au moyen âge: XXVe Congrès de la S.H.M.E.S (Orléans, juin 1994)*, 215–26. Paris: Publications de la Sorbonne, 1995.

Mills, Robert. *Suspended Animation: Pain, Pleasure and Punishment in Medieval Culture.* London: Reaktion Books, 2005.

Minnis, Alastair J. *Medieval Theory of Authorship.* Philadelphia: University of Pennsylvania Press, 1988.

Mollat, Guillaume. "Contribution à l'histoire du sacré collège de Clément V à Eugène IV." *Revue d'Histoire Ecclésiastique* 46 (1951): 22–112, 566.

Monk, Samuel Holt. "'A Grace Beyond the Reach of Art.'" *Journal of the History of Ideas* 5 (1944).

Morgan, Philip. "Cheshire and Wales." In *Power and Identity in the Middle Ages: Essays in Memory of Rees Davies*, ed. Huw Pryce and John Watts, 195–210. Oxford: Oxford University Press, 2007.

Murphy, James J. *Rhetoric in the Middle Ages: A History of Rhetorical Theory from St. Augustine to the Renaissance.* Berkeley: University of California Press, 1974.

Navone, Paola. "La 'Doctrina loquendi et tacendi' di Albertano da Brescia: censimento dei manoscritti." *Studi Medievali* 35 (1994): 895–930.

Nichol, Donald M. "A Byzantine Emperor in England: Manuel II's Visit to London in 1400–1401." *University of Birmingham Historical Journal* 12 (1970): 204–25.

Nuttall, A. D. *Why Does Tragedy Give Pleasure?* Oxford: Clarendon, 1996.

Nuttall, Jenni. *The Creation of Lancastrian Kingship: Literature, Language and Politics in Late Medieval England*. Cambridge: Cambridge University Press, 2007.

Owen, Dorothy M. *The Medieval Canon Law: Teaching, Literature and Transmission*. Cambridge: Cambridge University Press, 1990.

Owen, Edward. "The Will of Adam of Usk." *English Historical Review* 18 (1903): 316–17.

Palmer, J. J. N. "The Background to Richard II's Marriage to Isabel of France." *Bulletin of the Institute for Historical Research* 44 (1971): 1–17.

Patterson, Annabel. *Censorship and Interpretation: The Conditions of Writing and Reading in Early Modern England*. Madison: University of Wisconsin Press, 1984.

Patterson, Lee. "'What Is Me?': Self and Society in the Poetry of Thomas Hoccleve." *Studies in the Age of Chaucer* 23 (2001): 437–70.

Peters, Edward. *The Shadow King: Rex inutilis in Medieval Law and Literature, 751–1327*. New Haven, Conn.: Yale University Press, 1970.

Poole, Reginald L. *Lectures on the History of the Papal Chancery Down to the Time of Innocent III*. Cambridge: Cambridge University Press, 1915.

Powell, Edward. "Gascoigne, Sir William (c.1350–1419)." *Oxford Dictionary of National Biography*. http://www.oxforddnb.

Raine, James. *The Historians of the Church of York and Its Archbishops*. RS 71. London: Longman, 1879.

Ramsay, Nigel. "Scriveners and Notaries as Legal Intermediaries in Later Medieval England." In *Enterprise and Individuals in Fifteenth-Century England*, ed. Jennifer Kermode, 118–31. Stroud: Sutton, 1991.

Rancière, Jacques. *Mute Speech: Literature, Critical Theory, and Politics*, tr. James Swenson New York: Columbia University Press, 2011.

Reynolds, Suzanne. *Medieval Reading: Grammar, Rhetoric and the Classical Text*. Cambridge: Cambridge University Press, 1996.

Richardson, H. G. "Business Training in Medieval Oxford." *American Historical Review* 46 (1941): 259–80.

—. "Letters of the Oxford *Dictatores*." In *Formularies Which Bear on the History of Oxford c. 1204–1420*, ed. H. E. Salter, W. A. Pantin and H. G. Richardson, 331–450. Oxford: Clarendon, 1942.

Ricks, Christopher B. *Milton's Grand Style*. Oxford: Clarendon, 1963.

Rigg, A. G. "John of Bridlington's Prophecy: A New Look." *Speculum* 63 (1988): 596–613.

Sanderlin, S. "Chaucer and Ricardian Politics." *Chaucer Review* 22 (1988): 171–84.

Sartre, Jean-Paul. *"What Is Literature?" and Other Essays*. Cambridge, Mass.: Harvard University Press, 1988.

Saul, Nigel. *Richard II*. New Haven, Conn.: Yale University Press, 1997.

Sayles, G. O. "The Deposition of Richard II: Three Lancastrian Narratives." *Bulletin of the Institute of Historical Research* 54 (1981): 257–70.

Scarry, Elaine. *The Body in Pain: The Making and Unmaking of the World*. New York: Oxford University Press, 1985.

Schaller, H. M. "Studien zur Briefsammlung des Kardinals Thomas von Capua." *Deutsches Archiv für Erforschung des Mittelalters* (1965): 371–518.

Schwarz, Brigide. "*Statuta sacri causarum apostolici palacii auditorum et notariorum*: Eine neue Quelle zur Geschichte der Rota romana im späten Mittelalter." In *Studien zum 15. Jahrhundert: Festschrift für Erich Meuthen*, ed. Johannes Helmrath, Heribert Müller and Helmut Wolff, 845–67. Munich: R. Oldenbourg, 1994.

Sheppard, Lancelot C. *Lacordaire: A Biographical Essay*. New York: Macmillan, 1964.

Sherborne, J. W. "Indentured Retinues and English Expeditions to France, 1369–1380." *English Historical Review* 79 (1964): 718–46.

Simpson, David. *The Academic Postmodern and the Rule of Literature: A Report on Half-Knowledge*. Chicago: University of Chicago Press, 1995.

Simpson, James. "The Constraints of Satire in 'Piers Plowman' and 'Mum and the Sothsegger.'" In *Langland, the Mystics and the Medieval English Religious Tradition: Essays in Honour of S. S. Hussey*, ed. Helen Phillips, 11–30. Cambridge: Brewer, 1990.

—. *Reform and Cultural Revolution. The Oxford English Literary History*, vol. 2, *1350–1547*. Oxford: Oxford University Press, 2002.

Smith, Barbara Herrnstein. *Poetic Closure: A Study of How Poems End*. Chicago: University of Chicago Press, 1968.

Squibb, G. D. *The High Court of Chivalry: A Study of the Civil Law in England*. Oxford: Clarendon, 1959.

Storm, Mel. "Speech, Circumspection, and Orthodontics in the *Manciple's Prologue* and *Tale* and the Wife of Bath's Portrait." *Studies in Philology* 96 (1999): 109–25.

Strohm, Paul. *Hochon's Arrow: The Social Imagination of Fourteenth-Century Texts*. Princeton, N.J.: Princeton University Press, 1992.

—. *England's Empty Throne: Usurpation and the Language of Legitimation, 1399–1422*. New Haven, Conn.: Yale University Press, 1998.

Sutter, Carl. *Aus Leben und Schriften des Magisters Boncompagno: ein Beitrag zur italienischen Kulturgeschichte im dreizehnten Jahrhundert*. Freiburg: Akademische Verlagsbuchhandlung von J.C.B. Mohr, 1894.

Tait, James. Review of *Calendar of the Patent Rolls (1377–1385). English Historical Review* 13 (1898): 354–57.

—. Review of *Calendar of the Patent Rolls* (1396–1399). *English Historical Review* 25 (1910): 769–70.

Taylor, John. *The Universal Chronicle of Ranulf Higden*. Oxford: Clarendon, 1966.

—. *English Historical Literature in the Fourteenth Century*. Oxford: Clarendon, 1987.

Taylor, Rupert. *The Political Prophecy in England*. New York: Columbia University Press, 1911.

Traver, Hope. *The Four Daughters of God: A Study of the Versions of this Allegory with Especial Reference to those in Latin, French, and English*. Philadelphia: John C. Winston, 1907.

Tuve, Rosamond. "Notes on the Virtues and Vices." *Journal of the Warburg and Courtauld Institutes* 26 (1963): 264–303.

Ullmann, Walter. *The Growth of Papal Government in the Middle Ages: A Study in the Ideological Relation of Clerical to Lay Power*. London: Methuen, 1965.

Valois, Noël. *De arte scribendi epistolas apud gallicos medii ævi scriptores rhetoresve*. Paris: Picard, 1880.

—. "Étude sur la rhythme des bulles pontificales." *Bibliothèque de l'École des Chartes* (1881): 164–272.

Vredeveld, Harry. "Notes on Erasmus's *De conscribendis epistolis*." *Journal of Neo-Latin Studies* 49 (2000): 101–37.

Walker, Simon. "Between Church and Crown: Master Richard Andrew, King's Clerk." *Speculum* 74 (1999): 956–91.

—. "Rumour, Sedition and Popular Protest in the Reign of Henry IV." *Past and Present* 166 (2000): 31–65.

—. "The Yorkshire Risings of 1405: Texts and Contexts." In *Henry IV: The Establishment of the Regime, 1399–1406*, ed. Gwilym Dodd and Douglas Biggs, 161–84. York: York Medieval Press, 2003.

Wallace, David. *Chaucerian Polity: Absolutist Lineages and Associational Forms in England and Italy*. Stanford, Calif.: Stanford University Press, 1997.

Wenzel, Siegfried. *The Sin of Sloth: Acedia in Medieval Thought and Literature*. Chapel Hill: University of North Carolina Press, 1967.

Whitfield, Derek W. "Conflicts of Personality and Principle: The Political and Religious Crisis in the English Franciscan Province, 1400–1409." *Franciscan Studies* 17 (1957): 321–62.

Wieruszowski, Helene. "*Ars dictaminis* in the Time of Dante." *Medievalia et Humanistica* 1 (1943): 95–108.

Williams, Glanmor. *The Welsh Church from Conquest to Reformation*. Cardiff: University of Wales Press, 1976.

Wilson, Edward. "An Unrecorded Middle English Version of Petrarch's 'Secretum': A Preliminary Report." *Italia Medioevale e Umanistica* 25 (1983); 389–90.

Wilson, Edward and Iain Fenlon, eds. *The Winchester Anthology: A Facsimile of British Library Additional Manuscript 60577*. Woodbridge: Brewer, 1981.

Witt, Ronald G. *Boncompagno and the Defense of Rhetoric*. Durham, N.C.: Duke University Press, 1986.

—. *"In the Footsteps of the Ancients": The Origins of Humanism from Lovato to Bruni*. Leiden: Brill, 2000.

—. "The Arts of Letter-Writing." In *The Cambridge History of Literary Criticism*, vol. 2, *The Middle Ages*, ed. Alastair J. Minnis, 68–83. Cambridge: Cambridge University Press, 2005.

Wolfson, Susan J. "Introduction." In *Reading for Form*, ed. Susan J. Wolfson and Marshall Brown, 3–24. Seattle: University of Washington Press, 2006.

Woods, Marjorie Curry and Rita Copeland. "Classroom and Confession." In *The Cambridge History of Medieval English Literature*, 376–406. Cambridge: Cambridge University Press, 1999.

Wright, Sylvia. "The Author Portraits in the Bedford Psalter-Hours: Gower, Chaucer, and Hoccleve." *British Library Journal* 18 (1992): 190–201.

Wylie, James Hamilton. *History of England Under Henry the Fourth*. London: Longmans, 1884.

Yandell, Stephen. "Prophetic Authority in Adam of Usk's *Chronicle*." In *Prophet Margins: The Medieval Vatic Impulse and Social Stability*, ed. E. L. Risden, Karen Moranski, and Stephen Yandell, 79–100. New York: Peter Lang, 2004.

Index

Acknowledgments

Sean Curran, Jennifer Gurley, Charity Ketz, Maura Nolan, Katherine O'Brien O'Keeffe, Matthew Rose, Cassandra Sciortino, and Emily Thornbury read or discussed parts of this odd little book with me at different points. Michelle Karnes and David Marno read it all; both helped me undo some knots in which I had tangled myself. So did the two amazing press readers. So did my wife Chiyuma Elliott, who made everything wonderful except the book and its author. None of these should be blamed for anything that went wrong.

The dedicatee read it too, twice at least. A scholarly influence, senior colleague, professional mentor, department chair, tenure reviewer, intellectual sparring-partner, friend, and the best reader I've ever known, for thirty years she has been a figure both inspiring and commanding in my intellectual life. So it might be fair to blame her.